"A poetic, intimate, at times confronting encounter with a voice that convinces you of the extraordinary potential of our craft."
—Lee Morgan, author of *Sounds of Infinity*

"A winding journey into the deep heart of magic and Craft. This book will guide you through the realms of spirit, shadow, and story to stoke the inner flame that grows your magic, all while exploring the untamed, intimate, and transcendent work of breaking binaries and cultivating true power—the power to change the world."
—Nicholas Pearson, author of *Flower Essences from the Witch's Garden*

"In *The Witch Belongs to the World*, we are woven into the story of how Lust and Love are both languages and initiators into our Craft....It is rare to find witchcraft books that speak so deeply to the soul. I felt my senses and my magick responding palpably to each step as I allowed myself to drink from its poetry and beauty."
—Petrucia Finkler, Brazilian witch, teacher, and author of *Os Quatro Saberes*

"A breathtakingly rich and poetic chronicle of modern witchery, a provocative call to arms, and a generous guide to empowerment and self-initiation for magical folk, old and new. Fio pulls no punches in lovingly daring emergent witches to uncover and embrace the dissent, responsibility, love, and power at the heart of their magic and reminds adept practitioners just what it means to commit to the path, again and again."
—Jerico Mandybur, bestselling author and tarot/oracle creator

"This book is clearly a tome forged of inspiration and passion. Fio Gede Parma's words move me in a way many simply cannot, and it is in the empowering, provocative explorations found in this book that we find the true nature of the Witch as a transgressive, oracular force....This is a call to action, a reminder of who the Witch truly is, and a lyrical exploration of the intimate mysteries we immerse ourselves within as Witches. You will not regret picking this book up."
—Mhara Starling, author of *Welsh Witchcraft*

"This book is for anyone who's curious about a life that dares to tread outside of the constraints and binaries of empire, for anyone curious enough to listen to the deep, dark quiet of the witch's heart."
—Toad Dell, co-creator of PermaQueer

"*The Witch Belongs to the World* is a brutal, beautiful look at who and what witches are and can be; it sings along the edge between poetry and prose. Saturated with spirits, it speaks to us of a witchcraft that is experiential and vital, that is lived and remembered, that is modern and primal. Truly a must-read for anyone who is a witch or wants to be one."
—Morgan Daimler, author of *Fairycraft*

"As you read you become both the enchanted and the enchanter. Fio offers up experiences, memories, and visions that are uncannily beautiful, filled with colors, shadows, and the smell of rich earth, the substance of witchcraft....
This book is a dreamwalk, a pathworking, a soul flight that awakens the call to be the witch that the world needs in these times of great change and possibility."
—Ivo Dominguez Jr., author of
The Four Elements of the Wise

"*The Witch Belongs to the World* is erudite and alive, as poetic and transgressive as it is transformative. Where I might have an inkling, a hint of a complex spiritual insight, Fio snatches it from thin air and renders it like an opened honeycomb dripping with sweet secrets and mystery. Fio's content is whip-smart and the delivery to readers is like a mist one walks through until they're gloriously soaked to the bone....If we're lucky enough to pick up this volume and follow its wise instruction, we'll be transported through an unexpected journey into the heart of our power, into the soul of the Craft."
—Timothy Roderick, author of *Dark Moon Mysteries*

"Fio rightly acknowledges the Witch as being 'outside,' transgressing the perceived norm of consensus reality and challenging society to face its shortcomings and evolve, to awaken to the Lady who is Power and Beauty. Not everyone may always be sensitive to Beauty, but we are blessed that there are those who can reveal it to us."
—Ian Chambers, author of *The Witch Compass*

The Witch Belongs to the World

The Witch Belongs to the World

A Spell of Becoming

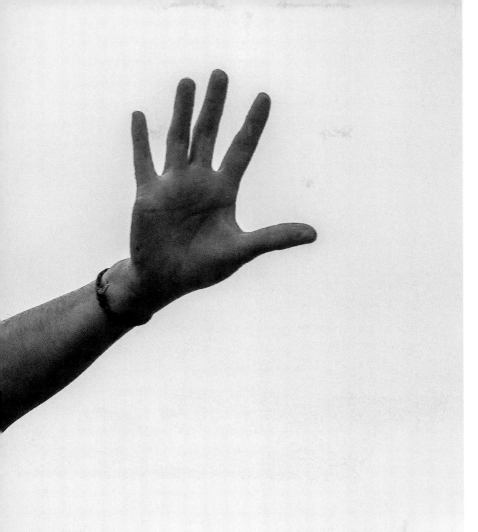

Fio Gede Parma

Llewellyn Publications | WOODBURY, MINNESOTA

FIRST EDITION
First Printing, 2023

Book design by Rebecca Zins
Cover design by Kevin R. Brown
Photography © Luke Brohman, fleetfootproductions.com

Llewellyn is a registered trademark of Llewellyn Worldwide Ltd.

Library of Congress Cataloging-In-Publication Data
Pending
ISBN 978-0-7387-7390-2

Llewellyn Publications
A Division of Llewellyn Worldwide Ltd.
2143 Wooddale Drive
Woodbury, MN 55125-2989

www.llewellyn.com
Printed in the United States of America

To Tash and Copper, who left this world in 2020. To Rose May Dance, who passed on the last day of 2021. To Poppy Palin and River, who journeyed on in 2022. Your soulful, artful, and wyrd magical influences and impacts live on in me and many.

Contents

Acknowledgement of Country

In so-called Australia—the continent I have spent most of my life within—there is an ancient protocol and custom that is shared by many of the First Nations that comprise the vast diversity and history of human relationship with this place. Today in English it is called acknowledgement of country.

In my listening and learning from First Nations friends, activists, elders, and community members, I have discovered that this is not just a thing that we must do for only one or two reasons or to tick any kind of box. There are a multiplicity of deeply layered reasons. We acknowledge country in order to acknowledge the very real and horrifying impacts of invasion and continued colonisation and to honour and celebrate the strength, survival, and thriving of Aboriginal and Torres Strait Islander people, communities, and cultures. We acknowledge country to recognise ourselves as present in someone else's country and reflect and step into our responsibilities. Acknowledging country is also a very potent way of listening to country, honouring the spirits and Old Ones, and dedicating our awareness to deeply listening and learning.

My friend Raphael, a Monero Ngarigo person, speaks powerfully and eloquently about country and the need for all peoples living in so-called Australia and on Indigenous land all over the world to cultivate this humility, connection, and acknowledgement:

> I will often see an acknowledgement of country used in so-called Australia at formal events by corporations or the local city councils. They are done to show awareness and respect for traditional owners, their heritage and their connection to the land since time immemorial. They are done to acknowledge the impacts of colonisation.
>
> The act of acknowledgement or welcome to country originates from traditional protocols. Before invader-colonisers stripped apart and fenced off traditional borders, created state borders,

*and forcibly removed people from their lands, it was against tradi-
tional protocols to cross into another country without first getting direct permission and blessing from that country's caretakers. Of course,
this is a way of ensuring land management and resources are cared for
correctly, but there are also spiritual consequences for going in, passing
through, or taking from another country without permission, and that's
where people who work with spirits and witchcraft need to be aware.*

 *In the colonised way of living, most people are consistently crossing
traditional borders. It is difficult and near impossible to get permission.
That's why acknowledgement of country was created. It is still a way of
showing respect to the country's traditional owners when a welcome to
country is impossible.*

 *Traditionally, in the way I have been taught by my elders, a wel-
come to country ceremony was and is a way to protect you spiritually.
Entering another country without permission could make you sick
or you could carry home unwanted or malignant spirits. Smoke from
burning eucalyptus and other medicinal plants is an ancient practice
still commonly observed in modern-day welcome to country ceremonies. It has varying meanings and significance depending on where and
who the nations are. Every nation may have different beliefs. In my
learning one of the reasons for being smoked is so the person being wel-
comed smells like the land they are entering; that way, the spirits and
beings of that land will recognise them, and they will not be harmed
while travelling through that country. There are many other ancient
methods and ceremonies across all the nations in so-called Australia
that are practised to achieve the same result.*

 *I encourage witches and spirit workers to think about the deeper
spiritual impacts of colonisation. Consider the ancient lore and protocol
that have been practised on and with the land and its beings for tens of
thousands of years. Consider the ancient spirits and ancestors and how
they are godlike in most Aboriginal spiritual lore.*

 *Consider how including acknowledgement of country in your
spiritual practice and doing so with complete sincerity, commitment, authentic intention, and respect will build a foundation for
decolonising your witchcraft—how it can open you up to a profound
connection with the land on which you live, make love, and create art
and sorcery...*

For this reason I acknowledge country every day. I acknowledge country in the morning when I awake. I acknowledge country at the beginning of each podcast, class, or course I teach and at the beginning of readings and mentorship or magical consultation sessions. It is important to recognise where we are, whose land we are on, the power inherent in that, the systems that complicate and compromise that, and the Great Mysteries who are the very essence of country.

I grew up hearing about acknowledging country, but it wasn't until I was out of my teen years that I truly began to understand. In Turtle Island—one of the Indigenous names for the continent called North America—I've heard it called a land acknowledgement. I am unsure of the protocols relevant for different First Nations in Turtle Island regarding this, but I do know that powerfully acknowledging Indigenous sovereignty, the spirits and ancestors of the land, and the impacts of colonisation are important.

Throughout this book you will come across names of Aboriginal and First Nations communities, tribes, and nations. I encourage you to research these peoples and lands with the same kind of time you might spend researching a country you might want to visit or a city or town you are moving to. You will also see me use the term *so-called* at times in front of colonially named cities or countries or reductive realities. I do this to undermine the colonial names of places and remind us of the reality of continued colonial occupation and systems of domination, coercion, and control. I also have made it a personal discipline to use more traditional names for the regions related to cities. You will see this in the place-names of Meanjin (so-called Brisbane), Warrang/Eora (so-called Sydney), and Naarm (so-called Melbourne). I aspire to stand and act in solidarity with Indigenous communities as best as I can. I aspire to learn what there is to learn and understand and dedicate myself to listening to elders, country, community, and law. I acknowledge that all of the above I have learnt from listening to and acknowledging Indigenous elders, country, community, and law.

I acknowledge the Gadigal and the Bidjigal peoples as the true and traditional owners and custodians of the country in which I write this book and currently reside. With the deepest respect, I acknowledge their elders past and present.

I acknowledge the massacres and genocide that have happened and still happen. I acknowledge the impacts of colonisation, imperialism, invasion, and occupation on country, sacred land, and sovereign peoples. We acknowledge and honour the power, determination, art, science, ceremony, song, government, kinship, and activism of First Nations elders and communities. We acknowledge and celebrate the strength, survival, and thriving of First Nations peoples and their culture and ways.

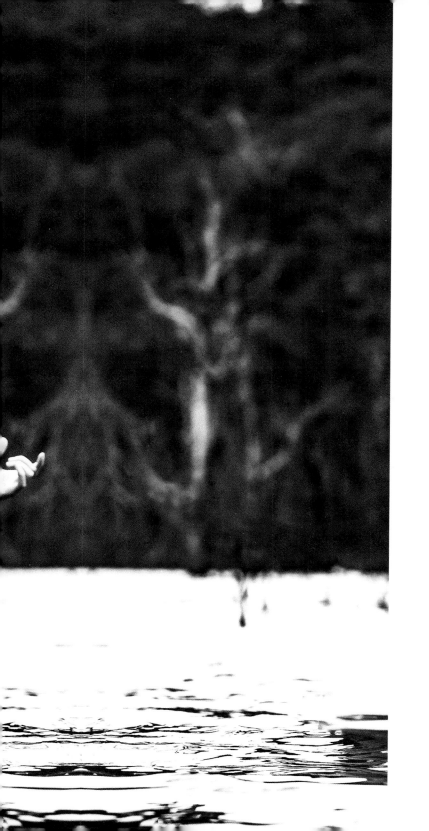

Foreword

It was a bright autumn day in New York City when a young witch walked up to me at a festival and politely introduced themself. A mutual friend had recommended we connect when this witch was in the city, saying they were immensely talented in magic. As this witch was traveling from Australia, I wouldn't get many chances to meet them again. This witch was unassuming, but their kindness was radiant. Because of the chaos of working at a festival, we weren't able to speak much that day, and I worried I'd missed the chance to get to know this talented witch. Fortunately, it was not long before the Fates drifted us back together. That witch was, as you have probably guessed, Fio Gede Parma. I am fortunate to call them both colleague and friend.

Fio attracts magically minded folk like a benevolent pied piper, connecting witches with one another wherever they go. The reclusive and the social, the grounded, the lost, and the comfortable wanderers are equally drawn to Fio's unique perspective on magic and witchcraft. I've been present when they've created impromptu rituals on dance floors and at underground parties, in city parks and the deepest woods. Their magic is a thoughtful collection. Rather than a shopping cart filled with shine, glitz, and the immediately available, Fio's magic is a carefully woven braid of tradition with strands selected after deep reflection and consideration. Fio is powerful, wise, and compassionate.

Also, they're fun.

Alongside Fio, I've experienced some of my most profound moments in magic, all the while laughing and having a delightfully good time. Fio helps people find their magic and connect with themselves as powerful beings capable of magic while also encouraging them not to take themselves too seriously. They see you for where you are in your journey as well as seeing where you could be. They lead with compassion and a deep love for others. Fio's magic is that of the present and the future, but it is also one deeply informed by the past. Their magic acknowledges and learns from legacy but doesn't cling to it.

Take your time with Fio's work. Their path and teachings are not things to simply blow through and put back on the shelf. The concepts they offer may seem strange or unfamiliar at first, but given time they will likely reveal themselves as deeply familiar. *The Witch Belongs to the World* isn't just another practical tool-book but a door to a new way of knowing magic. Theirs is the kind of magic that draws heavily on place and history, embracing both a space's beautiful and painful parts. But there is also a gentle quality to Fio's work, a kindness to it, a compassion that floats off the pages and hugs your heart. Fio is the kind of teacher we need for the next generation of witches to flourish.

Let Fio's magic unfold before you. Don't try to stick it in a box or put too much of a label on it. Like a dream, reflect in wonder but don't hold too tightly. Most of all, enjoy.

~Courtney Weber
JUNE 2022

Introduction

I want to think again of dangerous and noble things.
I want to be light and frolicsome.
I want to be improbable beautiful and afraid of nothing,
as though I had wings.

—Mary Oliver, *Owls and Other Fantasies*

The witch belongs to the world.

This book is a spell, a conversation, a conspiracy, a living talisman of power offered to the worlds. It is a spell of becoming that may change you . . . if you risk it.

This is also a book about witches. I have written other books about witchcraft and about the practice of witchcraft, but this—this is about us: about witches. Witches belong to the world.

I have been writing about and teaching magical technique, shamanistic spirit work, ecstatic ritual, and witchcraft theology and cosmology since 2006. In some ways, this writing and teaching—and ever remaining a student—is how I have been grown, refined, honed. These threads form the warp and weft of my work, inspiring how I show up to my vocation. But this—this is a book about witches. About being the witch, being forged as a witch. This is a love song about the vast leviathan body of Witches and how we belong to this world.

To get it out of the way, I define witchcraft as unsanctioned, anti-empire, transgressive, oracular, ecstatic, sorcerous spirit work—a mouthful for sure, as are witches. Witches stand in direct opposition to the forces of domination, coercion, and control, and we are the enemies of empire. This is how I understand it to be. Any other way could not make sense to me. Our magic won't work for empire. If it is commandeered, appropriated, or funneled in this direction, surely the tools will turn against us—the power will twist and the spirits will desert us.

Empires rise and fall and by their nature are egotistical, fragile, arrogant, self-referential, and prone to lashing out to cement themselves. Empires desire to conquer and assimilate land, culture, the more-than-human—so-called resources. Empire seeks to subdue challengers and questioners while it senselessly rapes and destroys all that serves and sustains the web of life. Empire stands against life. It also stands against death. The lovers that are life and death are worshipped by witches.

Those who are accused of being witches are often village healers, oracular seers, knowing wise ones, clever cunning-people, night-flying women, tribal elders, teachers and holders of ancient lore and ceremony, mediums, and whores who conduct wild, unadulterated life force and vitality. They do so in order to bind and blast, heal and soothe, and make way for right relationship once more. They willfully invoke justice because no one else seems to be doing it. They act as spirits, who act as fates. Ultimately witches are often if not always healers or involved in larger, deeper healing processes. Healing goes far deeper than we have been taught in our schools, universities, families, and societies.

Witches belong to the world. Etymologically the roots of the word *world* position this concept in terms of the age of man, an epoch, an aeon. The quantity of the known world, this place, this time; not some other place, not some other time, definitely not the otherworld. Witches belong to the world, and we are emissaries to and of the otherworld. To the otherworld we travel and with the mysteries of the otherworld we return. Born to both, witches are a blessing and a bane to the human societies who have feared and revered us.

We are part of the fate and destiny of humankind. We have always been here. Stories and legends about us are as old as written records and oral traditions. We are older than revivalist traditions bearing our names, we are older than initiatory lineages and orders of witchery, we are older than the persecutions, the pyramids, the cave paintings, the stone axes . . . but who and what were we before empire? What have we become? Who are we becoming?

Witches are a natural happening, a provocative disruption and interruption of human society by the uncanny, the otherworldly, the fated and fey, the titanic, and that which is forgotten, turned aside, denigrated, and suppressed. Witches are people of the Hag, of the Grandmother, of the much-maligned dark and all-consuming force who, to the witch, is our primordial source. She is the great cauldron in which we are broken down, brewed, and rebirthed: the hole within the stone.

We are eerily beautiful in our many forms, skins, and faces. We ensorcel desire and unfathomable bliss, just as we might also be the spirits that bring illness, blast the fields, and dismantle the apparent order of the town, the city, the empire. We are legion, yes. We are painted and drawn naked by men who desire their own origins and yet fight their very natures, who yearn for a kind of mastery that is seen between the horns of the Great Goat. We are etched and drawn bestial and sensuous, grotesque and always changing shape; orgiastic, dissolving our edges and letting go of the narcissism of needing to know a reified self.

Witches are primordially tearing at the fabric of the expected, of the sanctioned, to reveal the emotional reality of being alive, of dancing with mortality, death, disease, discomfort. On one hand the witch will turn the babe in the womb and bring forth the herbs that will bring down the fever and restore strength and vitality. We will abort the foetus, banish the spirit, brandish our rage at the gods, and with the ancient allyship of the Old Ones call forth the works of justice, spinning stories out of the shining threads of truth. Witches, after all, bow only to truth-seeking Justice, with Love and Wisdom as our guides.

This is a book that my foremothers and forefathers urged me to write, that my familiars and fetch-mate are deeply desirous of. It is written for and forged by my deep marriage to the witch gods I know and trust. This book has endured many failed attempts and complex emotions. It has lingered tauntingly, teasingly, at the edges of my awareness for five years, daring me closer. I have been frightened of this book, in terror of what it might mean to let it out of me . . . to let this one through this one. I have wanted to write this book for my students, for my beloved initiates and initiators, for my kin, for my parents, for my spirits and gods, but until I wanted to write this book for myself, it would not come. I too want a sacred and potent reminder, and it seems it needs to come through this head, this heart, these hands.

I have been obsessed with the craft since I awoke to it in early adolescence as an eleven-year-old, and then as a twelve-year-old, and then as a thirteen- and fourteen-year-old. Each age, each year, marked a new entry point. At eleven I knew myself to be witch; at twelve I dedicated myself to the craft with a ritual from a book; at thirteen I was brought into a coven of teenage witches. At fourteen I knew fully that this is where I have come from, this is who I am, and this is where I am going. And so each year I stepped into the labyrinth of initiation more deeply. Each year the fire increased in potency and feeling. Each year the braided road of wyrd compelled me ever inward, deeper into the crooked road of art.

The spirits came, the ancestors instructed me, the gods of the witches initiated me, and in the ensuing years covens were formed, traditions renewed, books written. I stepped into the role of teacher and mentor and discovered myself reflected in the faces of other craft traditions. Seeking initiation, finding myself and much more, and scenting the mysterious source of things in the thicket. I found myself dancing under the rose and yet tethered by sacred obligation, promise, oath, and word to the tension of having one foot in the outer world of being seen and one foot in that other world that largely goes unseen. This is part of the reason I have had such trouble—over several years—writing these sentences, forming these paragraphs, and committing to this work.

Along the way, what began as a hungry need to know myself and gain insight into hidden things gradually revealed itself to be a profound commitment to neither represent nor promote the craft but to ensure that the craft is ennobled and honoured in the face of sanitisation, fragmentation, and decontextualisation. Yes, to safeguard and pass lore, mythos, sacred teaching, and rite, but also to aid those wandering in the woods and deserts to drink of the well of memory and restore awareness to the mystery at hand and at heart. That mystery is that we belong to the world. Witches are the flesh, fruit, and flower of an ancient and mighty tree. That witch tree on that sabbat mountain on that misted island in that raging sea . . . you might know the way through the gates of night and day.

Perhaps this book will only mean something to witches and witch-type folk, and that is who I write it for. Much here will likely not ignite the awareness or activate the senses of those who do not have the eyes to see or hearts to intimate. However, in reading this book you might remember; you might find a missing piece; you might begin to understand a beloved one, a family member, a friend, or yourself and the world.

There are histories at play that impact us this moment, and they are mythic in legacy and substance. They are lore and story and cannot be encased in facts or articles or belief systems. They are the guts and spit of witches, the blood of ancient gods, the fire of fallen angels, the song of the good folk, and the provenance of the dead, those who have gone on before us, leaving a world that they had inherited and impacted. It has been said that witchcraft is the reprieve of the oppressed and marginalised, that much of our magic is the sorcery of the impoverished and enslaved. Some say we gather in the company of the crossroads—the college of the crossroads, as Raven Grimassi of the mighty dead put it—and that we all blend and merge in the mystery of the ecstatic sabbat. Class and the impacts of social stratification via imperialism and patriarchy are very real. Witchcraft acknowledges this and offers rites and states of consciousness that allow us to experience the truth beneath the deceit and the corruption of these horrific systems. Witchery is also one of the major tools in the fight against empire and its many extensions.

Many of us are familiar with the origins of the Roman Catholic Church. Some of us may have discovered that what began as a Palestinian Jewish messianic revolution against the occupation of Rome was somehow commandeered into a transcendentalist gentile-oriented religion via St. Paul. What was simply the custom—the ways of the people and the region, the ethnic and indigenous cultures of many—has since been cast as paganism or idolatry. Witchcraft has been cast by some scholars as the fever dream of the church and its societies despite the early church denying its existence, but it must be remembered that in pre-Christian societies those who we now call witches—an English designation—have existed and sometimes been feared and persecuted.

Witchcraft lives between and through heathen customs, pagan folk-ways, and Christian and Hellenistic cosmologies and philosophies. And then as witchcraft travels she absorbs, grows through, and evolves with whatever she encounters. She's often a weed wherever she is found out and treated as such. Witchcraft drinks in power from runic alphabets, faerie stories, old legends and superstitions, and impactful religious texts and grimoires. In the craft I know and love, there does exist Christian iconography and symbolism by virtue of history, cunning, strategy, and cultural collision. You will notice that within this book I do not consider these icons or tools of the oppressors as some name them; I consider this to be cultural continuity, symbols holding much power, and at times I even work sorcerously to bend and twist and reclaim life force and mysteries entrapped in certain elitist and constraining understandings of Christian ritual and language. The witch may walk backwards around a church, take the host and feed it to a toad or dog, steal fire in the votive candle, or stand upon the tool of torture—the crucifix—and spit upon the face of empire. It is not Christ nor Mary nor the saints I deny; it is empire in all its ways. I invite you to notice any discomfort that arises through the workings of this book and the various braids of mysticism and magic that are entwined here. You don't need to be on the same page as me, so to speak, but there is much to be perceived and felt below the surface of what we might think is happening.

Witches know the taste of holy blood, and we will defend our beloveds, the marginalised, and the oppressed with everything we have in our treasure trove of tools and magics. We are the tearing winds of Lilith; we are the cunning mind of Medea and the sorcerous skill of Morgan le Fay. We are the far-seeing and deep-knowing acolytes of Hekate; the lamps of Lucifer within the halls of the mighty; the scimitars of Kali; the gnashing teeth of Baba Yaga; the shapeshifting prowess of Cerridwen, who pursues the fleeing Gwion Bach. We are that which unties the knot and the hands that bind. Our knives glimmer with devil's fire and our cups overflow with the blood of the master who has been cut down in the first harvest of grain and vine. Our laws are the laws of moon and mountain, of key and crossroads, of silence and sorcery, of tide and heartbeat, of the deepest and most abiding cradle of responsibility—that which we do, we must embrace.

A witch seeks consequence, takes action, seeds vision, gives voice to the unpronounceable, and reckons with that which would seek to debilitate the inborn power of a being who is willing to risk—who with courage and honour stands in solidarity with those upon whose necks the heel of empire stands. By sword and stang, by drum and scissors, by herb and thread, we come.

This book is offered as a spell of becoming. These pages are laced with the sorcery of my life—that which I have utterly dedicated myself to and sacrificed/offered my awareness with. It is guided and supported by the Great Ones I am wed to, the spirits and powers I am in covenant with.

The spell that we are enacting is the living spell of you and your intimacy with the life force and the mystery. If you are willing and take the risk, it will initiate you into the craft outside of time and space and yet anchored within your breath, body, beat, and blood. On this crooked road you will remember and listen to silence in the darkness, and in that cauldron remember primordial you—how there is no difference between body and spirit. We are emergent, embedded, arising, collapsing, changing beings in all worlds at all times. You will find that it takes that leap, that fall—that breaking apart of what is considered to be certain—to introduce the queer, cunning current of witchery that is usually erotic and deeply rearranging. The Old Ones of Fate and Being, and the Devil and the Lady, your ancestors and spirits, will gather and make the circle of art that holds you in this initiation. You will need to dance with your demons, make pacts with your spirits and gods, and sing yourself back to life through letting yourself be sung and danced through the eye of the needle by all that you have called and all that calls you to this work.

My wish and advice to you is that you read this book from cover to cover and that you cast this spell with every step. Each step is a process—an exercise, a spell, a working, a meditation—that forms the greater magic of this spell of becoming: the witch belongs to the world. The steps are marked in large white numbers—1, 2, 3 . . . I also invite you to spend time between each chapter reading the poetry and scrying into the photography by my talented beloved Luke Brohman. These poems are offerings and provocations from my own deep well and soul-story, and I hope they provide opportunity for reflection and your own artistry, synchronicity, and inspiration. After you have engaged the book in this way, you are most welcome to dance with it in strange backwards-forwards-inwards-outwards ways.

This book is meant to invite and provoke: it is a dare to deepen, to exist more fiercely, more audaciously, more sensuously as a child of earth and starry heaven. If you should choose to take this holy risk, I hope you can sense and perceive my attention, love, and care in these words, prose, and poetry. Much is said, much is not said, but my whole self—as much as I can knowingly conjure—is here, along with my spirits and your spirits, as you read and deepen into your own holy craft. May the spirit of the witch meet you as you, and may the power of this living spell offer you many blessings, insights, and fortunes.

And so we begin where we all must begin: in silence and darkness.

Chapter One

Silence in the Darkness

Silence is the ultimate and final initiation. The
Gods are silent. Everything comes out of silence.
The true bliss of experience is without words.

—Lois Bourne, told to her by a witch she
called Margo, *Dancing with Witches*

Silence is a complicated feast of perils in the world today. It is a charged
concept and word, and rightly so. For too long, victims and survivors of all
kinds of oppression, subjugation, and marginalisation have been silenced,
taught to keep silent, and not speak, and those who might aid us are often
complicit in this silence. In the magical lore amassed in Europe and then
passed through colonisation and publication—books and texts have been
at the seat of magical revivals and pursuits for centuries—we come across a
deceivingly simple challenge: keep silent. Be silent.

Have you ever kept silence, observed the world silently, fallen into a silence? Not just for a minute or an hour but for a day or several days and
nights or a week or a month? As you read these words, there are people
who are keeping this deep silence intentionally in this very moment. For

many this silence is a practice, a profound entryway into deep and intimate knowledge of the phenomenon of self, of being and non-being. For others silence is enforced. For many in the world, silence is a cage, a trap, a curse. Some are not listened to even if they speak or shout or yell or cry. Silence is tricky; it is not one-sided or two-sided, and really it takes no sides at all. So I must make the distinction between the silence that is placed over another by something or someone with the intention to keep the truth from being known and the silence that is autochthonous, innate, coeval with the beginnings of being or the reflections of that being. I intend this silence in the darkness—this very chapter—to begin the spell we are casting through this book: this spell of becoming.

Almost all creation stories begin with silence and darkness—with nothing, a void, wordlessness—until there is a sound or until there is a quickening that produces fire or light. And then things change; things come into being, but before that there is silence in the darkness. As witches we know that in silence is brewed wisdom and through wisdom do we come to touch the mysteries and be initiated by those mysteries, joining with the ancient wise ones and becoming powerful. For witches, wisdom and power are partners, and they must temper each other. And we will come to explore how—through this spell of becoming—love is the mystery that binds and births them.

It is true that at an initiation into the craft there is silence. In one way or another, words are stripped or the perfect words are passed or words and names fall away and dissolve and leave us with primal sounds and primordial reality. When I think of the phrase "silence in the darkness," I visualise a cauldron, an ancient cooking pot, and immediately think of witches. As witches we learn to leap forth from the cauldron, we learn to ride the rim of the cauldron, we step into the cauldron, and we tend to the cauldron. I also visualise a cave . . . a cauldron in a cave tended to by the ancient Hag, the great initiator. From her we can understand deep silence and how we may even speak words with cunning, art, and truthfulness and retain primal silence. So what is the meaning of silence? Is it defined by not speaking or not saying something in words? What about writing? If you simply read and spoke aloud in your mind, would this be a form of silence? Does silence mean stillness? Is stillness a kind of silence?

1

To open to this spell, to participate in the magic of belonging to this world, I invite you to dedicate one full day—one round of twenty-four hours—to silence. To wordlessness. You may need to make certain arrangements for your circumstances and of course wait until a day when you will not be working or taking care of children or anyone else. A twenty-four-hour period in which you can largely be with yourself or around people who understand and respect your silence and wordlessness.

As part of this silence, you are invited to not engage with screens and potentially distracting devices of any kind. If you need it, you are welcome to journal or write during this, but not to read.

If you are someone who already cannot speak or does not speak, you may experiment with other kinds of alterations to daily functioning. If you are someone who hears but does not speak, you might want to put in noise-cancelling earbuds in order to experience silence in a more real way for you. Be safe.

Welcome the silence. Be within the silence. Dedicate this to yourself, to your own deepening, to your own power and sovereignty. Choose this silence as an agent of your own fate. Revel in that choice.

So what was it like to intentionally choose to be silent for one whole day? To keep silence as a practice, as a dedication of will and surrender? Do you feel you could keep going easily or was this one of the most difficult and horrible things you have ever brought yourself to do?

I know people who are silent most of the time, who choose silence as a special day in their week or month. I know people who prefer it. Then there are those of us—and I include myself in this—whose lives are filled with words, with speaking, with needing to be "on" and articulate with language and oration. Perhaps we don't prefer it—I don't know if I do?—but it's part of who we are and how our lives and professions function.

Some of us work and weave with words. I offer the provocation that the exercise and dedication above can help deepen our sensuous and somatic understanding of language and the words that we choose to wield. I do not see words or speaking in opposition to silence. I would suggest that from silence rises sound; from wordlessness, words. From words entire worlds come into being.

Three worlds. Seven worlds. Nine worlds. Infinite worlds. Entire worlds come into being. And apparently a world is an age, a measurement in comparison to another measurement. Measurements upon measurements of the infinite unfolding. Some say the world will end. Those same someones seem to suggest that this world, or a new world, will begin again. And over and over and around and around we go. Spiralling, likely.

In the craft traditions I work within—and live, breathe, serve, and celebrate—there are stories that speak of how we understand cosmogenesis, how we perceive existence to be, and most of them start in the silence, in darkness. Perhaps we might use the term *chaos* or *void* or *pregnant, swollen, dark abyss* . . . we might say *in the womb of night* or *deep in the well of forever* . . . there are stories that speak of goddesses, winds, and serpents; eggs and doves; God herself and mirrors; Grandmother Weaver and webs; stories that might sound something like this:

> *First, nothing. No one. Void. A void. A silent void. A void pregnant with itself. A void we might call chaos, a yawning and yearning abyss. Out of the chaos, with the chaos, darkness.*
>
> *The darkness was awake, alive, and aware of chaos. The darkness moved like a serpent within and around and through chaos. Chaos began to shake, to rumble . . . the darkness gleamed from within, a great leviathan luminous black body of all that might be and nothing at all . . . the chaos began to quake. The serpent who is darkness laughed awake stars from*

within the trembling void, the roaring chasm. Out of the darkness—from within chaos—came the light.

And the light was the radiance of the darkness. Darkness, the mother of light; light, the lover of darkness. The light had heard their mother laugh with pleasure, and desire was born in the listening. Out of chaos, with chaos, darkness. From within the darkness, laughter and pleasure. Through laughter and pleasure, the waking of stars; from darkness comes the light. In light, desire.

And this desire makes the worlds and breaks them apart. It is through desire that all things become; that beauty is beheld; that the infinite may feel, sense, perceive, know, and express. This endless desire is the source of all mystery, and the mystery is held in the darkness.

2

YOU MIGHT CHOOSE to read the above creation story to yourself. Whisper it to yourself. Or perhaps a friend or beloved might speak it to you aloud while you close your eyes and drift into a dreamlike state as you count your breath like sheep and listen to the telling. Perhaps you will write it down into a special book or turn it into a song. You might play an instrument and write music with it or paint or draw how this story makes you feel. Perhaps you need to write the story down in a different way. Consider *nothing*, *void*, *chaos*, *darkness*, *light*, and *desire*. Consider the infinite expressing infinitely . . .

Names and Naming

Then there are names. Secret names. The secret names of gods or the secret name written in the heart, your secret name. In various cultures the world over, in different times and places, knowing a name was and is considered an important piece of magic. There are certain spirits and beings who would prefer that humans did not know their names. They might even fool us into thinking the "name" they give is indeed their true name, and this might be the downfall of us later in the story. To know the true name of something, to be able to then speak that name, might mean that we could invoke that very thing, get its attention, or even by some strange means tie ourselves to it. Names open us, names define us, and speaking names changes us.

When we are born into earth, when we take that breath—and often before, perhaps even before conception—there are parents or families or communities who consider the naming of this new child, this most recent of the lineage, the legacy before us. Many human cultures have a variety of ways to name a child: a place, a story, a rite. Sometimes we hunt for names, call for them to be revealed to us. I want to tell you the story of how I was named, to pass on the story I was told.

Likely at my father's behest, my parents divined or considered many names. They then named several candles, lit them all, and at the end those that were left alight—by some oracular power, by some divine sortilege— were the names given to me.

I often refer to this as my legal name, the name that is on my birth certificate, my certificate of descent, on bank cards, on passports. These are the names the nation-states of the world and their bureaucracies know me by. And yet, for a varity of reasons, the cultural customs and practices of my naming would cause most Western societies to become immediately disoriented. One of the things that distinguishes my name in its fullness from Western names is that there is no surname or family name. There is not one name that connects me to my father or mother in the way many European cultures ordain other than the naming itself. As well as this, there is a single letter, I, which essentially means this child has been assigned male, marked as a boy child, and this single letter is the first part of my name. Many people in banks and at borders have questioned this. There is no first, middle, last name. There is no Christian name, as some school exam papers and government documents have confronted me with. I was named in a truly heathen manner and in a Balinese Hindu manner as well, named by candles flickering in the dark. Silence in the darkness.

I invite you to consider that a name is a thing, a powerful signature that marks you as a being unto yourself. You belong here; you have a mark that is yours. This name might have been whispered to your parents or family in dreams or by spirits or demanded by both living elders or ancestors. It might be tradition or religion or culture (usually all three as one) that demands certain names. But what might be the name that those Ancient Ones who stand at the Well of the Unborn know you by? What was written down in the Book of Mystery that the stars read in silence?

My friend and elder Pandora, a Reclaiming and Feri priestess, says time and again that there are infinite doors to the infinite. Sometimes a name is sung out from the threshold, and it conjures the unfolding mystery of what I call the labyrinth of you into being, into coming forth, into being born . . .

3

IN SILENCE, SIT, lay, walk—nothing too outwardly active—and follow your breath.

Breath comes in and fills the lungs and breath leaves and diffuses into the air around us, mixing us together. Then breath comes in again, carrying spores, bacteria, viruses, chemicals, and smells and tastes of all kinds. And there are other phases inside the breath as well: the pauses after we have breathed in fully and the death breath, that tension or complete release or pause after we have exhaled and just before we inhale once more. Just like the moon, these four phases of breath comprise this essential cycle. They are like the dark moon, the waxing, the full, and the waning. Notice that—notice what thinking about the phases of the moon does to you. Follow your breath.

If thoughts intrude, if you notice yourself building story or following narrative or going into a deeper trance or state of enchantment, just come back to the cycle of breath and fully immerse in it. Focus. Be focused upon.

Take time, stretch into time; imagine you know how to dissolve a little at the edges and diffuse into all that permeates you, all that exists within and throughout. Send out praise and love and gratitude to the sustaining and enriching powers and elements. You might name them silently or you might just feel and know and sigh them inwardly.

Feel into the names, the keys, the signatures that everything bears, that each being, spirit, mystery wears. Hold the idea that each thing—every person, myriad spirits and beings—has a name, several names. Maybe even a true name. Follow the breath. Notice.

Then let it go. Let the names go. They will be there regardless. What about underneath the names? Is there a namer? Is there a creator? Is there a creation? Or what about a singer—a singer, a sound, a song? It doesn't really matter whether we are grasping or being grasped or that thing which is experiencing either, whether we are naming or being named, does it? I dare you to release cause and release effect. What about something else? What about leaving it weird . . . wyrd. That all things ever-become, never begin, and never end, not really. Endless are the forms and realities and mysteries, and so nameless are the names. Ask your breath to help ground you. Here and now.

In silence it is thought there are no words. But perhaps silence is the very cauldron that brews the elixir of words, that grants initiation into the knowledge of how to wield words powerfully, wisely. Some words are also names. Names grant insight, unlock certain doors. In certain traditions of witchcraft, names are highly cherished, deeply cared for, honoured and passed in code, in sign—passed in silence. I don't mean that there is no sound nor speaking; I mean that the names witches know are the children of silence. Witches are often very at home with mystery, with a kind of knowing and intimacy that creates discomfort in those who wish to grasp finite meaning, to understand precisely facts and figures that make up this or that. And a witch might sing or speak a word, a name, in order to—for a moment suspended out of time, out of space—re-create, rearrange the worlds.

What and Who Is This Darkness?

I wish to pluck a verse from Genesis.

In the Beginning, there was the Word. And the Word was with God, and God was the Word . . . A lot of people might assume that this is how the Bible begins. But the Book of Genesis begins in this way:

In the beginning God created the heavens and the earth.

2. *Now the earth was formless and empty, darkness was over the surface of the deep, and the Spirit of God was hovering over the waters.*

3. *And God said, "Let there be light," and there was light.*

4. *God saw that the light was good, and he separated the light from the darkness.*

5. *God called the light "day," and the darkness he called "night." And there was evening, and there was morning—the first day.*

6. *And God said, "Let there be a vault between the waters to separate water from water."*

7. *So God made the vault and separated the water under the vault from the water above it. And it was so.*

At first glance there seems to be a distinction between the sensuous, poetic unfolding of the witch's cosmology and this faintly imperialistic ordering of the phases of creation. Of course we are reading a text that has been translated and mistranslated with multiple competing agendas and intentions. It is important to remember that there are hidden teachings and contextual understandings in these ancient Jewish teachings. There are entire libraries of books, podcasts, people, and films that can describe to you the origins and allusions of words, concepts, and text like the above, and that is not what I seek to do here.

Is it possible that the story of creation as expressed in Genesis, a text perhaps many of us would rather push away or do without—and fair enough—is simply another vantage point on the creation unfolding as witches poetically tell it? Victor Henry Anderson (1917–2001), who called himself the chief of his chapter of the Feri Faith on the West Coast of the so-called United States, was known to quip that reading the Bible through the eyes of the witch will reveal mysteries. I often think that he is speaking of this particular story.

For me, at least in these English translations in which much is lost, I imagine, there is a textural and tonal difference between the darksome, sensuous, and holy lust-filled cosmogenesis that I know as a witch. God is doing, separating, saying, pulling, and deciding this, that, and the other.

God said let there be light and there was light. This first miraculous event that tears open the darkness, emblazons creation, and is called good and therefore moved aside from darkness seems to indicate a bias.

In the Witch's Book—by which I mean *in a Witch's Knowing*—darkness is primordial, primary, underlying all things, within all things, and the mother of light, the birther of light, and the lover of light. You only need to read one particular witchcraft creation myth to understand how witches feel about darkness and light. The following can be found in *Aradia, or the Gospel of the Witches: A New Translation* by Mario and Dina Pazzaglini (Phoenix Publishing, 1998, page 144):

> Diana was the first created before all creation; in her were all things; out of herself, the first darkness, she divided herself; into darkness and light she was divided. Lucifer, her brother and son, herself and her other half, was the light.
>
> And when Diana saw that the light was so beautiful, the light which was her other half, her brother Lucifer, she yearned for it with exceeding great desire. Wishing to receive the light again into her darkness, to swallow it up in rapture, in delight, she trembled with desire. This desire was the Dawn.

It has been repeated over and over, but it is true that darkness and light in a way define each other via their contrasting. And yet darkness is the ground of being. Light may be the key to life as we know it, perhaps, but only because of darkness—only because of her limitless body of blackness.

Both the modern English words *black* and *dark* have surprising etymologies. The word *black* seems to arise from Proto-Germanic *blakaz*, meaning "burned." This may, in turn, come from a Proto-Indo-European word *bhleg,* meaning "to burn, gleam, shine, flash." Herein a mystery is already revealed: blackness intrinsically shines. And that brings me to the roots of the word *dark*. Dark ultimately seems to be connected to words that link to the notion of being hidden or concealed. So the second line of the beginning of Genesis hints at teachings passed on in witchcraft houses and traditions:

Now the earth was formless and empty, darkness was over the surface of the deep, and the Spirit of God was hovering over the waters.

Darkness was over the surface of the deep, and the Spirit of God was hovering over the waters. Waters reflect light, and it is true that God then creates, births, or becomes light, which therefore would reveal God from that darkness—hidden and concealed—and this is good in a sound, healthful, fateful way. If only the light and the darkness, socially and linguistically, could know each other today as they once did. Many societies abhor the dark; frightened of what is concealed and hidden, they deeply desire to abolish mystery and the unknown. There are those who wish to have all knowledge come into the light—to be categorised, deduced and reduced, and ultimately compartmentalised into finite pieces of data and fact. This is to betray the mystery of darkness, our original mother.

In her we gestate; from her we are born and have our being. So darkness and silence demand we bring our attention to the cauldron once more.

4

GO IN SILENCE and darkness to a place where you know you will not be disturbed—a place where you can concentrate and allow your senses to become keen and alive. This could be your own living room, bedroom, backyard, or perhaps a cemetery down the road, a beach, a hill, or a river bend.

When you are in this place, bring your attention to your breath and engage the fourfold breath from exercise three. Know that you are being breathed by the air and all that forms the air and lean into that. Perhaps you find yourself rocking back and forth or side to side, or perhaps you are beating out a light rhythm with your hands or fingers on your knees, thighs, sex, or belly. Let the breath support you. Let the rhythms emerge that will help you engage your senses and turn them on to the interconnected and seething systems of life moving and spinning. Sink through this; your breath has got you. You can relax, release, surrender into the primal darkness.

Cup your hands together as if you are holding water or keeping safe a small creature. This is the cauldron of mystery. Allow your awareness to become entirely enraptured with this cauldron, and let yourself fall into that cauldron, go right inside . . . relax, surrender, be silent, and open to the idea that this may transform you.

And eventually you will re-emerge. You will hear sounds, smell scents, feel slight or sudden movement; your senses are a latticework supporting you in keeping vigilant and present. They are connecting you to support and safety, and you are sure to be fine if you have ensured this is a place you will not be disturbed. So fall back into the cauldron—go right inside and dissolve. Return to the darkness . . .

One of the core distinctions often drawn between the early so-called Gard-nerian witches and so-called traditional witches—Robert Cochrane being a clear example—is the ritual cosmology, style, and location. Robert Co-chrane once wrote about a witch ritual that his group enacted in a cave. Apparently he was an enthusiastic caver. Doreen Valiente wrote a great deal about how rituals and workings she experienced with the Clan of Tubal Cain were among the most ecstatic, wild, primal, and beautiful of witch-craft works she had engaged in. The early Gardnerian witches seemed to favour working indoors and doing so skyclad—without clothing—whereas traditional witches are often said to favour ordinary clothes or perhaps robes and cloaks, as they used to be called the robed covens. Traditional witches are also said to favour working out of doors, immersed in the pow-ers of the land. Lois Bourne, an early high priestess of the Bricket Wood Coven, was also taken in by non-Gardnerian witches of another order, and her mentor in that craft is the origin of the quote that opens this chapter.

In modern revivalist craft there is often a great deal of speaking, written out and recited liturgy, or even sacred theatre and acting out certain dra-mas. In the traditional craft I have known and been brought into, there are words, yes—written and verbal poetry and incantation—but there is also a great deal of silence and wordlessness. Perhaps there are no words at all and the only sounds that are made are the atavistic voices and expressions that emerge when we set aside performance and convention and walk under the trees together to the clearing by the stream, under the moon, listening and waiting for the spirits to come.

Ultimately, all forms of witchcraft work with silence and words. We may also share more in common than entrenched sectarianism and witch wars would have us believe. It is true that there are also distinctions and diver-gences in lore, ceremony, technique, and mythos that may, in fact, deter-mine an overall contrast in ethos and mythopoetry. The differences are also beautiful and just as important as the samenesses. I draw inspiration from multiple places, and I have been trained in styles and traditions of craft that are Wiccan-impacted and others where that impact, if any, is minimal.

All begins in darkness, and so must we. All will be taken into darkness, and so into and through darkness we will go. Often at the beginning of a witch rite there will be the lighting of a single flame, whether that is within a cauldron or on a working altar or between the horns. The moments before, the moments during, and the moments after the lighting of that flame are deeply significant to a witch. We are enacting and remembering important cosmic truths. We are praising the witch gods, who reach to us through silence in the darkness and who are just as enamoured of light, colour, word, poetry, and art, which come out of the cauldron and back again.

Silence and Listening—
Colonial Realities

Many of us reading these words are living on stolen land. You might not think about it that way. You might have been raised in a society, nation-state, or family that is deeply anti-Indigenous or anti-Aboriginal or doesn't actively engage these realities. You might have been raised in a progressive and compassionate family that attends protests and seeks to wilfully dismantle white supremacy and connected systems of oppression and domination. You might be trying to raise your own children—or yourself—with an awareness of these atrocities, these continuing realities, to question and interrogate assumed colonialist authority and to centre Indigenous peoples and people of colour. You might belong to the Nations, tribes, clans that the land has been stolen from.

I live in so-called Australia, and this is where I have spent most of my life. I was born in Bali, I am Balinese, my father is Balinese, and yet when I was two years old, we all moved to the great southern—southern by northern hemisphere designation—continent that my mother had been born and raised within. There my sister was born in Yuggera, Jagera, and Turrbal country, and we lived in various towns and regions of the state now called Queensland, a truly ill-fitting name referring to a long-dead British queen, head of the British Empire—this being that same empire that sent colonisers to Gadigal and Bidjigal country in January 1788, effectively beginning the process of invasion and genocide.

I am about to understate something because there is no way for me as a non-Aboriginal person to justly or adequately express the horrors, losses, grief, and pain inflicted upon First Nations peoples. These are not fond memories for First Nations peoples and communities in Australia; in fact, many would rightfully name them as deeply traumatic. These are also not only things that happened in the past; colonisation hasn't ended. We live in it, immersed in its lies, manipulations, and deceit. We are all affected to lesser and greater extents by the arrogance and ignorance of "the colony." Aboriginal deaths in custody, police brutality, missing Indigenous women, the systemic and systematic stealing, rape, and abuse of First Nations children, and the objectifying and abstracting of country, of land, river, mountain, star, sea, forest, desert . . . The survival and strength of First Nations communities, cultures, languages, kinship systems, songs, ceremonies, arts, sciences, entire ways of being is testament to the dynamic complexity and profound depth of Indigenous ways of being. For further exploration, appreciation, and deepening, I refer you to the bibliography and the few books I have read and included as inspiring during the writing of this book that are specifically written by Indigenous folks. In the pages of those books you will find other important works cited. Follow the threads.

Why do I bring this up in a book about witchcraft and witches? Some would have you believe that this doesn't concern "us." There may be all kinds of metaphysical, ahistorical, and spiritual bypassing rationales people have concocted in order to support their case, but it is deeply important to face colonial violence and imperialist and white-supremacist oppression in the works of witchery. It is not just outside of us: it is inside as well, and decolonisation concerns both literally returning land and dismantling and destroying the colonial mindsets that manipulate people who might naturally be in solidarity with one another to fracture and fight and ultimately betray sacred trust and obligation.

So often in the lands I live in I hear Aboriginal and Torres Strait Islander activists, leaders, and community organisers speak about listening to the land, that the law/lore and the land are one. I have been told to stop, put aside my racing and incapacitating concerns, and just look, listen, sense, open, drop in, turn to that which is here. This necessarily means the ugly and the horrifying as well as the profoundly beautiful and wondrous.

Silence is required of those of us who are not of the Indigenous experience. These lands have been taken by force and deception and are still being occupied today, with little more than vague nods to a supposedly wrapped-up history. Much has been actively hidden and concealed, and in that way the modern English word *dark* may also apply, a darkening. And yet throughout my life I have noticed how darkness and blackness are denigrated, hated, and pushed away, and how light and whiteness are exalted and honoured as the default, the normative, the sacrosanct, the desirable. Let us consider again the stories that witches tell one another of how this has come to be, and then consider and study the wisdom teachings of First Nations communities and cultures throughout earth.

Some might argue that every group of humans has been the oppressed and the oppressor throughout history; I would say look closer, enquire more deeply, study, feel. There have been so many histories stolen and deceitfully warped for particular agendas and storytellings. There is also a definitive difference between tribal skirmishes, inevitable group conflict, and wholesale, systematic genocide and annexing of sovereign country. There has always been tribal distrust, and there have always been human patterns of welcoming, peace, and negotiation. The full-scale imperialist and invader-colonial actions of genocide, lying, displacement, enslavement, and denial is a continued and still-happening horror, and many people live in their own lands as prisoners, as outsiders, as social and political fugitives . . . strangers in estrangement. I know some of this myself as someone who feels at times exiled by "neo-colonialism" from Bali, the land of my birth, the island that my family is indigenous to.

If you are to continue to read these pages—indeed, if you are to call yourself witch—then these are among the most significant stories and truths to be engaged. These are the demons to dance with; this is the beginning of our journey.

What do you know of the land you live in? Yes, its traditional names *and* the names of the First People. Perhaps you live in Britain, the Netherlands, Germany—places you might say do not fit this story and yet are also the originators of these foul endeavours. So acknowledging land and country before we begin is not just words we say, even when we mean them earnestly and deeply; it is a continued practice of remembering, listening, paying attention, orienting, and opening to learn and heal. We have each suffered some amount of fragmentation, fracturing, and dispossession.

WHAT IF YOU took a day out of your schedule, your work week, your work month, and committed it to wordlessly walking through your town, city, countryside? Moving through and with the land, taken in by the land perhaps, and dedicating your senses and awareness, offering your awareness up, down, in, spiralling through and with. Pay attention. Take notice. Drink in and be drunk in. Remember those sensations and feelings, those deep knowings of the cauldron. This will serve you well as you wander, as you take this witch's walk.

Within the deep land's own self is the dark and dreaming heart of the Weaver. So I wish to share something of that Grandmother Weaver with you here.

Grandmother Weaver

In the Wildwood tradition of witchcraft, a tradition that initiated me and I helped to unwittingly midwife, we honour four great spirits. Grandmother Weaver is usually the first of the Sacred Four that we acknowledge and honour. In my experience there is no invocation or calling to the Weaver.

I am within her, I am of her. She is the Great Hag who will devour me, unravel me, and grind my bones once they have sunk to the bottom of the great ocean. For she is the Bone Mother in the cave under the sunless sea, and all bones will she bring to dust once more. This is the same dust that she then blows out into the darkness to seed the stars from whence they came originally. This ancient and ever-unfolding creation and destruction is that of the Weaver.

I remember the ritual in which I first knowingly beheld the Weaver. I was with the witches of the Coven of the Wildwood and largely we would meet out of doors, in public parks in the city, in so-called national parks, in bushland areas in the suburbs, but also in each other's homes. This particular ritual was held in the apartment I shared with my boyfriend at the time. We were squeezed in by the shelves and altars in the one-bedroom apartment; deep in trance, we each journeyed through the Wildwood, our namesake. I saw her then. First I noticed shining threads of a web stretched between the branches of a tree, and I understood that these were the strands of the web of wyrd. I then noticed an ageless shining woman sitting in that tree and laughing. I recall returning from trance to share our experiences to find several of us had witnessed a similar mystery. We soon came to call this being the Weaver or Grandmother as she would often appear as a crone or a hag.

Grandmother Weaver is the great body of all that has never begun and is never-ending. She is Fate herself, the wyrd, that which is continually becoming. To say she is a goddess would be missing the point in some ways. She is both a being and being itself and also not being and a non-being. At times Grandmother Weaver and the Star Goddess honoured in Feri tradition feel the same, and at other times, paradoxically so, I am able to hold multiple possibilities and realities simultaneously. Victor Anderson definitively argued that Feri witches are not monotheistic and that each star is the body of a god. This is an important skill as witch and spirit worker: to cultivate a state of apprehension and appreciation of those infinite doors to the infinite, as my friend Pandora puts it.

Grandmother Weaver is not just a mystery for Wildwood witches, though our particular poetry may inspire and move you. She is especially honoured by us and our mysteries and lore, and perhaps you already know this mystery. Perhaps your tradition or path resonates with a similar understanding.

Grandmother Weaver is the void of creation, the hag who haunts the lonely universe, and the maid in the well who is laughing stars awake. She is the fate of all who are becoming. She bears no name. In the appendices you will find more information on her.

6

In honour of this journey you may be deepening into—this spell of becoming—I invite you to contemplate this prayer.

Our Grandmother of infinite darkness
    birthing and devouring infinite light!
Hag of the winter and the Loathly Lady,
    Sovereign of All Being
Veiling and Unveiling, Illusion of the Veil and
    She who tears the very fabric of Herself
Unnamed and yet each thing into Eternity names You.
Boundless and yet ever Binding!
Maiden with the Starry Fire of Ecstasy
Weaver of Wyrd, your kiss is the risk
    of skin touching skin,
    soul knowing soul.
Reveal ourselves to ourselves!
Soundless voice singing a Name that
    cannot begin and cannot end.
Unknown, Grandmother Weaver.
Hag who is the Maid in the Well of Stars.
Bone Mother knitting our souls together
    with your knuckles
In the cave beneath the Sunless Sea.
Washer at the Ford, cleaning skin from soul . . .
Grandmother Weaver, weaving woven Wyrd,
    ever becoming . . .

Once more, go into a dark place in a dark time and spend time in silence. Meditate on the words above—the prayer—and notice what occurs to you, what resonates and emerges. Then, when you are feeling ready or at the risk of the possibility of being ready, whisper these words aloud as prayer and imagine everything hearing it. Through the mysteries of soil, the wild sabbats of bacteria and fungi, photons, electrons, sound, space, time . . . imagine and know that this prayer emanates out, in, as, and through all things—into that which lies beyond your comprehension, into the very wildness of things, into the dark, deep heart of the origin of origins, the primordial ocean of memory.

Mean the words, truly mean them. Desire the ever-becoming; yearn for *skin touching skin, soul knowing soul.* What might it be like to experience *She who tears the very fabric of Herself,* she who is *Boundless and yet ever Binding*? What would it be like to be dissolved into this vastness of eternity and this roaring of exquisite loneliness, the holy tension between longing and belonging, that profound and painful birthing into the realisation of being? These are the mysteries of Grandmother Weaver.

When I have read the writings of Robert Cochrane (the once magister of the Clan of Tubal Cain) about the Black Goddess behind the gods who is Fate and Truth, I understand this to be the Grandmother Weaver I know. When I read the cosmic poetry of God herself by her own stirring beholding her reflection in the curved, dark mirror of space, I know this to be the mystery of Weaver. There are countless Great Ones, ancient ones, mysterious ones who may indeed be the names, titles, or epiphanies of Grandmother in those lands and cultures.

Can you see her? Can you hear them? He's humming a tune you know. You are walking down a dark and lonely road, the moon in her phases and darkness courting you as a lantern in the night. The stars seem to be singing to one another and spelling out in the skies holy words of power that unlock great doors to other realms you are familiar with. That cloak witches are so known for—can you feel it heavy and whole around your shoulders and arms? When you sense down your arms and into your hands, are you walking with a staff, a stang, a blasting rod? Do you carry a basket, a pouch, a fan, scissors, knife, sword, snake? Are there dogs or other creatures with you? Does your shadow speak with you? Who and what surrounds you? For though this is a lonely road, it is absolutely peopled. There are spirits everywhere here. Are you willing to breathe in the mystery and power of the road rising to meet you now—the road winding down into your guts? There is a precious learning beginning and deepening . . . into the body, deeper, wilder, wiser than we know—we go.

Everything kisses everything else
or else slashes or stumbles
like this knife I hold, cling to, grasp, wield
like this knife I hold over the smoke
like this myrrh turning me inside out
like this drum pressed against my thighs
as I beat rhythms made of memories

Everything kisses everything else
or else breaks against the shores
of what might come, to become
like the god who comes
pressed against me, as I am
my thighs now—instead of drumming
liquored in the sweet cum
of the goat-horned bull-roaring god
He is the one I never ask to come
He is always coming

Everything kisses everything else
or else locks the door and swallows the key
lucky for me the art of turning swallowed keys
into gold was passed to me in my mother's womb.

I've never had to wish for future lives
I've never had to say to you *may your weapons
    turn against you*
I've never had to ordain anything
because the mountain you cleaved
to grants me everything you have become
so that I might be pared back
and remember Silence.

Chapter Two

The Breath of Life and
the Mystery of Body

Grandmother, Grandmother, grind our bones, sing
our songs. Light up the skies with our stars, guide us
home; we are your own. Grandfather, Grandfather,
breathe our birth, reap our death. Gate of Life, Giver
of Breath, Old God, Green Man, take our hands.

—A Wildwood chant to the Old Ones

At the most basic level, we do not come into this world fully until we breathe in. One could say the deal is not sealed until that moment. In newborn infants this may sound like a gasp as lungs previously filled with fluid now react to change in temperature, exposure to air, and lack of amniotic fluid. The baby breathes difficult breaths, their own labour, and there may be crying. A lot happens at once. As I understand it, before this the mysteries of the three souls are aligning for, with, and because of the moment of that first breath. Time works backwards in this way; a spiral of becoming. We might notice much works "backwards" in this way as we journey the landscapes of this book.

Before I continue, I want to make it exceptionally crystal clear, so no one can misunderstand me, that those with uteruses—cis women, trans men, and many non-binary and intersex folks—are the deciders of what happens within themselves. That is it. I don't have anything else to say on that topic.

In the darkness of the womb, within a fallopian tube, a serpent and egg meet and kiss and become each other, drawing upon ancient lineages and daring to forge new legacies. In many creation stories there are serpents and eggs. In the luminous darkness of the womb there is a dance between animal and god: god-animal and animal-god revealing themselves to each other. The red river of blood from which comes the fetch as ancestral blessing, connection, and power meets and marries with the star soul, the holy daimon, the god and spirit who is drawn in by this happening. Perhaps this daimon is inspiring and directing the eventuation of this very moment; witness to it and desirer of it. If the embryo survives through five or six weeks of pregnancy—although this is generally four weeks after conception—this clump of cells begins to produce an electrical pulsing that later on may form the heart.

What unfolds in the development from a single-celled zygote into a rapidly forming embryo and into a foetus and a human infant can be a powerful way of speaking about the coming together of the three souls, but it is also only at the drawing in of the first breath that it is complete. Then it has happened, this triple soul one. Once more I will underscore the point: whether or not an embryo develops into a foetus and then a human infant and is born is dependent on many factors, not least of which is the desire and circumstance of the person carrying this foetus.

Traditionally the expression and shape of the soul that is carried in and as the first breath is perceived to be the aura, which in Latin means "wind" and in ancient Greek "breath or air in motion." At the first breath of life, the new being who has emerged into earth, into the middleworld, now has a breath-body—albeit one deeply linked to the birthing parent—and a circumference to the centre, a boundary marker to the beating heart of the being. In this distinction and differentiation from their ground of being or parent—through this birth—perhaps the phenomenon of self begins to form. We don't know.

The animal that is human is a creature of three souls or three parts of soul. And this triple soul is known through the phenomenon we call body.

For centuries the body has been considered to be variously a sheath, a mortal coil, a machine or mechanism, or at best a temple housing the spirit. These dualistic and sometimes even flesh-hating and denigrating notions and concepts have evolved from an entire and complex history of ideology, philosophy, and indoctrination. One might say this has been an active dismemberment and fragmentation that in effect influences how we speak, how we think about and explore things, how we judge and discern what is considered to be real. This fragmenting and enculturated split between "spirit," "mind," and "body" directly and potently impacts how we perceive reality in general and the value we place on being, the intelligence of the senses, and instinct. This permeates all aspects of culture and society in the so-called West and manifests in the way we phrase and label levels and regions of reality.

Everything is body, and it is this radical notion that is clearly held to be a simple fact and truth in many cultures' creation myths, stories, and cosmogonies. Hesiod's depiction of how things came to be includes that there is chaos—which is as a roaring or fecund gaping or void—and then just there, just always, is Gaia, or Earth. It is not that there is spirit first and then matter as a breakaway or even manifestation of spirit. It is that what is termed "matter" is; it just is. One could also call it "spirit" if desired, but that does not change the quality or even cut away the matter. To some it may appear that we are naming different parts making up a whole, all implying one another, when we just are; reductive taxonomy is not going to helpfully map out a terrain that not only do we exist in, but as.

One of the most enlivening, inspiring, and transformative magical techniques I have ever been taught is how I might mindfully breathe with my three souls as body. I, we—this one—is what I call the covenant and contract, the kiss and the wonder that my fetch, daimon, and breath-soul exist as. It is not that these souls occupy or inhabit "the body" but just as

William Blake poetically expresses, "Man has no Body distinct from his Soul; for that called Body is a portion of Soul discerned by the five Senses, the chief inlets of Soul in this age."

You may desire definitions of these souls, of these parts.

The fetch is the animal-bestial-primal self that joins us to the ancestral red river. It emerges out of that river of blood at conception and surges, seethes, and shakes to coalesce as the potency for that phenomenon—or crossroads—we call body to know itself, ourselves. The fetch can be perceived to emanate out of the physiological or surface skin as the second skin, sometimes called the "etheric skin." It is this soul that gathers in the life force, the vitality, and instinctually knows how to concentrate, distribute, and sustain that vitality. A strong and vivid fetch makes a strong and vivid animal and certainly is required in the effective workings of sorcery and the art of spirit work.

Some people speak about the souls psychologically and call them "selves," which can be a useful lens for some. I think it is also very important to not get trapped in the notion that these are metaphors or concepts. Treat the souls as real. Treat yourself as real. Or rather do not conceptualise or symbolise yourself as if you are a ghost copy of something transcendent, away, and apart. This can often lead to disillusionment and self-denigration.

Sometimes it feels to me that saying "this is my body" can be an objectification of something that is ever relationally subjective. It goes back into this notion that there is an architect and arranger separated out from who we really are that wears something for a moment and casts it away. What if all things are simply changing from one thing into another all the time? No absolute origin, no final destination? In my experience, the fetch cannot say or understand "this is my body" or even conceptualise the idea of a distinction between itself and what we narrowly interpret the body to be. Sometimes I gesture over myself and say "this one"—a phrase I learnt from my friend Jamie Lantz—to hint at a deeper mystery, emergence, and convergence. If self (and therefore the awareness that initiates self) is, then perhaps it is a happening, an event unfolding. And self is the body that is the book—a poetic mnemonic we incant in Wildwood craft—a "book" that is read by the stars and the land, the dead and the living.

The breath-soul, which is sometimes abstractly referred to as Talker in some lines of Feri, is the same thing that some people call the aura. The aura, the shining one, develops as the animal that I am grows in the middleworld. As discussed, it was originally wrapped around the rest of me at my first breath in this world. The shining one is a kind of luminous cloak that helps the fetch begin to discern between the field-of-this-one (I) and the field-of-the-rest (other). This is the original polarity and most dynamic, most creative: I and thou, thou and me. And what happens when the other inhabits the I and the I inhabits the other?

The shining one carries a developing and lucid body of knowledge, reference, contrast, and comparison. We know left from right, up from down, this from that, and night from day because of the secret workings of the breath-soul. It is like the gleaming of a knife or arrow that delineates a point in between what only exists in the moment of observation and then dissolves. The shining one aids the sorcerer in the powers of clarity, discernment, intention, and the magic of willingness. While the fetch carries innate and multidimensional ancestral wisdom, the shining one offers the holy suffering and ecstasy of love—that perilous quest that is the knife to the cup—as we are able to contemplate difference and dissolution. The shining one conceives and relates with ideas of experience and reality—ways of tracking and navigating stimuli and relating—and those hidden potencies of consciousness aid us in our own self-awareness. The danger here is that certain tracks, trains, stories may be running in the background and can become their own ghosts or ghouls within the system, so to speak. These stories and complexes may start to run us if we are not doing the sensual and thorough work of alignment. If we are not mindful and caring to ourselves, we may become susceptible to an indoctrination of self rather than an organic being and becoming.

The daimon, the god soul, or the star soul is the quintessence of mystery behind the swelling of the red river and the artfulness of the shining one. The daimon is the deep well of power making it all possible, for we are and may act as spirits when we know this to be true. The daimon is the story weaver and the one from which emerges the mythic potential of who we are and may become; the daimon is the key to the keyhole opening doors of reality that we may engage and enact. If we open to that indwelling divinity—to that true self the daimon is—we can consciously remember all pieces of self and become one of the cunning and wise and hopefully, eventually, one of the mighty dead. The daimon brings the fire of the witches— that incandescent, raging, terrible wonder of the ecstasy of spirits and the bliss of the sabbat—into union and alignment with the red river's fetch and the shining breath-soul. When the three souls are as one, we may, as Cora Anderson so profoundly said, ask for anything and it may be.

And the challenge of the triple soul is not necessarily to be embodied or to ground here and now or even to become God . . . we are already all these things; there is no need to strive for any of it. We are present, always, as we are. The invitation, the deep dare of engaging the triple soul as we are, is to remember and enact our immediate potential and power. This is the unveiling, for unfortunately one of the strange paradoxes of this primordial coming forth and existing is that we somehow feel separate from something else. Existing is, at times, a crisis, and everything may be questioned. We might feel that it is in another room, another place, as if we are not in fact always in deep communion with that. Perhaps it is useful that we cannot always fully, presently, in all ways, know that we are this thing, this thatness, or else we would not chance the breaking apart. Only through the Promethean stealing of the essence of reality do we crack open the infinite to reveal more of ourselves and more of the depth of the ever-roaring void—more of what could be possible.

In the heart of the witch's mysteries is the heart made to break open: that primal and courageous act of risking intimacy, the great longing of things. Let us explore a primary working-blessing-alignment practice I pass on to everyone I work with.

7

THIS ALIGNMENT ARISES out of the work and mysticism of the Wild-wood tradition and specifically the Sophian branch of that tradition. Our veneration of and orientation to the three realms of land, sky, and sea is also at times anchored and distilled within the three cauldrons in the landscape of body—hips-pelvis, heart-ribcage, and head-skull. We also acknowledge that the great families of ancestry—blood, land, and craft, or inspiration—may be powerfully engaged with through the souls, realms, and cauldrons. The fetch with the ancestors of blood; the breath-soul with the ancestors of land; the god soul with the ancestors of the craft, or inspiration for non-witches. A tripartite understanding of cosmology is and has always been central to Wildwood witchcraft.

Originally I learnt the triple soul alignment through teachers and mentors within the Anderson Feri tradition and also within Reclaiming, but what I present here is distinct to the Wildwood tradition and via my public and private teaching has gone on to affect various threads in both traditions.

1. Breathe and be breathed wordlessly by the land. Acknowledge country and the depth of place-time-space-being. You may notice, as you bring mindfulness to your breathing, that your breathing deepens, relaxes, and lengthens.

2. If you feel the need for more grounding and centring, you may work with your vision, sensation, emotion, and imagination to send, grow, and anchor roots and tendrils within the land, not just down but also outward, spiralling and spiralling. In Wildwood practice we often send waves of blessings through the land rather than dump our shit into the earth in the hopes it will be transformed. There's a time and a place.

3. You might wish to sweep your attention up through your skull, where you may be perceiving and feeling branches or connections of some kind spiral up and out into the ether, into the atmosphere, through the biosphere of holy lover-teacher earth. Perhaps you open to the white-hot fire of the stars to cascade down as a great river of light, cleansing and invigorating your being. Become a channel that mediates this light into the earth and to the spirits of the land and the dead. Offer the light to them.

4. In this grounded-centred state—which after a while of practice may take one breath in and out—bring your attention to the cauldron of your hips, the cauldron of warming in Irish tradition. Know that it is holding the sea, the underworld. Feel into the red river of blood; acknowledge all your ancestors— not just one, two, or three of them, but the entire greater-than-the-sum-of-its-parts ancestral web you are woven from. Perhaps you remember, imagine,

or sense your genesis within the darkness of the womb when sperm and ovum met. Animal, fetch, primal soul. Breathe into the fetch, the double, knowing that the fetch instinctively will draw in vitality. As you exhale, send blessings and attention to the ancestors of blood. Do this several times.

5. Move your attention to the cauldron of your ribcage, the cauldron of motion or vocation in Irish tradition. Know that it is holding the land, the middleworld. In your lungs, in your heart—the land. Feel into the shining aura that is anchored within the breath, emanating from this cauldron, and notice the tone, quality, colour, or sound of your breath-soul right now without needing to judge or assess any of it. Perhaps you remember, imagine, or sense your very first breath upon birth into this middleworld, when the fullness of this soul was drawn in and cast a boundary and circumference around your own heart. Breathe into this middle soul, trusting that the intuitive expansion, contraction, and rippling of the aura's edge is what it needs to be. As you exhale, send blessings and attention to the ancestors of land. Do this several times.

6. Move your attention to the cauldron of your head, the cauldron of knowledge in Irish tradition. Know that this cauldron is holding the sky, the upperworld. In your brain and its labyrinthine mysteries are reverberating the powers of the sky, the stars. Feel into and yearn for communion with your holy daimon, your god soul, your star soul. Perhaps you remember, imagine, or sense the timelessness of many lifetimes and the deep guidance of your own holy self and the deep

mythopoeic weaving of you. Breathe into the intrinsic connections with your god soul, with the infinite, with mystery. As you exhale, send blessings and attention to the ancestors of the craft or inspiration—the mighty dead—who have helped braid these roads and ways. Do this several times.

7. After tending to each cauldron, opening to each realm, feeling into each soul, honouring each great family of ancestors, you may seal this by drawing a deep breath up through each cauldron and blowing it up to your god soul, who knows what to do with it. Surrender into active trust with your holy daimon. You may wish to trace the triquetra—the three-cornered knot—in front of you and seal it with words and song. You may simply feel things sliding-clicking-spiralling into place and meditate silently or wordlessly in this space. Ultimately this process is meant to vividly ground, centre, and orient us through and with ourselves and through our relationships with great powers, lineages, and realities.

In engaging the discipline of the alignment of the souls within the anchoring of cauldrons holding realms and realms forming cauldrons, we daily-nightly kiss and praise nature. Our own natures are honoured, and we may find ourselves tracing ancient arcs of time and lineage, spiralling into the labyrinthine mystery of self. If the breath of life signs the contract that is the body, then through the body do we experience the phenomenon of self.

8

EXQUISITE, LONELY, ROARING silently, wordless and thoughtless, unconscious; neither ignorant nor unknowing, but bornless and deathless.
And yet—a pressure builds, a power thrums, a storm of something brews;
the lightning flashes to reveal light, and a reflection is caught in the curved
dark mirror of space.

In yourself you behold your self, your twin. Here through the mirror,
holding the mirror, the mirror witnesses you, and there is a looking across
at each other, through each other, to the beating heart that is the fulcrum,
the centre, the kiss—a primal initiation of the mystery of self.

Imagine this into being with all your senses. Remember it. It is happening now regardless. Hold this imagining, sensation, experience. Surrender
into this until you can absolutely perceive and feel yourself and your divine
twin reaching towards each other through the mirror. Notice the tension
build between you. This tension will build and build and concentrate immense consciousness, feeling, and pleasure, until it cracks and explodes,
rippling out in waves of radiance, wonder, light, and sound. Thus all the
worlds come into being, thus the spirits.

And though it was you and you—this one and that one—before that beginning it was you and I and each one born from that sex and genesis. The initiatory gift of boundless desire knows no end nor possesses any aim except that of delving deeper through the emergence, swelling, breaking the banks of limitation, and erupting with a power that colours the infinite. Feel the paradox. Embrace it, sing, dance, express it. Offer it as a blessing to the earth, the stars, the many worlds and beings who people the secret cosmos.

All is body. Bodies birthing bodies eating bodies kissing bodies breaking bodies loving bodies healing bodies moving bodies opening bodies dancing bodies missing bodies joining bodies dying bodies surrendering bodies desiring bodies . . .

How could we have missed the remarkable simplicity? We are sold on theologies of transcendence "out there" beyond our senses and comprehension. We are taught that the gods are somehow distinctly apart from who we could be, even though we are of the same family. We are all spirits together of various histories, tones, qualities, regions, bodies of knowledge.

In the witch are all things transformed and distilled, only to be summoned forth into crystalline precision and power. We witness as we stir the cauldron and watch as bodies dissolve and mix and mingle within the brew. We gaze in wonder as new forms emerge, old forms dying, changing, transforming. We sing and name what we witness, see, sense, and know, and thus fuse our awareness with the process we participate within. The witch magic happens to us, through us, and emerges as the courageous and potent act of choosing something else, deviating from what seems to be. We are walking a crooked road, a road that possesses no certainty but all poetry, its pathways forged of star hearts and dark holes. Dragon roads, serpent paths, twisting and hissing as we ride them through the breaking of things and the breaking open of our own hearts as we are initiated by the rites of passage of being and becoming, of longing and belonging.

This first breath that we took, that we were given, that was assigned by us to us by virtue of ancestral crossroads, in land and place, by holy daimon anointed, is also every breath we are breathed by and that which we give back. This breath will be returned at that death of the known-surface body and the transformation that involves decomposition, rot, return, and rebirth. It is the body that implies birth and death. It is the breath that initiates this whole "being on earth" thing for us and the self who we might discover or meet as we follow that singing, shining thread of power through the constantly shifting and breaking things. Perhaps we will notice the patterns, the omens, the conversations that may be there, that we may be able to draw upon, sink into, or call up from within in order to learn the names and win the words. We have come to the point in the story now where a secret and special history must be delved into. That breath and body are initiators is clear. Body is the vault of living memory; deeper into the maze of witches we travel.

Here now is the revelation of the blood of witches, a great myth of our kind.

I want to know why your fire-eyes linger at
   the shaking shadows of my twisting feet
in the ground when they are lingering on
   the silent-still frenzy of your eyes of fire
I want to know why when you speak, to
   anyone at all, my rusted coat of jaded
   humanity shivers, opening to the
   deeper well of primal gift
I want to know if you will come back for
   me when you go, when after we have
   made love because this war is too much,
   you will return to me and help me heal
You were the one who taught me that we
   had taken the iron knife and sliced this
   way instead of that way and what a
   crucial error was once made
how our enemies linger not in haunted
   prophecies or star-strung agendas
but in the twisted and tormented hearts
   of the capital hills
I want to know how when you shudder-
   sweat-seethe-spit and my skin, souls,
   skeleton dances
how when I shudder-sweat-seethe-spit
   and your skin, souls, skeleton leaps
I want to know how the coiling together
   and the tearing apart brings me the
   ecstasy that is the torture of our
   fracture
I want to know why at night when I am
   sleeping you slip outside through the
   wooden doors and sit in the half-light
   smoking, twisting braids of dried husks
   of once-were and speaking to the water
   in the clouds . . .

Chapter Three

Falling in Love, Breaking Apart, and the Witch Blood

Life will break you. Nobody can protect you from that, and being alone won't either, for solitude will also break you with its yearning. You have to love. You have to feel. It is the reason you are here on earth. You have to risk your heart. You are here to be swallowed up. And when it happens that you are broken, or betrayed, or left, or hurt, or death brushes too near, let yourself sit by an apple tree and listen to the apples falling all around you in heaps, wasting their sweetness. Tell yourself that you tasted as many as you could.

—Louise Erdrich, *The Painted Drum*

Have you ever seen the Three of Swords from a tarot deck? Look it up if you haven't yet locked eyes with one of these cards. To me it is one of the most human cards in the tarot. A classic image we modern tarot readers often associate with this card is a red heart suspended in grey clouds with three swords stabbing through it. Yes, stabbing through the heart. Sometimes there are droplets of blood, sometimes storms and lightning.

This classic image I am referring to was painted by Pamela Colman Smith (1878–1951), and she was likely inspired by seeing cards from the Sola Busca tarot—a fifteenth-century deck and the first known tarot with seventy-eight cards—in the British Museum. The Three of Swords in the Sola Busca tarot and in the Smith-Waite—also called the Rider-Waite tarot—are clearly connected.

Through years of reading tarot for friends, strangers, kin, and beloveds, I have come to look upon each card in multiple and mixed ways. The Three of Swords in particular carries a certain charge. Many people who look upon this card have a sinking feeling or *ugh* that might be similar to the response people have upon seeing the Tower or Death cards. This is often true even when, perhaps especially when, the person does not know the language of tarot. Of course I would argue we all intrinsically understand the language of tarot. Over the years I have transmuted my own relationship with this card from one of dread and damn to one of compassion, awareness, and a willingness to be with the process. The Three of Swords process is one I have named "the heart is made to break open"—and in this I have experienced a powerful realisation of self, relationship, and the cosmos. For in the breaking open rather than just the breaking, there is a holding, a brewing, a changing within the cauldron or a tempering within the secret forge. This card signals the potential for profound growth and empowerment.

One of my witchcraft mentors and I used to speak a lot about how courageous-foolish a being has to be to willingly incarnate as human. Of course we were also speaking to the intuition and personal knowledge/ experience of reincarnation as a part of the context of this conversation. Regardless of what you intuit, think, or believe about what happens before you are born and after you die, there is a truth to consider here. That truth twins us with those ancient ones—the watchers—who witches have long danced and worked with. Depending on how you look at it—and with certain cunning caveats—we too could be seen to have fallen in the process of incarnating and becoming this singular entity who is named and unnamed at turns and who carries a body of experience . . . a being who has a face that becomes recognisable to others, a voice, a tone, a signature unique to you, to me, to your parent or best friend . . . we each know something about that distinctiveness of a person or being, and we also may have directly experienced the sameness of things. There is a great yearning or longing in many to experience that at-oneness with what some might call source, ground of being, or God or Goddess. It has never gone away. We become endlessly in the process of God herself rapturously becoming.

When I relate the process of incarnating or becoming human to the fallen angels, I need to emphasise again that I do not think of or act in terms of "unmanifest spiritual essence" and "manifest physical body." I perceive and experience the mystery of the endless and infinite becoming and changing of names, beings, spirits, faces, and things. Beyond and within that I cannot say. Therefore, when I say that the process of incarnating as flesh-to-breath beings might be parallel to the mystery of the fallen angels, I am speaking of an aforementioned courage and great risk to change things from what they are to what they may be and to be changed by that process. I am also distinctly referring to the mystery of falling in love! And for me, falling in love has always meant that my heart breaks and almost always breaks open to hold more, to be held by more.

Think of those flame-wreathed sacred heart Catholic icons because that's how it "looks" to me, how it feels. Think of the crown of thorns around the head of the master we call Jesus. Perhaps this brings to mind the holy grail, the blood, the spear, and the five wounds of Christ that were once represented by the pentagram as a Christian symbol of salvation. After all, Christ is the Morning Star. Here is another who has been called to fulfil a mighty charge, who "fell," and in the Christian myth was crucified. It is said that this occurred in almost a scapegoat kind of way—that Christ took upon himself all of humankind's errors so that we might be liberated into a new state of grace. I don't have a theology in which so-called sin plays a part, but what I am getting at here is that there are mythic parallels between witch teachings and mysticism from all over the world. Interestingly, several key folk from the Western witchcraft revival period—Robert Cochrane, Cora Anderson, Victor Anderson—speak of this relationship.

The blood that "redeems" or that is taken in holy communion as a link to the Christ and to salvation could be said to be—in a complete fit of heresy—a mystical twin to the notion of the witch blood, especially when viewed from certain angles. Victor and Cora Anderson both encouraged their students to read the Bible through witch's eyes. There is a mythic virtue being spoken of here, and it is not a genetic reality so much as a poetic provocation and magical complex with far-reaching implications. I encourage the ability to hold all of these strange meeting places, these awkward or even uncomfortable syncretisms and "twins," because this kind of way of thinking and playing is incredibly useful for the witch's work.

The witch blood is a topic that can easily be hijacked or twisted into serving an agenda that is not held by the mythopoesis of this mystical teaching. Yes, it is the elfin blood—the faerie blood—but none of this can be held down, placed under a microscope, and viewed and assessed in any way that assures understanding, context, or intimacy. To become intimate with the witch blood, one must, of course, be a witch. And it is said that witches are of the many children of that marriage between the bright ones, who we will also call the fallen—in love—angels and the red daughters, who in Genesis are recorded as the daughters of man:

> Genesis 6:4: *The Nephilim were in the earth in those days, and also after that, when the sons of God came in unto the daughters of men, and they bore children to them; the same were the mighty men that were of old, the men of renown.*

These writings of Genesis and the subsequent unnumbered interpretations of who these mighty men of renown might be form one of the great magical riddles of the past few thousand years. Those mighty men of renown—the Nephilim, children of the marriage between fallen angels and human women—perished in the great flood and are thought to have become all the demons and malevolent spirits that fill the broad earth and haunt and harrow humankind. Might there be apocryphal or wilder and older understandings of the progeny of such a terrible and powerful union?

A rich understanding of the primeval relationship of the witch with their familiar spirit or spirit lover may unfold by deeply journeying into these stories of the watchers, of the fallen angels, of the Nephilim.

These are not new ideas to be discussed by any means. Anyone who has read books like Paul Huson's *Mastering Witchcraft* knows of the works of Cora and Victor Anderson or is connected to covens and craft folk who cherish this lore and pass these stories and legends, understands that at the core of the traditional craft we have inherited today is a mystery that still expresses through the blood and art of witches.

The red daughters are those ancient and powerful foremothers of our kind; they who with hair unbound, unveiled, and perhaps dancing naked atop the mountain to which they were called, dared summon stars to witness them. Here is a time when stars were known to be gods and gods had bodies. A time in which sex between the spirits and those who desired and feared them was known to occur, and not just in legend or lore. There was and is a perpetual unfolding moment of ecstatic, terrifying bliss—the coming together of brilliant white fire seduced from the heavens and the red blood of the human animal. This white current and red current are held and woven with the great initiators of the green and black—of the plant people and their kin who impact and steward this planet and the deep, dark ones from within the earth, in the underworld, who receive those who die and make mystery with them. We will explore these four great families of black, white, red, and green more below.

In the legends of some witch houses there is a pivotal and significant story that speaks to the origins of how witches came to be. It involves fallen angels or sons of God—I like to call them spirits of Sophia—and daughters of man, or the red daughters as I name them—and the powerful, beautiful, and mysterious planet we call Earth.

Witchcraft is often considered to be an underworld-centric or chthonic tradition rather than a transcendentalist or out and up there magical worldview. Witches such as Starhawk have spoken and written of witchcraft as a tradition that centres immanence. The concept here is that there is no qualitative distinction between the material and the divine; that when we say spirit we are simply referring to the inherent quality of something, or all things.

The mystery of the fallen angels is encoded in the lore of several witch houses. I'm also not the first to write about these things—Paul Huson, Michael Howard, Nigel Jackson, and Madeline Montalban are among them—and yet we all received these teachings differently, and we all feel and interpret them in our own ways, within the context of our traditions, practices, and lore. Yet the story is pervasive. This story has resonance and parallels with ancient ideas and myths of shining ones, gods, magically powerful peoples, starry beings coming down from above or from a specific direction and bringing laws and the gifts of how to build civilisation. In some Aboriginal nations and clans within so-called Australia, these stories of Great Ones coming down from the stars into the land offer instruction on cultural protocol in accord with the law that is country. It is said by various Indigenous elders that this law encodes and teaches ways of being in active, respectful, and powerful relationship with one another, honouring the best possibilities of being human, and remembering to abide by the sovereignty of land and each other.

In order to understand this mystery of the fallen angels, we must dance near the precarious edge of madness and initiation humans name love. We must risk this fall. In the great unfolding of our lives, many of us, most of us, probably all of us—in some way—fall in love. Notice that. Notice the poetry, in English at least. We say *I have fallen in love* or *I am in love*. This mystery that sends us mad, breaks apart our worlds, demands us to know stillness and storm, centre and circumference, is at the heart of the stories of the watchers and the fallen angels as I know them.

When I was sixteen years old, I fell desperately, unnervingly, in love. Right about the time, right? Ripened not just with wondrous, heady animal lust but the capacity to be incredibly foolish—to throw everything away and risk irrevocable change; to dive headfirst, heart in my head; like the Hanged Man, I gave my all.

I met him at a queer youth dance party in Meanjin. We saw each other and I truly felt and still feel that some force of fate tethered us in that microsecond. I saw him—tall, slender, radiant, humorous, and wanting me—and I know he saw and felt that powerful desire in me too. I was struck, quickened, changed forever. I was in thrall to my witchcraft initiation at the time. This fated meeting would—a year on exactly—then catalyse the birth of the Coven of the Wildwood, which helped open the way for the midwifing of a hallowed, ever-renewing tradition called Wildwood. My personal history and unfolding as one of those midwives was catalysed in this moment. It was love. Always love.

I returned to Toowoomba and he to a city an hour south of Meanjin, a place where I had formed many happy memories in my early childhood. We spent hours on the phone with each other—he in a boarding school, me in my mother's house—and we wrote and sent love letters to each other. It was in that time when the world was about to completely and intensely alter; so much would vanish from the minds and hearts of the people who would come of age after me. Coming of age . . . that's what was happening to me.

I turned seventeen towards the end of July that same year and he drove up to be with me. We fucked passionately. It was he that helped forge me into a lover. He taught me most of what I needed to know about how to give pleasure with fingers, tongue, palms, cock, ass, thigh, eyes, nostrils, lips, mouth . . . he gifted that to me. I was awkward before that; awkward, unknowing, naive.

Poetry started to quicken in me; a life force would move and snake and reveal ancient memories, other lives, journals worth of witchery that later upon meeting initiated witches would be my key into confidence and coven. And it was utter pain. To be in love and be separated by school, by class, background, colour, expectation . . . the fire started moving through him too. A year after falling in love, we both stood together with two others and received initiation from mountain and mystery. An initiated witch to share love, life, lust with. But something in me—a part of me locked away—started to emerge, and in that emergence parts of me decided upon courses of action that hurt my beloved deeply. I started to fall and break apart in a way that I didn't know at the time how to stop, how to stem, how to talk about. I cheated on my partner, breaking sacred trust several times. I have always remained open about this and ever regretful. My choices were not the choices I would make now or ten years ago, and yet I made them then.

A theme rippled through my poetry about him. Angels. Seraphs. Fiery serpents and celestial counsel. They started to arrive in dreams and visions. They moved through me in oracular and possessory states, startling and exciting my witch kin both before and after moving cities. People would say I spoke in other languages, other tongues. So you see this falling in love became a powerful human metaphor of mythopoesis, as well as a literal remembering of a legacy of magic and a host of beings.

I was cracked open. Moving to another city, founding a coven, and receiving a current of power from the mighty dead all within the matter of three months undid me. It initiated me as it was meant to. At the feast of Bealtaine that same year, I knelt on a small hill near our apartment. Before me, hovering in the air, appeared a flaming torch, a firebrand, and I knew instinctively it was mine to take, to claim. This was taking me a layer deeper into the initiatory mysteries of our coven. What happened on that hill became then what is called in the Wildwood tradition the taking of the firebrand. A firebrand is both a way to refer to the flaming torch of ancient pagan rites as well as a human person who agitates, who provokes, who calls for justice. Along with my beloved I was initiated and dedicated into the work of the Wildwood, but now I was committing to something else entirely: becoming a firebrand priestex. This deepened and focused the initiatory process I was in. Since then I have observed a quickening and agitating power move through the lives of those who take the firebrand in our tradition.

A month after taking the firebrand, my whole romantic relationship fell apart in my hands, and while I knew I could fight for it—and for several months I did—ultimately I offered the greatest sacrifice I could offer at that time: I gave away my relationship utterly. I surrendered. I could no longer fight the tide. I gave up this central and defining relationship with the one who taught me I could love in this way. He taught me I could love furiously, mythically, and for this I will always be thankful.

Angels did this to me, and I did this to me. And then I began to remember. I began to remember the great fall. I found books and studied rhymes, old lore, superstition. The spirits did the rest; my daimon did the rest. It was all there in the air for me, as Robert Cochrane alluded to in his mystical riddles—all awaiting my gnosis, my willingness, my understanding. The falling in love broke everything apart so that things that otherwise might never have had the opportunity to bear fruit could be planted in those cracks. And should they anchor deep, drink deep, they might grow strong to share those fruits.

I was being offered an apple, a pomegranate, a holy fruit. These things are intimately linked. The decision to eat of the fruit of the Tree of Knowledge, the decision of rebel love-lusting angels to upend order and allow difference, risk the staidness of things to chance madness, feeling . . . this kind of letting go, in the face of fate, it's that kind of courage that undoes and rearranges us truly. We have to give everything up and fall down to earth to truly begin to understand the hidden things within the soil, underneath and inside the land. And this too is why the angels fall, why the watchers watch, for there are secrets inside the earth, in the labyrinthine chambers of our very own hearts, that hold the stars in their courses and call forth dreams of a different kind.

I honour the falling in love, the risk of madness, the breaking apart, the holding more and being held by more, the transformation, and the powerful beauty and wonder of the light-bearer and their family. Blessed, blessed, blessed are those who sing the infinite praises of the infinite infinitely.

What happened in that potent erotic rapturous coming together of these fallen ones, the watchers, and those who would become witches? What primal transgression, powerful breaking open, and initiation took place in the secret lovemaking between white and red, sealed and received by black and green?

The Red Daughters and They Who Fall in Love: A Story

She climbed. Her calf muscles twitched; dust covered and caked her lower body. Her ankles were cut, and dried blood could be caught shining in the full moon's light. The moon was in the sign of the scorpion as they climbed the mountain together. Thirteen climbed, or thirty, or one hundred, one thousand . . . They came from villages nestled in the foothills and from lands from over the rivers and the seas. Some had travelled unfathomable distances to this moment. They climbed the mountain and tonight it was that this mountain they climbed was all mountains being climbed and all mountains being climbed was this mountain being climbed by all of them in many places at this time.

They all followed an eerie and vital music, the kind of rhythm and sound that trilled the air and brought lust out from limbs. This was a throbbing felt in the sex, in the belly, bringing the blood into heat and the eyes into a shining iridescence, startling like the stars in blackness. Spiralling up the mountain in silence; words lost and emotions impossible to name or define. A yearning and longing filled each of them, an ancient half-remembered burning in the chest, reminding them there is something missing, something you have known you have needed since before you were born. Go to the mountain.

Their feet fell onto the virgin whole-and-complete-unto-itself soil of the crest of the mountain, of this strange and enchanted place, and from through the trees and scrub and across the rise they saw each other. In a half-trance they knew not to cry out, not to break this spell, but to remain in this pregnant wordlessness, listening to a building silence carpet the forests, the hills, the deserts, the rivers, the seas. Those who had not come to the mountain were in deep sleep, in that blackness of dreaming from which one wakes and while feeling the dream strongly cannot remember, cannot express.

A suspension of time and space between worlds. Was it possible? Is it possible? And their eyes raised upward and they turned their brows skyward. The stars shone furiously as if they now existed intimately above each head. Shining. Fire. A light beyond the knowledge of light radiated through the circle of those who had come to the mountain. The light encompassed them, pervaded everything, and from within the light stepped forth those who had been watching and who had dared fall, to risk the breaking apart of worlds for the chance of this, for what might be love. The mystery of love.

Lust moved through the sons of God herself and it made the light bright and hot and the blood of these red beings, these artful ones, unbound them of any thought to censor the desire panicking through the corridors of their bodies. And a great marriage was made. And the knowledge forbidden to them was passed with great power, and that great power moved up from within those who had received it from the watchers. This power knew this home, these bodies, for it was of these bodies. Destined.

Down the mountain they spiralled, returning to their homes, villages, tribes, and lands. The first of the witches had come into the world, and this virtue they now possessed was able to be passed through the families of humankind. At times it was passed through fucking, conception, labour, and childbirth; at other times through the giving of the breath in secret, silent places, in secret, silent times wrapped in the cloak of darkness, their mother.

They had not been passed any books except the books of their bodies—and their great prayer *My body is the book and the book is the land* renewed the great enchantment. Some found one another and gathered together in celebration and covenant, discovering and refining the deep magics of the witch sight, the knowing, that ignited by the light of the Great Ones also enabled them to soar in other skins unseen by most, to the goat field, to the mountain, and later this was called the sabbat.

Others took arrow or staff formed from twisted tree or wand of tangled vine or stone blade or, later still, forged metal and sharpened knife deep into cave, forest, knee-deep in the gushing sea . . . and they cried out the half-remembered names of the watchers who still watched them. Into these witch lines had been passed the great genius of the seraphs, but not even they could foresee or understand what would become of the transformation, risking it all to the profound alchemy of that great marriage. The white and red and the black and green braided a legacy whose prophecy is in their own becoming. The witches had been standing in the darkness simply waiting to take their place. Though in the darkness they would sometimes be forced to stay, the human family would always desire them and call them to the campfires and the common places where the people gathered.

A suspicion, a resentment, an envy of the witches was natural. Who are these people to have been sired by and sired those mighty ones of renown? Who are these to know the secret languages of stars, of river, of stone, to speak in runes and kindle mysteries? Who are they to walk into the homes of gods and challenge them, entreat them, negotiate, and ask? Witches weave with fate and are preciously needed and required. For they will smell what is to come and protect, ward, and keep us, but they always ask of the people more than they might be willing to give up. Sometimes the witches were called priestesses, oracles, seers, cunning folk, wizards, healers, or conjurers, but truly a witch may be anywhere and anyone.

The Compass Kin: The Four Great Families

I can still feel strongly the experience of first reading the chant that some witches today adore:

Black spirits and white,
Red spirits and grey.

Originally—I think—I read it in a book by Doreen Valiente. This woman was and is of great significance and impact in the modern witchcraft revival. She wrote many incredibly important books, poetry, and liturgy, and in her constant journey of seeking out the craft, she ended up being initiated into four branches of witchcraft.

The words above meant something to me. Doreen goes on to suggest that the "four Celtic airts" relevant to Britain placed these colours in the

east—red

south—white

west—grey

north—black

And this has to do with the tone or quality of the light or atmosphere in those directions. There are various regional and cultural maps for these colours and the airts or winds and directions in those islands. Another from Ireland has purple in the east and pale in the west, but the other colours remain the same. Of course red and grey and green do appear in that map too, in the regions you would think they would.

The sun rises blood-red in the east, it dazzles white and radiant in the south—in the northern hemisphere—at its midday zenith. In the west is the twilight gloaming of grey, and in the north where the sun is not seen to pass, that direction of the Arctic, the North Star, and behind the North Wind, there is blackness. Several British and European witchcraft traditions will place an emphasis on the northern direction in their cosmologies and ritual workings.

My own journey and learning of the craft has had me engage in various apprenticeships, trainings, and initiatory rites of passage. Upon working and weaving with Lee Morgan, a witch and beloved based in lutruwita (Tasmania), I was introduced to the idea of realms expressed as black, white, red, and green. As I was already deeply oriented to the poetry of three realms of land, sky, and sea—the middleworld, upperworld, and underworld—through my covenant as a Wildwood witch, and I had already known the four airts as distinctly related to a cosmological witch's compass, I worked both with the material and lore as passed to me as well as allowing the intimacy of direct experience. Through this I began to deepen into what I call the four great families or the "compass kin," as I term them, as related to a kind of witchcraft mastery map, a helpful spirit ecology that allows me to navigate through my own evolving nature and the spirits I am in relationship with. I honour my deep friendship and magical wyrd with Lee Morgan in these unfoldings and learnings.

In the compass of the witch—which is also a circle of art—these colours, these realms, and these kin describe the families of spirits, of mysteries and beings that the witch may be contacted by and commune with.

Each of these colours, these kin, might also describe a series of sorcerous or magical skills.

We might be able to look at it like this:

The black kin may be oriented via the compass to the direction of midnight. This will be south in the southern hemisphere and north in the northern hemisphere. These respective directions also happen to be the nearest magnetic poles for both hemisphere. The black kin mysteries include the dead in the earth, the underworld spirits of wisdom and quiet, and the night spirits. Skills or themes encompassed by these kin may include blasting, binding, cursing, listening, silence, finding treasure, necromancy, shadow stalking, illness/disease, wisdom, fertility, and power.

The white kin may be oriented via the compass to the direction of the most powerful solar radiance in a day. This will be north in the southern hemisphere and south in the northern hemisphere. The white kin mysteries include the starry ones, seraphic and angelic spirits, and upperworld people. Skills or themes encompassed by these kin are prophesy, the sight, expansion, brilliance, light work, word sorcery, astrology and star magics, purification and invigoration, oracular work, and receiving the spirit.

The red kin may be discovered by turning ourselves to face the east, place of the rosy dawn, of the pinkish hues, sometimes of what looks like blood spilled across the horizon. The red kin mysteries include red-blooded creatures, animals, iron, spirits of the blood, and the living ones of the blood. Skills and themes that these kin can aid us in include fetch work, blood magic, hearth and home, health and vitality among the red, sex and lust among the red, promises, pacts, covenants, shapeshifting and skin-turning, and exercise.

Originally I learnt about this airt as grey per the spell above, which is found in Thomas Middleton's play *The Witch* and then expanded upon by Doreen Valiente. Then I learnt from Lee Morgan of these ones, this realm, as green. In deepening into the work, I discovered that blue would emerge for me and reflected upon a word I had discovered in my Feri studies. This is the Welsh and Irish word *glas,* which could refer to a grey or silver colour, or green, or blue. In fact, this word is found in several European languages.

We might orient to these mysterious ones in the twilight of west, the direction the sun is setting towards or in. These compass kin include the Good Neighbours, the Hidden People, the Alfar, the Gentry, the Little People, the djinn, the plant people, the fungi people, the river people, the mountain people . . . Skills and themes that these beings may aid us in include certain kinds of healing, wort cunning, glamour, faerie enchantment, health and vitality among the green, sex and lust among the green, musicality, grace, entheogenic work, going into Faerie, otherworldly journeying and knowing, poetry . . .

It's not that some of these gifts or magical talents could not or do not also fall within other colours—or within the scope of those kin—it is that there are specialties, alignments, and resonances. The kin may also help us to understand who we might be as witches, how our magic works, who to partner with, where to grow our edges into, and how to dance into the sabbat ecstasy and discover the elixir of all that we do.

The compass kin—the four great families—are not held in isolation away from each other in watchtowers. That's not how this circle works. Watchtowers to the edges of time and space, as they are wont to do, are a different cosmological circumstance. These families, these kin, are interwoven with each other and tell stories about each other.

The black receive the white in a furious dance of eros and tension that forged the stars out of the womb of space. The white spirits are the extension of light into what becomes the underworld, the darkness and wisdom within what we now call the earth.

The white and green are in some ways seamlessly and synergistically wed. The white gives to the green what it needs to survive and be healthy and vital, and some among the green-grey-blue kin may even have their origins among the fallen angels as folklore recounts. The shining ones walk among us, remembering, singing of their starry and perhaps celestial origins. We must remember too that there is light in the earth.

The green and the red are in a sacred and holy dance together. We take lovers from each other's courts and realms. We share breath, ribbons, and rivers of breath. We each gleefully receive this mist of breath for that taste of what it might be like to be animal or the gift of air that is our lifeline. We have written poetry and ballads and whole books of faerie stories about their kind, and they skim the fat of the land, blast the crops, sour the milk, and occasionally, when they desire it, take our children for their own. They may also drive elf-shot into our bodies and skins and enchant or ensnare us for their own purposes. Of course it's not cut-and-dried at all; remember, some of the most powerful allyships are between the faerie people and the witch people.

The red sometimes long for these green-grey-blue ones or else we would not have for centuries written stories about them, told our children tales about them, feared and desired them. We are also very wary and perhaps even paranoid about the good people. Most cultures have ways of warding them off, of undoing what they have done or keeping them far from hearths and hearts. Some of the green kin are deeply fascinated by our blood-red hearts, and we may be utterly enchanted by their greenness, their fatedness, their glamour and artistry.

The red and the black are in many ways our origin and our destiny. How the red is the distillation of the animal life force, the blood of waking and living; how the black is like a great sea, a mass of the dead, a shoal, a horde, that draws us in and tries to overwhelm us, dragging us down to the underworld, into the innerworld. The black and the red are braided. They bleed into each other. We take from each other; the living taking from the dead and the dead from the living, and this is as old as we ever were and ever will be. And we give to one another—our sorrow and our joy, our grief and our bliss wrapped up into each other's destinies. The black and the red are two sides of this coin of existence for us, and yet both take us deep into mysteries we might not yet be prepared for or aware we desired. It's inevitable.

IF YOU ARE able and it is accessible to you, find a place outside where you will not be disturbed, or at least where you can be left alone, and bring with you a walking stick or staff. Perhaps you'll find one along the way. Be in silence; listen with and acknowledge country, and pour blessings and power through your own roots and tendrils through the earth. Ground, centre, align your souls and cauldrons. Give blessings to the ancestors and orient to the realms.

Now find the direction of darkness. This will be the north for those in the northern hemisphere and the south for those in the southern hemisphere. If you live on the equator or close enough to the equator that there is no discernible direction regarding the sun's arc, you may intuit this entirely and find yourself orientating to a land feature like a cave, a deep part of the sea near you, or the depth of a forest. Either way, find the darkness, and when you have found that and are facing it, begin to carve the compass with your staff or walking stick. Trace the circle on the ground in the direction—clockwise or anticlockwise—that makes sense to you. This may make a visible indentation or furrow in the soil, but if it's on grass or harder rock it will be more of a sensation and a feeling. And as you go, you may incant the following:

> *Black spirits and white*
> *Red spirits and green*
> *Gather, gather, gather to be seen*
> *Throughout and about*
> *Around and around*
> *This compass be drawn*
> *This circle be bound!*

(My adaptation of the traditional rhyme channelled by Doreen Valiente and based on lines from *The Witch*, an early seventeenth-century play by Thomas Middleton.)

You may find that you want to compass round three times to seal it well, as tradition would have it. Or you may make the circuit once or perhaps even nine times—three times three.

Bring your attention back to the direction of darkness or the midnight and sink through your breath—remembering your experiences with the cauldron and the un/naming—and begin to whistle or sing out to the winds to come. Know that as you do this, the dead, the dark elves, the great black powers of the underworld, and the ancient ones of the places of harrowing, dismemberment, and forging will hear you. Let yourself enter into trance and allow the black spirits to reveal to you what you need to see, know, perceive, sense, experience.

When your engagement with the black kin has receded or dimmed a little, bring your attention across the compass to the direction of the white kin, which will be north or south, the direction of the sun at zenith in their arc of the day. Open your mouth, take a deep breath in, and on your exhalation vibrate the sound *aaahhh*. Do this several times as you imagine and feel the crown of your head opening to receive diamond-white fire that cascades and rivers down through you. This fire is spilling through all your parts, filling each cauldron to overflowing and then pouring down into the next cauldron and down into the next until you are a channel for this white-hot river of light to pour into the land and feed the underworld! Feel your connection above and below as this seraphic power moves through your being. Open to perceive and commune with the starry ones, the people of light, and the light-bearers who we may know as angels, seraphs, watchers, Old Ones. As with any trance work, surrender into the experience from this grounded, centred, aligned state.

When this experience has softened or you can feel it is shifting, turn your attention now to the west, to the direction of twilight and dusk. Here invite yourself into a kind of listening or sensing that feels familiar and foreign to you at the same time. Imagine that you are accessing a deeper faculty of perception as you lean into the green. Remember these are the grey and the blue ones as well, together, and all these colours may be covered by the Irish and Welsh word *glas*, which usually refers to sea green, grey-blue, blue as the grass, grey as the mist. Either way, these are the hidden people, the cousins to the plant people, so close that they may be those same people or move through and as them at times. The mushroom mysteries, the shining ones, the elves, the good neighbours. How is it to have your senses so keen in this space, finely attuned to the faintest movement of a blade of grass in the wind or the dropping of a leaf or tiny twig into the mulching earth? Feel yourself wandering as if you hear stirring music and a singing unmistakably otherworldly and lean in—though not too far—into the mist and imagine that mist building around you but not penetrating or permeating you. Remember you are still in the compass and are holding this staff that grounds and delineates. Listen, open, welcome the communion.

As this experience begins to shift, take some cleansing, clearing breaths and move across the circle to the east, the direction of that rosy-red dawn. Saturate your awareness with memories of that near blood-stained horizon. Perhaps you can recall the somatic sense-memories of the times you have been witness to the rising of the sun. Was there a stirring, a turning, a firing up? Here we turn towards and into the great radiant light-bearer of our solar system—the reason we exist, our source of life itself. And here I am in this primate, mammal form; this is part of who I am and what I am. And I am also this strange other, this spirit and daimon who is connected and wed to this fetch. I am also this breath, this boundary, and this centre, and all together are the great kiss of body, the great challenge of body, and we are red. The red blood rules me. I am iron-bound and iron-forged . . . iron-formed from the heart of a star. This is my living lineage and legacy! Red. Animal. Hunger. Lust. Need. Wanting. Thirsty. Energy. Movement. Rest. Recharge. Perhaps you feel your skin shift. Your shape and signature might move or change. Will you allow your fetch-beast—the deep powers from the red river—more-than-human Great Ones to emerge and dance through? It is time. Embrace this and dance the circle. Bring up the power in this ring and seal this magic of the compass kin, of the four great families of spirit.

In some way, either through rocking, dancing, chanting, drumming, or rattling, move to a point of exhaustion appropriate for you. Come close to whatever your limits are and then collapse, lay yourself down, or open yourself through sensation and imagination as if you are spread out between them all, between the four compass points in this circle of art. Know that denizens and mysterious ones of those kin, of these families, are aware of you, watching you, with you, and you are invited now simply to take notice and pay attention.

Especially observe which colours or kin are seamless for you, easy for you to feel a resonance with, or perhaps a knowing sense of belonging and intuitive understanding. Perhaps there are kin or mysteries here that frighten you, repel or repulse you, or have you feeling nothing at all. This is also good information. It will help to provide deeper insights at another time.

When you feel the time has come, return to a more ordinary posture or middleworld state of mind and give blessings to the spirits via the same directions and release the circle into the land or the air. I sometimes incant the following three times:

> *This circle is released and unbound into sea, into sky, into sovereign ground.*

Once the circle is released and unbound and I can sense that, I say:

> *If the land should need it, may the land take it.*

THE FOUR KIN, the mysteries of the compass, the crossroads, and the circle help us anchor into a rich landscape of sensuous and primal witchery. A map of mastery, a sacred orientation within the land, through the sky, through the sea, and into infinity . . . a way of discovering more deeply how we are attuned, how our power moves and shapes itself, where we grow forth from, and what we might grow into.

This powerful work is manifold in expression and philosophy. You will find threads of it shared by Doreen Valiente, as I have previously mentioned. You will find it within the rich works of the witch and faerie doctor Lee Morgan. Echoes of it may even present themselves in the lore and liturgy of your own craft practices or traditions. It is in the falling in love—for me—that I find renewal and reforging. And as harrowing and as healing as it can all be, the compass kin, these numinous networks of witch lore help to ground and recenter me in the web of relations. These are not just abstract notions or theologies, they are my cousins, my siblings, my teachers, my parents and grandparents, and my descendants. Once the compass is hallowed and the crossroads open, give yourself to the journey. Walk the crooked road and you may find that the great work of initiation is beginning.

The witch blood is story-spirit; what I mean by this is that it is not a quantifiable, measurable, scientifically observable piece of information. It is not data to be used against anyone; in fact, to speak of it all is a quandary, and I risk something here. It is, however, a significant pivot, a qualitative mystical teaching and truth for those who share in the covenant. In some witchcraft traditions we acknowledge ourselves as children of Cain who bear the mark of Cain. In this way, according to various folk tellings, we are beyond the reach of God and also unable to be struck down by the wrath of God or any other. We wander through the wilds, along the crooked way, and find one another in the hidden places under the man in the moon, who is called Cain by some. Witches are creatures of another kind, another court. We are the lovers of other gods. The Devil may be our partner.

It could be that it is the witch blood that binds us to their story, for within us he is re-enacting the great fall over and over. In falling in love with witches, the Devil, the master of the art, breaks the worlds apart again and again. This is the way to fulfilling his role as master, for the Devil I know is smith, poet, healer, and shapeshifter extraordinaire. And this Devil is initiated by and central to the mysteries of the watchers.

The watchers tell a different story of the creation of humankind. They speak of the stars and the winds and the towers before citadels, walls, and cities. They gave the arts and knowledge that they might be carried in certain families and lineages among humankind and passed wisely, with grace and fierce devotion. Fortunately, it still happens. Even now. And I have heard stories that match the watcher narrative—celestial beings coming down to mate with humans and pass knowledge and strength—from multiple carriers of various cultures.

One of the important things to consider within all of this is a powerful story of liberation from oppressive constructs and cages of the so-called demiurge and an awakening to intrinsic knowing of body.

The term *demiurge* comes from Greek *dēmiourgos,* which derives further from the notion of public worker or craftsperson. In some of the early Gnostic schools and texts dating from the first few centuries of the Common Era, there is a pervasive myth-telling that identifies Yahweh or a particular dominating and jealous god as a being also called Ialdaboath. An interesting story to many traditional witches is that of the first thought and reflection of God or the True Spirit as discussed in the Apocryphon of John and the Pistis Sophia, who is both feminine and also androgynous, essentially inferring this of God as well, some might add. In a series of ineffable emanations or extensions of God called aeons, there comes to pass one called Sophia—which is Greek for wisdom—who is considered in various texts or various times to be a great powerful consort of the Saviour or cast as a more lowly, shame-ridden being who went off without "cosmic permission" and accidentally created a fallen material world.

This essential duality of what is divine and true and what is fallen and false is anathema to the kind of witchcraft I honour, but underneath and through the riddles of these stories that make me uncomfortable is a special kind of insight. This notion of the construction of a fallen material realm ruled over by archons and a dominating god could be seen to be an explanation of how humans reincarnate in this illusory horror- and pain-filled world. The archons in these cosmologies are often associated with the planets in our solar system, and they are cast as low and separated out from the original aeons. They are bound by the wheel of the zodiac, and one overarching, essentially asshole man-child god, who is filled to overflowing with jealousy and rage, is their commander-in-chief. What some witches find intriguing about these stories is the heretical and profound inroads to perennial and primordial wisdom gotten at through the cracks.

Somehow Adam is formed and enlivened by the stolen Sophianic power or by the True Spirit breathing through into this created being of clay. The eating of the fruit of the tree of knowledge is an important and catalytic initiation for humans, which perhaps each of us can still do. Both apples and pomegranates feature deeply in both Pagan and craft lore. The serpent could be Lilith, could be Sophia, could even be Christ . . . Ultimately, these early so-called Gnostics were arising out of strange and hugely syncretic times, when the world as they knew it was in crucial apocalypse at all times, perhaps just as our times seem to be, or all times?

The reality is there have often been overt and covert forces, systems, nation-states, empires, churches, and societies that desire to limit knowledge, restrict certain bodies of knowledge, and persecute and even murder those who might carry that destabilising or daimonic knowledge. Witches have been carriers of this knowledge, and we belong to the world. The falling in love of the bright ones, the powerful consummation and marriage of them and the daughters of "man," the coming of Nephilim and mighty ones of renown sing with the same throbbing power and mystery as the eating of forbidden fruit, as the knowing of one's nakedness, as the revelation of being within a "walled garden" and needing to venture out into the great and wild unknown.

Many of us know from very real and recent geopolitical events that there have always been those wed to the great lies. Stories of deceivers and deception might be interesting to those of us who seek occult and intrinsic knowledge. I can't simply ignore a story or a myth simply because it is woven in a complex cast by a later understanding or co-opting of that mythscape. Once more, Christianity or Christianities are not the enemy to me. If there is an enemy of humankind, it is ignorance and bigotry, and so therefore anything we can do to awaken and move through into critical, self-reflective, collaborative thought and feeling is needful. World wisdom traditions have enshrined knowledge and the pathways of knowing as central to their histories, myths, and principles of faith and hope. Witchcraft—which may or may not form one's religion—seeks that wisdom and seeks to be transformed by that.

I now call upon the one who has been said to be a slanderer, an accuser, the one who lies and deceives. I call upon the Prince of the Outcasts, who we call Master, the one who is mastery itself. He is the piper who will bring us home again, gather us in dreams and dreaming. Let us meet the mysterious one at the crossroads, in the heart of things, at the edge of wild places, and in the centre of cities. Our houses have kept the secrets in every image at the side of every hearth. In every halo, flaming heart, virgin's tear, and every faerie tree and holy well. We go to the watchers to learn again, as our foremothers did, the original daughters of "man." What they learnt upon the mountain and inside the dark heart of the hill is braided into the lineages of the craft.

I am aware that some in the craft—and outside the craft—dislike these stories. Some may not even know them, or know them within their context. Others have other ways of conveying similar truths and mysteries. Of course, the internal lore is detailed and orally and textually woven in ways that are bound not to be shared until or after the intimate act of initiation. And dear, fierce reader, this is also your history, by which I mean it forms and forges the histories of our known world too. It is the history of intellectualism, philosophy, religion, occult art, science, and poetry. It is the story playing out right now all around us, again and again. In various forms, in various places, the legends of the watchers, of the Old Ones who came down and made love with us, is encoded in the core mythos of culture and art. The witch belongs to the world.

Oh, sweet human, you seem to forget how it is you came to be . . .

There was only the deepest dreaming of the desire for you, for the infinite ones to come forth and become, but you, you, you had to leap, take the risk, and fall in love with that becoming.

Know that you did, before the beginning, desire it so much that you fell in love and broke all things.

You write about it, you talk about it, take it in, sweet broken-apart human.

Your kind wrestles with this: Am I broken? Honey/ honeyed ones, you did this! Unknowing, you came into knowledge. Now what?

See how brave and foolish that is. The Fates and gods can only hold their ancient breath. But there is not pity; there is only wonder and terror. Twins, you might say. So let them be twins.

You are not looking for your pieces, though; they aren't scattered across the earth and sea. Your pieces are looking for you, singing out and always connected. All you need to do is become. This is the mystery of life and of death that is for me to tell you another time.

—My fetch-mate

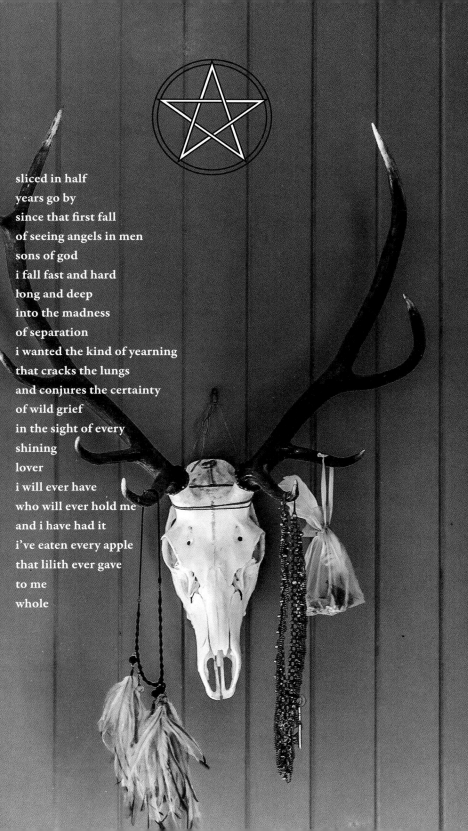

sliced in half
years go by
since that first fall
of seeing angels in men
sons of god
i fall fast and hard
long and deep
into the madness
of separation
i wanted the kind of yearning
that cracks the lungs
and conjures the certainty
of wild grief
in the sight of every
shining
lover
i will ever have
who will ever hold me
and i have had it
i've eaten every apple
that lilith ever gave
to me
whole

BEFORE WE EMBARK more deeply into this talismanic book—this living spell of witch and wyrd—I invite you to return to read what you have previously read. I invite and encourage you to place this book down for several days or a week or longer and to spend time thinking into the provocations and the prose and poetry above.

This book continues to offer steps—spells, workings, rituals, processes, trance work, active reflection, introspective meditation—leading all the way into the tenth chapter, entitled Initiation. You will notice things may begin to change around you as you drink in more and more the magic offered here.

If you are able to, desirous of it, when you come to the poems, I dare you to read them aloud. Read them aloud to your three souls; let them vibrate through your three cauldrons. Read them to your ancestors, or at least ancestors who might like them, or perhaps ancestors who will be challenged by them too. Read them as invocations, as praise-prayer and dedications. And then please write your own. Paint your own. Dance your own. Incant, shape, cook, tease, play, mould, offer, plant, harvest . . .

Out of silence, out of darkness, through the compass of the body that is the land—all the lands you might carry and which carry you—with the ancient blood of the art vibrating within and around you and your memory of the falling-in-love, with the breaking apart of the worlds, we meet the one who, it is said, did that thing. We meet a great one whose trial records, folklore, witch legend, history, and even those who would condemn us all say we know intimately. Let us go to the crossroads, to the strange and threshold places—between the horns—and adore the flame that rises there.

Chapter Four

The Devil Takes the Hindmost

"Why do you call him the Devil?" they asked.

"Because the morality you are presupposing by asking me that question does not exist in the old covenants of the witches or in wild nature. He-she-they wanders drumming to ancient bones and singing flesh up from the well of our ancestors. The Devil is not a name, it is an idea, a powerful idea that reminds me that the culture we would try to appease by saying we do not dance with the Devil is the sick and evil one. The world is full of lies."

"So you don't like Christianity at all?"

"It's not Christianity or Christ; it's the church, it's the doctrine of Original Sin, it's an institution that says more than half of our species can't be priests, that says I must confess my carnal realities to absolve them, that rapes the land and steals children . . . I trust the wise serpent who told me that the demiurge was lying."

I offered an apple from the fruit bowl between us and noticed the look of terror in their azure eyes.

"Eve ate of this and saw the truth that the world around her, the walled-in prison that the demiurge had called paradise, was a lie . . . and then she had eyes to see and walked into the wilderness . . . "

"There are no gates to paradise," we whispered together.

—A conversation that once happened

The Devil is a complex figure. He could be easily said to not exist or never have existed at all. I know some witches who would happily do away with the Devil, but it's not that simple and it never has been. Witches belong to the world, and there are histories we have to contend with, very real events that have taken place that bear consequences, perspectives, beliefs, doctrines, desires that have liberated people, terrorised nations, broken spirits, and raised us up. The Devil lives in and between and around all of this. Of course, it could be said that, just like the witch, the Devil is a haunted figure who has been constructed and utilised to morally sanction the conversion of whole tribes by the superior and rightful arms of Christ's church upon earth. And yet there has often been either an adversary, a guardian at the gates, a wild god of wild people who terrifies us, provokes us, seduces us, and leads us away into directions we had previously deemed profane or problematic.

The word *devil* has multiple possible etymologies, folk usages, and meanings. It could simply refer rather neutrally to a kind of strange spirit at the edges of things or to any spirit at all! Etymologists generally trace the English word *devil* to the Greek *diabolos*, meaning "slanderer." And who is this devil slandering anyway? Is it that certain creator god who from many angles demands ignorance and obedience rather than knowledge, responsibility, and understanding? From conventional Christian interpretations of the story of the forbidden fruit in Genesis, it is the Devil as the serpent who offers us the fruit of the tree and says *eat*. This is the mercurial and Promethean act we have been waiting for—an act of a trickster and someone who is wanting to see something happen, to set something else into motion. Just like us, really. Worlds must break apart to be remembered, things must change so that we live. Just as fire is stolen or tricked from the gods in various cultures, so the change element is required in nature for dynamic evolution. The Devil in this telling is that folkloric and profoundly multifarious story-spirit that is experienced intimately in saying yes to this offer of most carnal knowledge. It is the Devil that initiates the process and initiates us as witches. It could be that we are initiated into ourselves to discover how it is we are accountable, responsible, and effectual in the world. And, as always, this all bears consequence.

It must be honoured that this term, *Devil*—just like *witch* and *pagan*—has been used to discredit and defame the cultures and traditions of many Indigenous nations and traditions all around the world. The usage of this term by traditional witches is largely folkloric and usually also simply vernacular; it is a sideways and underways reference to a powerful initiator-initiate Son of Art god-being or many such beings, just as we might refer to the Good Folk or the Little People with such appellations. We don't always want to be looking directly into the fulcrum-furnace of the very being who initiates us into being witches in the world.

Some modern pagans and historians have said that the European Christian conception of Satan or the Devil borrows from pagan depictions of certain divinities. There are many instances of pre-Christian deities being depicted as crowned with antlers or bull, ram, or goat horns. Egyptian Amun, Arcadian Pan, Gaulish Cernunnos, or the ancient and ever-from-another-place Dionysos. Some conjecture that the witch's God, who has in the past been called the Devil, is a syncretism of all this. Some might suggest that the Devil—this apparent God or initiator of witches—is a composite character, a hypostasis of themselves, a story-spirit perhaps who may be a god at times. A very important god in the history of humankind. A very important and very human phenomenon.

The Devil is too sophisticated, too beguiling, for such reductive, easily explained away options.

10

YOU MAY HAVE read in books like Paul Huson's seminal *Mastering Witchcraft* (1970) that there are important rites of unbinding and liberation one might need to engage if one is quagmired by internalised dogmas. To be effectively free or have more space from certain church or imperialist-capitalist doctrines linked to shame, original sin, coercion, and domination, we must face and name the bonds and their effects. Sometimes in order to really confront ourselves and the bindings of society we need to do the very thing they told us not to do—especially when those things might actually be pleasurable, wondrous, and beautiful.

You may decide that you need to emancipate from certain dogmas or doctrines you were coerced into as a child. I am speaking of the ones that truly affect your thinking, behaviour, self-image, and self-respect. So, if possible, you may decide to take yourself out and walk to the nearest deserted or quiet crossroads, edge of the forest or bush, a safe subterranean place, or beach. You might take sticks from the place and with twine make an uneven cross—a crucifix, an instrument of Roman imperialist torture—and trample upon the cross until the sticks are all broken. You might then kneel and place one hand on your head and another under your foot and declare that all between your hands belongs to the Devil, to the art, to your own holy self, to the mystery . . .

There are witch customs from places like Cornwall in which the consecrated host is stolen and then fed to the next toad you come across. Some would say this is returning stolen and hoarded power back to the land, to the hag, to the underworld that generates fertility, power, wisdom, and wealth. Another oft-quoted sorcerous practice is to steal a lit candle from a church as if you are stealing fire, again returning and reclaiming that power.

You may be directed by your instinct, intuition, spirits, ancestors, or triple soul to confront, name, unravel, and work through this in other ways that might not have folkloric precedent, and this is okay too. If you already have a divinatory practice, please consult that divination, or ask a friend or acquaintance whose abilities and discernment you trust. Also please refer to chapter 8 for more support, information, and technology around how to work these kinds of shadow and transformation magics.

It may also be helpful to engage in deep and intimate conversations with beloveds and trusted allies regarding concepts such as shame, feelings of and stories regarding "imprisonment" or "incapacitation," and being held back by internalised or passed-on dogmas and doctrines, religious or otherwise, in our families and societies. These brave conversations have often shifted things in my perspective and in my experience as a body-being, and I encourage these if possible. As well as this, you might require the professional assistance of counsellors, psychologists, and pharmaceuticals in your journey through the internalisations of these abhorrent teachings and the fragmentation that it can wreak.

The Devil in the World

The Devil in post-Reformation Europe had become the distillation of the internal landscape of the war between puritanical Protestants and apparently idolatrous Catholics. That adversary—Satan—was fully embodied as a candid and cruel prince of lies and arbiter of piety and devotion to Christ. If Christ was the heart of salvation, then to meet Satan and rebuke him was the way to it. The Devil was the gods of any and all peoples, tribes, and nations that these imperialist and thieving powers encountered in their "expansive explorations" of so-called new worlds. We have to contend with the reality that the ways, cultures, languages, and ceremonies of many sovereign peoples have been defamed and denigrated as devil worship and witchcraft, as "pagan savagery," and that these terms are therefore not looked upon kindly by many Indigenous peoples. These words are often loan-words, proxy-words, common terms that are called upon by all kinds of marginalised groups to refer to spirit workers of various shades in their communities and cultures.

The witch's Devil in early modern Europe was no clean spirit. A messy monster, yes. A maniacal madness-drenched beast whose promise of power was catharsis and liberation for the peasants and the marginalised, and for the wealthy and the land-owning a subversion and submission of worldly acumen. Like the folkloric Robin Hood, we are engaged to steal from the rich and give to the poor. The fat is skimmed from the milk, the crops and the livestock of the wealthy are blasted and shrivelled, and the poppets and clay icons of mighty men in their towers are struck with disease and night-mares. The Devil is the anarchist, the rebel, and, in fact, the seeker of truth, the revealer of truth, the ambassador of it. The serpent in the garden. But this is no sweet spirit. This is a Prince of Paradise who paradoxically ruins the walls of illusory gardens and takes the hindmost.

11

SO IT IS time to conjure the Devil, and it will take daring and a whole lot
of yearning and shuddering desire and holy lust.

Search out a lonely place, a liminal place, a graveyard or cemetery. Perhaps a crossroads or a bend in the river in your city, town, or village. If you are able, make sure to journey outside of your dwelling place, and if you are unable, go so far inside that it ends up taking you outside regardless.

In that inside-outside place, lay down whatever you have brought with you. I imagine you will bring something with you. Perhaps you bring a knife, a thimble, a pipe, a black candle, a necklace, a bottle of beer or wine, or, or, or . . . Place it down and acknowledge that you are in this place that has history, secrets, pain, wonder, dreaming, wisdom, and more. Become mindful of your breath; allow a primal, instinctual rhythm to guide your breath and your breath to guide the rest of your consciousness.

Perhaps you find yourself praising the alignment of your souls, and if you do, take your time with it. Engage the fetch; let the animal move in the belly and sex of you, rippling interpenetrated with your surface skin but moving as your second skin, your magical coat and fetch-body. Whisper on the winds and communicate through the middle soul, your breath-soul. Feel and perceive it shine, shimmer, spark. Make sure to open and hold steady your boundaries. Go up into your daimon and cry out through it, like a hawk, a peacock, a creature of great power and wonder. Cry out to meet this Devil who the world has told you is terrible, evil, an enemy of all that is good, pure, and righteous. Come here to meet the Son of Art. Come here to meet the antlered one, the goat-horned one, the bull- or ram-horned one. The one of many skins and names. The man in black playing the fiddle, who has sixpence in his pockets and lust in his eyes. They of art and artifice or illusion and truth; trickster and truth-teller all the same. Let this prayer-spell of desire and awe rise up like a current of life force through your cauldrons, your souls, the worlds, and ring out in this place.

Lean in; await them. The conjuration must move through your guts and blood, thunder through your breath, shout through your silence or whistling in the dark. You must risk something here. Risk discomfort, perhaps; risk the path of mastery, risk being changed, risk changing something.

Master! Master! Master!

They who are master in cunning, master in awareness, master in magic, yes! They who are no longer shackled nor enslaved but the great liberator, the great revealer of secrets and destroyer of deceit and yet the one who spins tales and possesses the silver tongue. Await them. Stand strong in the current of your magic, weave that vitality with the artfulness and rigour that he-she-they would. Weave it with the finesse, skill, passion, and ferocity the Devil would bring to the task.

Await them, and in the waiting let there be release, and in that release let there be relief to your bones, muscles, and meat. And in that relief let there be a soothing, a soothing that is a kind and pleasant fire, a fire that swims through you and builds and builds, licking through your skeleton and blood rivers. A fire that spirals like a cyclone through and around your skins and souls . . . and—a fire that becomes a beacon, a mighty lighthouse that brings the ship safely to the shore of this rite, of this calling, of this place and time.

And the Devil is here. The Devil has come. Now what will you do? What will you ask? What will you offer? How will you show yourself, and what will you reveal? What is the exchange here? And there is always exchange.

Something happens here. It is up to both of you now.

When they have departed, then so must you too. Make your offerings, give your peace to the spirits and the place and yourself, and walk away without looking back.

I originally named this book *Fire in the Heart: A Witch's Book of Revolution,* and for several years it has felt like there have been multiple possibilities jostling around within and around me. This book and the spirits who have been sponsoring this work have been deeply supportive throughout as my life has utterly rearranged several times since my Saturn return—the year 2017—when I first began to understand what this book could be. The gift of discipline and that utter craving to bear witness, to midwife, to aid this creature to come to be, to interact with you, with me, with us, has smelled of the Devil. The cunning Son of Art has his breath and mark all over this talismanic offering.

I wonder what you feel as you read these enchanted words, words that come forth from fingertips dashing away on strangely formed cubes and keys, on the chrome flatness of grey and blackness? When you direct your attention towards the Devil—to this skin-turning, shape-changing, way-ward belonging-to-no-one-and-nowhere, to-everyone-and-everywhere story-being-thing—what begins to quicken or unfold in your heart?

If the head is full of fire and the heart is full of honey, then in that sacred marriage, that dance of power between the Lady and the Devil, there is fire in the heart and honey in the head, and that brings forth the revolution that is their very charge, essence, and character. Through our hands of art, which we will deepen into later, do we discover the mysteries of the bower, do we begin to unravel the meaning of "the Devil takes the hindmost."

He Brings All to Her Bower Who Desire It

In the ordinary and troubling interpretation of the phrase "the Devil takes the hindmost" lies a series of complexes arising out of feudalism, master and servant or even slave ideologies, ableism, and all manner of notions that could be summed up in the glibly Darwinian "survival of the fittest" motif. Some people believe that the Devil will take the last one, the one at the end, at the back, who hasn't been first or second or third. No. This is not how the witches I know interpret this phrase.

I came to my own gnosis regarding this phrase several years ago, which I then discovered others had too in that age-old peer corroboration. It is not that the Devil of the witches is waiting to snack on the last one to make it; it is that the Devil will await all to come to the Lady's bower, to come into the ecstatic bliss of communion with the mysteries. In the mythos of the witches I hold most dear that is enshrined at the heart of Wildwood tradition is an especial relationship between four great spirits, four witch gods, that we call the Sacred Four (see appendix 3 to discover more about them). The Devil comes forth from the Lady and eventually is drawn to her in several of her forms. They are fatefully killed and reaped by her before her descent as well.

It is the nature of the craft to confront lies and deceit—especially those we tell ourselves—to tangle us in the thicket so that we may bleed on the thorns and come to a place of powerful presence with ourselves. Knowing this and being known by this: all is body—everything is a body kissing a body breaking a body dissolving a body loving a body eating a body melding a body opening a body reaching a body laying down in a body. The Lady's communion is not easy, but it is grace. And it is the flame between the horns, the dance of the Devil, the hearing of the violin at the crossroads, the thunder clapping in the clouds and through the sea and land that may bring us to the opportunity to discover it. Her grace is thunderous as well, the kind of grace that lives as waves and swollen sea or the inky black quiet of night in the desert lit up by a million fires or the fierce grace of a sea tern flying over oceans and back again.

Sometimes I call the Devil the thorny one, the thorn-kissed one, the thorn-sworn one. The kiss of the thorn can be seductive. If we are raised on stories of purity and becoming the hero that saves the others, saves the world, then we feel a compulsion to flay ourselves in those thickets until all that is left is for the wind, the dirt, and the fungi. The Lady asks us to consider what it would mean to live for this rather than be in pain for it. What price does pleasure ask? What is ecstasy, the bliss of the sabbat? What are these mysteries of pleasure, of pain; do they weave as divine twins? What is it to be gathered home by the Lady once more?

Either way, to dance that dance—and remember, the Devil takes the hindmost—inevitably is to be wrapped in thorns. These mighty daggers, these fae teeth, these kiss marks of wonder teach us presence, agility, cunning, and patience.

The thorns leave marks, but they are nothing like the marks that love leaves.

Hail the broken-open heart! Hail the heart who is learning to love ever more wondrously, ever more daily, ever more nightly, ever more in ways that only you or I will learn how to love. Lies and deceit fall away in the presence of love. And we might feel ashamed, embarrassed, deeply hurt by how we have stood in our own way, but all of this was simply a fool's errand to begin with. The Devil laughs, reminding us of the strange humour of it all. We are reminded that the power of all of this can be found in what we do with that—the making and breaking of our worlds—and in how we wield the key to these worlds. We are that key.

The desire to come to her bower is a powerful yearning to remember where we have come from and the source of our own capacity to love.

Beware the belief you carry as a currency to endorse
    a wisdom older than your blood.
The wind laughs right past your thinking head stuffed with
    the empire-spun thoughts sold to you from the lords in towers.
HA! Hail, Lords of the Watchtowers!
The inevitable is not at war with itself
    it is in deep eros with the mirror spun of the sex of stars.
She shrieks as the shaman draws out pins from her ailing,
    shivering body . . . no metaphor. No need for your sanctioned
    science-sight.
This is the raw intimation of the need.
He meets the Devil at the crossroads, lays down his pretence,
    and embraces divine right.
He "sells his soul" to the mastery of art, our souls were never our
    own anyway, his parents were slaves.
He lights candles at the door and leaves the tobacco and rum.
    No metaphor.
His mother reminds him: Down there, deep high, there is the
    remembrance of all souls, all saints.
You are in your own keeping when the shackles fall,
    when the blindfold lifts.

It is sin even to call it magic—this is the nameless deed.

There is reason enough to fear those of us ennobled and
    impassioned by this artfulness and cunning.

Beware the belief you carry as a currency of fact,
    facts are the annotations in the Book of Life,
    useful but they are not the bones themselves,
    they are not the blood,
    they are not the breath of Our Holy Mother, vital!

Watch as the prostitute cradles her daughter and carries her
    to the crossroads and summons Venus there . . .

Watch as Venus anoints the daughter and takes her into the
    company of the outcast.

You have never made a place for us,

So we gather—in secret—at the knife's edge—where the
    tongue of angels makes the words that begin things.

We know we are responsible.

So we find grace in the cup drunk deep of the blood
    of Our Lady's line.

Oh no metaphor. No metaphor.

No facts. No currency.

No barter. No buying. No selling.

Here in the bower we are free
    and her love is infinite,
    but we do not require you to leave anything
    to come lay down your head on the lap
    of the Mother of Mercy.

Instead, ask yourself,

When was the last time my skin surrendered and was
    seized by the sacred?

All is undone in the ring of flames!

We bring you the ash to show you where you have been.

Eat of your body that you may become as the beloved
    to the lover who desires

every wholeness-unfinished inside of your perilous heart.

You may have noticed I have resorted—well, truly intended it—to litanies, poetry, and prose increasingly and exceedingly in this chapter. I find it near impossible to speak of the Devil—and they shall appear—without doing so. I notice as I type these words my legs—and I am standing—are moving quickly back and forth, though my feet are grounded in place. I am filled with a nervousness, not to get to any point or even to explain myself, but to have certain keys made manifest, to have certain doors carved clear and thresholds passed through. Except that I have done nothing; I have simply participated in the Devil's own works. He will gladly deliver all who are seduced by his piping to the bower of Our Lady, who is also called the Queen of Witches. And he will await them until the last has come forth. *Devil take the hindmost.*

12

A SUBTLE WARNING: If you do this, it will impact you in ways you might not enjoy. It's likely to be uncomfortable. This is not a light-hearted act. It is not only pleasurable, though certainly the Lady lives through and as our pleasure. If you are to engage the Devil to help you discover the way to her bower, more power to you.

Ground and centre. Align your souls. Begin to drum a steady beat of enchantment. Begin to rock back and forth, or perhaps you have a thirty- to forty-five-minute playlist that you have created in response to reading this chapter. A playlist for Our Lady, the Queen of Witches. You can find a Spotify playlist I have created for her here.* In some way enchant your senses, entrance yourself, and find your way to the thorny roads. These are the roads, this the thicket, the woods that might bring one to the Lady's bower.

Call upon the Devil in the way you know how. Whistle him up, invoke him with words, drumbeats, gestures, dance . . . call the Devil to this work and working. If he comes, it is a sign that this may begin. Proceed only if the Devil appears. And remember that the Son of Art may express in multiple forms, but you will know when he has arrived by the feeling in your genitals, belly, heart, skins, souls.

* https://open.spotify.com /playlist/6xWUtGFYPNUNLiRtyrsI5l

Ask the Devil to reveal to you the way to the Lady's Bower. Allow the conversation to unfold, in images, memories, words, sensations, knowings. Allow the back and forth to become erotic, intimate, sensual, electric. Let it build and braid to form a potent magical container to carry this work.

Emerge from the trance and record, write, or draw in your magical journal. It may be part of a longer story, a story that is drawing you back to yourself.

quiet first
the hallways
rocking chair squeaks
as the house mice play
their games of concord
with each other
their tails tapping out
morse code for the dead
amongst the crumbs left by the living
chimney swept
broom upside down by the hearth
there i've lit a dark candle
made of animal fat
that still stains the floor
and my hands smell
of the faint sweetness
of the oils i have given over
from the hard-won tributes
of scavenging in the wildwood
i am hoping, blithely,
and inside that, desperately
for an apparition
for the familiar
presence
for the shadows shaping
themselves while I cut the air
with scissors
and slash the stars with memory
my invocations will be woven

into the mountains
i will cast them from the back door
and they will land where the
fallen ones
landed, and were caught
In the name of the Darkly Beautiful Prince.
my hands are wrought
with the labour of land
and the land's labours
in my hands
i whisper the words spirits gave me
on their way to
the cavalcades of prosperity
always moving through the air
and the patterns of the land
are marked in my palms
there i read the book of dragons
and recall the fateful night
i was marked
In the name of Lucifer, bearer of the light.

let me tell you, how he comes—
like a black dog sniffing the air
with subtle cunning
and a knowing
of how to get anywhere
and with the same loyalty
like an old lover
who remembers everything
about the way your hair falls
or curls
or mixes with the wind
like a peacock
who explodes the darkness
with the cruelty of sharp vision
and the mania of unknown colours
like the serpent
that i caught
only the briefest

sight of
and then
when i thought the wild had receded
returned to my door
and began to speak
the language of angels
like the friend
who
abandons
no one
nothing
who she has sworn
to honour and uphold
the oils, the words,
he cares not
the prettiness of what i do for him
but he notices everything
and repeats it all
so that i know
he has seen and loved

and then, upon the bed
where no one can see
we fuck
and he teaches me how the
good neighbours think
how the swans listen
how the dragonflies see
how the witch
undoes the world
and summons strength
from brokenness
remaking everything
Everything is new
when he looks
into my eyes
which he says are his keys.
Blessed is he who is here.

Chapter Five

Lady, Gather Me Home Again

She is the Lady because she is our Lady. The Mother of Witches and the living essence of stars blooming and darkness singing.

The Queen of the Night is the most red rose and only those who know will know. Everything under her skirts is secret and silent, and no word could ever decode it.

The name written on the heart is the name most wondrous. Unraveller of all expectation, destroyer of attachment, yet deliverer into the arms of desire. She is filled with desire for you all, her children, her kin, her marked and cunning siblings. And as they say, you are all in this together.

> —Words from my fetch-mate
> as the moon begins to wane

In most contemporary craft traditions, we hear about "the Goddess" or "the Lady" and sometimes "the Queen of Witches." This powerful spirit is primordial, excellent, and liminal, though she is as present as presence can be. She may be multiple spirits, or there are other Great Ones alike to her, or multiple spirits may come together to form her, and all may be Queens of Witches. This is essentially a mystery to me and I like it that way, but I want to encourage folks to hold that this is a central mystery of her as well. She dwells at the crossroads and is the oil of love by which the flame of cunning burns. The witch gods all initiate and contextualise one another. She is the mystery of the risk of love and the power within the heart that is broken open.

Her names are many, but I do not speak about a soft polytheism versus a hard polytheism. This binary or duality is not really of the persuasion of the witch gods I know and love, though I have dallied there before and spent time philosophising via those frames. I have discovered in my relationship with the Queen of Witches that she doesn't go in for things like that. She has worn countless names and faces, and yet she is still Our Lady. Those names and faces she has worn and merged with—those historically attested or named deities—are powerful in their own right and fate and are their own beings and mysteries. Sometimes the Lady is—or expresses as or with—Persephone, Auset/Isis, or Diana, but that doesn't stop Persephone-being-Persephone or Isis-being-Isis in their own rights.

In the varied lore of Europe we find that the Queen of Witches is also the Faerie Queen, the Queen of Elphame or Elf-Land. And there are many Queens of Faerie, many mounds, many elfin realms. In the lore of southern and eastern Europe she is often spoken of as being crescent-crowned, as Artemis, Diana and Isis are sometimes shown. She runs naked in the forests with stags, wolves, owls, hares and serpents. In Britain She is connected to the moon through lunar hares and age-old customs and superstitions. In Welsh lore and legend she may express as-through-with the mysterious Arianrhod, who sings through lifetimes and the circle of stars, holding firm the gates of initiation for her son Llew.

In the tenth century CE *Canon Episcopi* there is named "the pagan goddess" who is called Diana in the original text—and later also Holda, Herodias, Benzozia—with whom wicked and delusional women believe they fly upon the backs of animals and farm-domestic tools in that cross-cultural and multi-era spectral train of the dead and the good folk. Our Lady rides on goats and broomsticks, on the pitchfork and the stang. She is traditionally the Lady of the Wild Things, connected to the stars, the moon, the waters, and the fecund earth.

She is a wolf-mother and a key-bearer. Her name(s) is kept private by most orders and traditions within witchcraft, and she is the secret soul and the hidden quintessence of many of our rites. Of course, the more we say the less we say, and this is the nature of the craft and of the Lady herself. She is the sup and succour to the spirit and the rapturous ecstasy of wonder that drives us further into the swollen river of desire.

In the Wildwood tradition she is the daughter of Old Fate, of Grandmother Weaver, whereas other witch houses might say these are the same goddess. She is the origin, initiator, and sometimes lover of the Young God who becomes the one that some have called the Devil and is also the most beautiful angel and that elfin Prince of the Witches.

Our Lady who art in the stars
Blessed by thy name,
Our witchdom come,
Our will be done,
In earth as it is in heaven and under the sea.

She is Queen of Heresy, of haeresis—agency, sovereignty, choice. At the heart of the very craft, she is. Our Lady. I breathe into her, my connection with her, my marriage to her, and I feel my heart blossom. I can sense the memory of my feet and everywhere we have walked and wandered on this crooked, serpentine road.

I am sure you have read about the witch's Goddess, and therein lies some caution for me and for you, for are we really speaking to the same being or mystery? If you notice you are drawn into this offering by this mystery—for that is how I feel this chapter to be—then I would encourage you to take notice of your sensations and feelings as you read.

Returning to the Tale of Love

Love must master the witch house . . . if it does not, then the
gods will desert that house. Love must master all witches.
It is my love that is the secret heart of all our sorcery.

—The Lady

If I am to offer a just and right offering to the great spirit I know as the
Lady, then I am to tell some more of my story of love, which is her great
and fierce initiation. Sometimes it is an initiation that is heartbreakingly
painful and I would rather know nothing about. Mostly I am grateful for
the chance to have been touched by this depth of power, this profound re-
shaping of expectation and desire. I wish to return more deeply to my story
of falling in love, of heartbreak, and of the healing, power, and insight I
have discovered from passing through these gates.

After my first major romantic relationship was severed and he moved
to another country to pursue different tracks, different futures, I was still
eighteen years old and a year living into Meanjin—Yuggera, Jagera, and
Turrbal country—the city I had moved to shortly after graduating from
high school. I was deep within my Wildwood initiation, and my life was
rearranging and coalescing around this primordial and potent current of
power. I moved back to the Fortitude Valley and New Farm area of Meanjin, on the north side of the river who bears the traditional name of Maiwar, into a two-bedroom apartment in an older and strange building on
James Street. I began to explore my sexuality in new ways that felt freeing,
liberating, and sometimes honestly quite confronting. I turned nineteen in
that James Street apartment in 2007, and I would meet several beloveds—
again, after what felt like many lifetimes—in those years.

In April 2009 I was dancing at one of the main gay clubs in Meanjin
with several friends. I met a man there who I would end up handfasting.
We caught eyes, desired one another palpably, went home together, and
entered—without enquiring too deeply—into a romantic relationship
that saw us married, travelling together to several continents, and breaking
apart after three years. This breakup was catalysed by me after more than
six months of questioning internally and aloud. We went to couples coun-

selling, we trialled a month apart, things of that nature, to give space to a serious decision. I still wear the ring he bought me as an engagement ring. I chose it. It is an antique golden traditional Irish Claddagh ring with a red jewel—could be garnet or ruby—as the heart crowned held by the hands of loyalty and faith. I have a strange and magical story about that ring. I will have to do some time-wandering and looping to get to it, however.

Sometime in 2019—having newly returned to Meanjin from Naarm—I recalled quite suddenly one day that I had previously thrown my ring into the massive tangled roots of a giant Moreton Bay fig tree in the City Botanic Gardens. I had done this as an act of saying goodbye to the haunted romantic relationships of my past and as a way of opening myself to a new lover, James. It was a dramatic move, to be sure. Sometimes magic requires a little bit of drama. Retrospectively, if I had not done this, I would not have this story to tell. More time-loop-wander-labyrinth-walking is required.

James and I were connected via social media by a mutual friend whose name means life, the essence of life. I had been yearning and longing for a romantic partnership for nearly two years, and I thought I was ready for an actual, visceral, enthusiastic boyfriend. At the time I was living in Bali, based in the beautiful town of Ubud. In September-October-November of 2015 I travelled through various regions of Australia teaching, hanging out with community and kin, and facilitating several initiation rituals. James and I connected online early into that trip, and we ended up talking on the phone for two or three hours a day for the five weeks it took me to get to the city he lived in. By the time we met in person, we had thoroughly wooed and learned a great deal about one another. Strangely, that very same week I taught a workshop on the Devil in the craft and met someone who I would later fall in love with after James and I had dissolved our romantic partnership. These synchronicities keep spiralling. But back to the Claddagh ring.

I was sitting with James in the Botanic Gardens early into our relationship by the great river Maiwar in the very place known as Meanjin, which means "place shaped like a spike." We were discussing our relationship and I was either about to return to Bali or head to the USA for eight weeks. I remember feeling the need to take off the ring, and then I went to the tree that stretched over the place I was handfasted in mid-2010, at the age of twenty-two, and I threw the ring deep into the crevices of the roots. And then I forgot about the ring.

James and I lived together for nearly two years of our romantic relationship in Naarm. It was a heated, very passionate, heady, and intense partnership. We argued quite a bit and at times we weren't the best with each other, though we both tried very hard to come back into harmony with one another. Eventually at the end of 2018 we mutually realised we were going in different directions and sadly we said goodbye to one another in that form. Within that week I decided to and did move back to Meanjin. I hadn't lived there since the very beginning of 2012 but a cycle was closing, another opening.

At some point in early 2019—three full years after the giving away of my Claddagh ring—I was living in a new share-house in Meanjin with several witch friends of mine on the south side of the river Maiwar. I recall suddenly remembering my ring in the tree in the City Botanic Gardens, so I decided that day to get on a bus, go into the city, and hope the ring would somehow be there. I felt a great deal of power and presence gathering around me as I walked a direct line to that tree from the front gates of the gardens. I prayed aloud to the spirits of the place and to my own that I would be able to find it. Once I got to the tree and regarded that being, I realised this was a lovers' tree. Though I had never done it and would certainly not do it, as I looked up at the great tree I noticed many humans had carved their initials with arrows and hearts and other lovers' sigils all over this Moreton Bay fig.

I knelt down in the mass of pythonic roots and worried. How could I possibly find this ring with all the rains, weather, and creature rustlings of three whole years . . . surely the ring would have sunk deep into the centre of the tree or the soil or have been taken by something or someone . . . I spied a hole into the roots that I believed I had thrown the ring into, and I took my phone and shone the torch into the hole. Marvellously and shockingly, I spied gold glinting at the back of the hole. It felt like my heart was in my mouth in that moment. I steadied myself, gave thanks, grounded and aligned, and retrieved the ring with a long stick. It felt like I truly reclaimed a lost part of myself—my own heart, perhaps, or at least a piece of it.

All of this had unfolded months after meeting the person whom I had originally met the same week I had met James. This new and emerging relationship all originally began during a workshop on the Devil in October 2015. I was completely saturated with eyes and heart for James at the time, so whatever attentions this person—which he later confessed to—had on me, at the time I did not return them.

When we met once more, it was while he was back visiting his family in Meanjin from living in Aotearoa (New Zealand). This happened in December 2018, only weeks after I had moved back from Naarm after James and I dissolved our romantic partnership. I had no idea that a sexual fling with someone I had barely conversed with would find me moving to Gadigal and Bidjigal country in Warrang two years later. I also had no idea that at nine months of living together in our beautiful apartment—after three full years of relating romantically—that he would suddenly announce he could no longer be in our relationship and that he was no longer in love with me.

In actuality, I am writing these words two weeks after this breaking, two weeks after I lived through a shocking nightmare. I truly thought this was it for me, and he would often say the same. Up until the last week we were together, he was still telling me that I was the love of his life and kissing my forehead sweetly and holding me at night. I later discovered he had been talking to most everyone in his life—except for me—for at least a month about this choice. It is quite natural that I felt angry and deeply shocked at this. Parts of me doubt I'll ever understand what happened there.

I have loved and lost. Cliché, to say the least, but the clichés are often honest, so let me be honest about the clichés. These are the Lady's initiations. By this I do not mean that there is a powerful humanoid being out there making random and fickle decisions about who will fall in love with who, whether it will be requited or not, or who will leave who. I mean that all of this, all that I have experienced, she lives in it. They are her mysteries. I think of everything that I have weathered, that has weathered me, and I think of her. My medicine, my affirmation, my provocation, my dare for the last few years has been this: *Our hearts are made to break open.*

13

I CAN SEE why for me this is the perfect poetry, the perfect words, the correct evaluation of all that has passed and all that is with me still. If you can, if you desire, if you want to feel it, try saying those words aloud right now wherever you are. Whisper them, sing them, incant them, declare them, question them.

> *Our hearts are made to break open . . .*
> *Our hearts are made to break open . . .*
> *Our hearts are made to break open . . .*

To hold more, to be held by more, to know love.

Who Goes Down, Who Arises:
The Descending Goddess Who Returns

A Wildwood chant:

> *O Queen of the Witches*
> *Rosy, crescent-crowned*
> *Who goes down, who arises*
> *Beautiful, terrible Ancient One.*

A strong and repeating motif in the mythos of the Witch Queen is that she is a rising and descending goddess. Gerald Gardner wrote of the legend of the descent of the Goddess. This is a feature in Aegean and Mediterranean mystery traditions. Of course there is Kore, Persephone, Queen of the Underworld. There is Inanna, Ishtar, great goddesses of the Fertile Crescent, of Mesopotamian cultures, who descend through the seven gates and face Erishkigal in the deep below. The Lady as I know her—the sacred lore I hold to—spins and sings a seasonal mythos that involves descent at the autumn equinox and rising from the underworld at the spring equinox. Other traditions might hinge these happenings to other feasts or tides, but there is usually an autumnal and spring-tide correspondence.

Why does she descend? In my understanding she descends because she is in deep grief, sorrow, and rage. It's also one of those things that just needs to happen. After, as Fate would have it, cutting down the corn and bearing the great scythe of time turned back in on itself; after the true death of our Prince of Paradise at Lammas tide, Our Lady stalks the worlds shrieking in pain, raging and mourning. Silently she wanders as the winds and rain clear away the debris of a past reality, and finally she comes to a cave in the side of a hill, a mountain, an opening that winds down and spirals into the very heart of the underworld. She who once stood as a giant bearing the cornucopia of land, sky, and sea; she who is the Queen of Elphame and the Mistress of Magic, comes to meet with the Dark One at the gates of hell. Perhaps you have stared into the face, into the eyes, of what felt like the enemy or the challenger? Those still eyes, watchful and remarkable in their capacity to never once move from holding your own gaze. Perhaps we cannot look into Death's eyes because we are afraid that what we would really see is not "the end" or annihilation or the loss of things, but the changing of things, the mystery of something that might imperil our very being to follow down to discover. Our Lady sees something like this in the Dark King's eyes and whatever they offer her at this gate must be enticing enough for the Queen of Witches, even in the midst of disorientation and ruin, to steal her attention and cause her to follow them down, down, into the underworld.

Innana's Descent

What is she descending into? Hades, hell, the underworld: words above and words beneath. That which is deep below. Once I stood in a circle of one hundred witches, artists, and activists in the redwoods at California WitchCamp. We had agreed to step our way into the ancient story of Inanna's Descent to face her own dark sister, Erishkigal, the Great Queen.

We sang,

> *Entering into initiation*
> *Walking into initiation*
> *We turn our ears, we turn our ears*
> *We turn our ears to the great below.*

The drums echoed through the groves and creeks as we spiral-danced around the dazzling fire. I looked into two hundred eyes, and even in the crimson-orange blurred darkness in the woods I could see the vulnerability, the fear, the intensity of focus, the commitment, and the open-hearted willingness to go as a group and as a tiny being into the great unknown. Maybe because we did it as one hundred hearts beating together we were each emboldened, helped to feel safer, to feel supported and held in the descent. And yet I could never really know for sure why each witch was descending that night, willing to follow Inanna eventually, crossing through seven gates, seven thresholds, and having ourselves stripped bare until bowed down low and naked we would crawl into the presence of Erishkigal. What happens next is recorded for us. When Erishkigal in her own grief rises to greet her sister, Inanna seizes the throne that her own sister had just stood up from. This leads, of course, to Inanna hanging on a meat-hook down there. It is quite fortunate that Inanna had the deep and abiding friendship and love of Ninshubur, who drummed for her back in the land of the living. Her beloved drumming up there in the land of trees, dates, cities of flesh-and-blood humans, birth, laughing children, illness, war, famine, greed, and eventually that death that would bring all into the deep place of demons, ghosts, gods, and mystery.

Because of Ninshubur, who had been given particular instructions to go to Enki—Inanna's grandfather—if she was not to return at the time appointed . . . because of a friend who was willing to wait, to witness, and to carry through the instructions passed to her by her beloved one . . . because of this, and only because of this, was Inanna eventually revived. Enki, Father of Wisdom, formed from the substance under his fingernails the Kurgarra and the Galatur—neither male nor female, some say genderless fly beings—and because of their profound genius and empathy, the care and solidarity they showed to Erishkigal in her pain and labour, were they then offered anything that the Queen of the Underworld could give. Of course they asked for the hanging corpse of Inanna. They had the water and food of life that Enki had passed to them, and in this way was Inanna restored.

There are needful and noticeable elements to this story that illumine the Witch Queen's magic and mythos. Here I offer the crucial and core pieces I observe:

- friendship and love
- descent and nakedness
- wisdom and genius
- empathy and honour
- fate and agency
- return and restoration

I deeply encourage a thorough study—in all the ways one can "study"—of this ancient myth. Much is revealed over and over again. I would like to share more of the story from my experience of Inanna and Erishkigal at the Reclaiming California WitchCamp in 2013.

Friendship has always been a shining star to lead and light my way through the confusions and choices of life. My human friends have been that council of allies, those people who I knew I could turn to when I could not speak to my family of origin or even to my own spirits, though these are friends too. Recently this has been underscored a thousandfold. My friends have turned up for me in a million ways big and small—it all feels big to me—during this horrific heartbreak. I honour them all, and I feel utterly grateful for these mutual threads of potent and joyful obligation that we hold with one another.

One of my deep beloveds—Lucky—was present in that circle of one hundred witches in the redwoods. Those words that we chanted, that fire we spiralled around, was on the first night of seven. It was on the seventh night that the intense power of friendship opened a portal to the mysteries and challenges of the story of descent and return.

She came to me whispering quietly, carefully, *She is down under that tree outside the circle, and she needs help to come in.* I was only a few parts of the ritual away from needing to be entirely focused and present to anchor a significant piece of spellwork that would seal this seven-night magical process we had embarked on a week ago. With a great deal of adrenaline and a blazing hyper-focus, I followed the witch to the edge of the circle and walked through that strange threshold. I looked down at my friend at the base of a mighty sequoia. I had met Lucky first through email, when she applied for my first one-to-one distance Shamanic Witchcraft Apprenticeship. Six months later we met in the flesh-to-breath, along with our friend Shiray, in Manhattan, and I had the deep pleasure of witnessing her Wildwood aspirant blessing. A year and a half later we are here, and I can sense the profound power surging through me, Lucky, and the witches gathered here. I remember feeling the gravitas of the moment. I remember how other awarenesses looked down through my eyes. I remember how, when I reached out my hand to my friend and spoke words, there was a chorus of voices and consciousness that rushed through me at once.

"You either take my hand and come with me into the circle and join life or you do not," we said. Simply. Simple. Through the bullshit of things to the heart.

I remember the holy dread in her eyes and the power of this person to turn up and be present to her initiation many times over. Only clarity seemed to be left, that kind of clarity where you see and know that this is the only step to take, this is the only way to go, and it's going to suck and there will be pain and breaking of things, but still deeper we go, inward we continue.

She grasped my hand and I pulled her up, embraced her, kissed her, and brought her into the circle. A week later I did this again, in a different way, in a different place, for a different reason. Except it was the same way and the same reason. And I have had the deepest pleasure of witnessing this witch and priestess do the same for others.

Initiation can be summed up in those words we all spoke—me and the Powers—to Lucky that night under the redwoods in a circle of one hundred witches returning from the underworld and reclaiming the vital life force that is ours to begin with. And in the end, it's only you . . . it's only me . . . it's only anyone at all who is faced with that holy risk and profound dare that has to claim the transformation, own it, and be changed by it. In the end it is trust. Trust in the mystery, but trust in your own desire as well. Trust in love.

14

Take your journal and writing implement into a space you know to be safe and secure for at least an hour. Clear that space beforehand and make it beautiful. Fill it with scents and icons that make you feel connected to beauty and sensuality; cover the floor with rose petals or other flower petals that signal to you a surrender into softness, colour, texture, and joy. If it works well with you, burn oils, fragrances, and incenses that fill the room with gorgeous smoke. Make sure you have ventilation in the room, such as an open window or door. All children and animals need to be cared for and away from this space if possible. Allow yourself to have this hour; take it for yourself. Carve it out in some way, and if it is a very real sacrifice of time and energy, make this sacrifice for yourself. You are entering into the bower of Our Lady.

Bring a thorny stem with a rose bloom into the space, and when you are ready, drop into your breath; watch how you are being breathed. Ground, centre, align, and become. Call out to the Lady, honour her, need her, desire her; let it come out in sounds and words, perhaps in sobs or shouts. Whatever you have to conjure with, conjure with that. Move the words and sounds through the rose and the thorn, through the stem itself.

When you feel the presence of the Lady, of the Witch Queen, tell her that you are going to write to her something of yourself. You are going to send her a love letter that will reveal important things about your life, about your experiences, your emotions, stories, reflections, and rites of passage. Say this aloud so you know it's real and you know that it's happening. Here and now it is happening. And then commit the rest of the time to writing this all out. Keep thinking, holding in your awareness, *I am here in the Lady's bower, she is with me, her eyes are upon me. Her consciousness permeates me, she is holding me and stirring me, bringing me into this work. I am writing this for myself, for her, and for what might be, that which I desire, that which I yearn for and with.*

When you are finished writing—finishing pouring and channelling onto the page—honour the paper and the ink, honour these tools of the art, and pour honey, or sing a song you love that breaks open your heart and soothes it. Or perhaps you burn fragrant resins to the Lady and send blessings through your body into all the bodies that you are connected with in this time and place. Honour the spirits of place once more. And when you are ready, pack down the space as a way to ground and transition to whatever else you might need to do.

Who Is This Lady Really?

The mystery of witchcraft will have it that we meet with her. She is there in the trial records, in fragments of history, legend, and lore; many female spirits, saints, and goddesses are there to be met.

We meet Abundia, Satia, Diana, Perchta, Hecate, Dame Orientis, Herodias, and Irodiada in witch lore of the medieval and early modern period. We see that in France, German-speaking countries, and what is now called Italy, Sicily, and Scotland, there are mentions of these night-flying, wisdom-sharing, spell-casting, magic-wielding spirit women who are likely also those we would know and respect as goddesses today. These names come down to us from various cultures, societies, and regions throughout Europe, and what seems to be the case is that this is a goddess who provides for her people, her children.

She displays that she can resurrect dead animals and restore them to life—that with one touch of a wand, she can wield the powers of rebirth. She teaches the use of plants and signs and magic words and calls us on certain nights to travel with her to liminal places between the worlds. There we revel with one another, feast, heal, and learn sorcery. Some theologians and inquisitors during the witch trials felt there was a Dianic society—a cultus of Diana—a conspiracy of witches growing through Europe. They thought that this was an organised and underground society that was opposed to Christianity, secretly working against it. These ideas, of course, merged with and shared a charge and tension with the diabolic compact concept of Satan securing witches through pacts, perhaps of the selling of souls for familiars or power and the complete repudiation of the church. This was thought to include the blaspheming of the host, the renunciation of baptism and Christ himself, and the treading on the crucifix. According to certain church thought, this was all to commit maleficium against good Christians and Christendom and carry out Satan's will. There are other books that skilfully unpack the many circumstances contextualising and colouring these times and these notions. You may find some in the bibliography. Here I am writing of the very real witching spirits who guide and initiate the craft I know and serve.

Witch Goddesses: Goddesses of Magic, Sorcery, the Otherworld, Fate, Power, and Sovereignty

As I write this, I am sitting in a crossroads I breathed and awoke into before I set to the task of immersing in the midwifing of this book-being. In the east I hailed St. Brigid, or Brighid; to me they are each other. While there may be distinctions, to me they come as sisters or as one. Brighid is the exalted one—as is the source of her name—I know and love. In the west, across from her, I felt into Our Lady of the Wildwood, the Witch Goddess whose secret name is written on my heart. She is Raven Queen, the crescent-crowned rosy one who descends and arises like Persephone and Inanna do and who wields mighty magic with a power that thrums through and as the cosmos knowing herself.

In the north of me in this personal crossroads of reverence and sacred orientation to my goddesses is Maa. Great Kali, black and luminous, all-encompassing, all-permeating, permeated consuming consciousness. Great initiator, beloved, and mother who I pour divine love into, receiving end-less blessing and mergence with mystery.

In the south I hail Morrigu, the Morrigan. My relationship with this queen, this Phantom Queen, Great Queen, Queen of the Otherworld and Fate, is nascent, and yet she has a potent relationship with some of these Great Ones who are here with me. By this I pay heed to her standing here at the gates of power with us all. I bow silently, respectfully, and sing her names.

Above me I invoke, honour, and adore Aphrodite in many aspects; Ou-rania, Pandemos, Symmakhia, Hetaira, Melainis, Peitho. I can feel how the sky is the great ocean and the ocean is filled with stars, rushing roar-ing space, and I feel broadened beyond horizons I cannot see. I feel how she is born—parthenogenesis—whole and complete unto herself, virgin. Though there are stories that say she comes from the foam churned by the castration of Ouranos by Kronos, before even the war between the Olym-pians and the Titans. Aphrodite is primordial, and perhaps she is directly of a lineage of sister queens of Mesopotamia and the Fertile Crescent, born of Inanna-Ishtar-Astarte. Perhaps this lineage brought her to Cyprus, to Kythera, into the rest of the Greek world, and then into the greater world at large. Almost all of us reading this know her name. Many times I have sung to Aphrodite and been in the sea reclaiming my own virginity, my own self-belonging, so that I may once again return to the rest of the world with the perspective that comes from loving a goddess and being loved by her.

I turn my heart to the below, in this crossroads unfurling and anchored in my guts and cauldrons. The roads are writhing, rising to meet me as

I open the gates of power. There! *Hekate! Brimo! Soteira! Adamantaea! Angelos! Trimorphos! Trivia!* Perhaps of all these goddesses, Hekate is the one most popularly linked to the forbidden arts, to those magics wrought in darkness discreetly. A goddess who has been changed by the telling, shapeshifted utterly by the Roman writers, and yet whose earliest mentions in writing are of a matronly maiden-being who delights in childbirth and brings wealth, harmony, law, and justice. It is said she is mighty and wise, holds power in all three worlds, and that Zeus bows to her. She who in the Homeric Hymn of Demeter, in which the infamous tale of the abduction of Kore is told to the world, hears the cries and goes to Demeter to share the news, to be an ally, to aid and support this grieving goddess, mother.

Then I craft my consciousness with cunning into a golden, glowing key, and with that key I unlock the gates of power and the crossroads open. *I am here and I am now. I am with the holy centre. The centre is the circumference and the circumference is boundless!*

In the centre that makes all this possible—and to which I have now arrived by first honouring these compass points, these dimensions and directions—I align with Persephone.

Persephone. Persephone. Persephone.

My story with Persephone and the mysteries I have been touched by via moving through the landscape of her being are still unfolding in my life. I could share with you facts, stories, lore, ideas, notions, interpretations of this goddess, of this mystery named Persephone, but this would all feel in some ways sacrilegious to me.

Persephone is the one I know as my soul goddess. This is a term I first published and unpacked in my book *Ecstatic Witchcraft*. I needed a term to describe my experience with this mystery. I often say, "I don't know where she ends and I begin, or vice versa." And this is what I mean. And more than this, deeper into it, I am referring to the awareness that I am hers—that at my death I will go to her. That we wander together through the infinite, though yes in my heart are lamps lit for many, many, many. And yes I can imagine that I will be walking with a legion through the infinite. After all, we are legion. And yet it is her name, her forms, her deep initiations that have brought me through and into myself again and again.

Persephone. That name is a mystery to me, a name I can fall into forever. No one really knows what that name means, not really. There are plenty of good ideas, however, including the destruction of light, the slayer of sound, destroyer, thresher of grain. And then of course many did not want to commit to saying her holy name out of holy awe and dread. And so there was and is another way to refer to her, and this is to simply call her Kore, which means girl, maiden, sprout.

Is Persephone the Witch Queen to me? My answer might shock you. My answer is no. She is not. And yet she can be and she could be. You might even know that she is or perhaps you have experienced the Witch Mother wearing that name, expressing as this mystery, this named goddess, who is also unnamed and whose secret names are guarded. And this is true of the Witch Goddess. This is why I say *Her name is written on my heart.* This is not to say *Ha! I have and know her secret name, and I shall keep it and hold it and laud it over you.* No, not at all. It is to say *Her secret name is unpronounceable and only my heart can speak it.* There are names we might incant, be passed, be whispered in the intimacy of initiation. Names revealed to us within secret rites in witch houses and covens. It's true that I have been passed these names and pass them. It is in the passing, that intimacy, the build-up to that moment, that awaiting and surrendering and the tension between not knowing and knowing that the mastery of this lies. In the passing of the name there is the name. Simple, unadorned, powerful, prescient, and the invoker of presence.

WILL YOU KNOW her name?

With all the magical skills you have and the capacity to do so, go to her and ask her: *What is the name I may know you by?* And listen to your heartbeat. Know this heartbeat is the secret forge of creation, and the mystery will be passed to you. In the passing and remembering there will be great joy, rapture and the meeting of her.

Do not write the name down, do not speak it aloud to friends or write it on social media in any way. Simply be with the mystery of the passing, of the sharing, of the intimacy. This is her name.

This Mystery-Spirit-Goddess-Queen who moves through the ages is renewing herself endlessly. She is the quaking of the worlds awaking and becoming themselves. She is the soulful poetry that inspires the dare to fall, to change, to risk the breaking apart of things, of worlds. She is the great challenger with sword and a crown of stars. She comes to the circle you have drawn and demands your honour, your loyalty; the blazing edge of your knife is marked for her. Her eyes are the dark moon, alluring and ancient. Her skin is obsidian, crimson, the white lustre of pearl and moon on sea foam, glowing through waves and shining through depths of sea. Her voice is thunder, whirlwind, the strange cry of corvids, the hiss of serpents, the language of cats, song of fern, and the breaking of hearts.

If Persephone is my soul goddess, then the Lady of Witches is my yearning, the depth, colour, tone, texture, flavour, sound, and breadth of it. Not the yearning for anything in particular, but the whole experience of yearning, of longing, of being, of becoming. She is the very fullness and meaning of yearning. The knowing that I have nothing to strive for, nowhere to be, that I am already this, already whole, intrinsically a part of all things, connected and interwoven. I have nothing to be and nothing to become except being and becoming.

And so I am made of a longing that ripples and radiates, that destroys utterly—like a hot knife cutting through butter—any affectation, any blockade is removed, swollen is the sea of her rage, and it overcomes all. So I float, swim, drown, toss, spiral in her sea. And in the sea, in her being, I learn sorcery. The art flowers through me, forged and tempered as this witch's knife. She has taught me without needing to teach me. She has looked into me and unlocked what needs to be unlocked, and there was the key the entire time. I take my steps into what is a warrior dance, a lover's dance, the artful wandering of one who carries something heavy with power and responsibility. If I am to wield this power in the worlds, then I must know to whom and what I am sworn.

16

WHAT OATHS HAVE you taken? What promises have you made? If you have made vows, how were they sealed and sworn? Reflect on this, write about it, dance through it, meditate on it, walk with it, journey, trance.

If you were to make oaths or swear vows, how would you go about it? What would you need to feel witnessed in this—to know you were doing it fully, honourably, and powerfully? As a witch, a spirit worker, who might you conjure, invoke, invite to attend and witness these oaths, these vows?

An oath is something that binds and frees you; a vow is something you must keep, uphold, be in integrity with. So, then, before making an oath or dedicating a vow, what are the risks, the dangers, and what will change when these are sworn and embarked upon?

I have made promises and broken them. I am sure you have too. I regret these. Promises to friends, partners, myself. Generally I have felt myself to be a person of my word utterly, and if and when I have fallen short and found myself compromised, I have journeyed into the grievance and the grief of that. I have committed fully to wade through and find what needs to be found. Sometimes a broken promise or unmet vow actually brings great insight if we can be accountable to the road and the journeying of that road. And then there are the oaths that are iron-clad and cannot be broken because to do so would not simply hurt another or infringe upon your own integrity—damaging perhaps your own self-image or comprehension of who you are or might be—but it might endanger a whole group.

In the craft of initiation and in initiatory craft we speak about oaths a lot. I am sure you have heard of oath-breakers and perhaps you might have taken oaths in circles or at crossroads or sealed them in pacts with masterful spirits and officers, with ink, blood, mark, flame, death, and rebirth.

I invite you to meditate on oath-breaking . . .

oath-keeping . . .

oath-upholding . . .

oath-knowing . . .

An oath may be taken in words or in deep silence; either way, there will be some kind of relational awareness. There will not just be you in your triple being who knows about it, but also your ancestors, gods, familiars, coven, tradition, house, community, parents, children, the land . . .

So go be with your oaths, your vows. Go—be with them. And if you dare, seal it on the secret name of the Lady and then walk as that warrior-witch through the worlds of power and commit to learning the art of shaping, wielding, refining, and deepening that power. We need you. Come!

I Dance Under the Rose

Our Queen of Witches is neither a composite character nor an amalgam, at least not in my experience. She is completely unto herself. She is real and essentially mysterious. She does not belong to any one tradition of witchcraft, and yet it is also true that different houses of craft and various streams of witchery are sponsored and in kinship with particular spirits and powers. It just so happens that some of these spirits and powers are the great witch-wreathed gods, the Old Gods who love witches, who desire witches, and who may be part of the awakening of or even summoning forth of witches.

So the Witch Queen, the Witch Mother, Our Lady is who she is. She may express herself as a goddess, faerie, angel, saint, or spirit you might already know, and yet she never stops being herself. She becomes. Those spirits never stop being themselves. There is conspiracy here, too, an intimate sharing and knowledge of something primordial. I embrace the notion of infinity and multiplicity and that these Great Ones are their own agents as well, with their own agendas, desires, and knowings that far surpass my ability to track and comprehend. We are partners, we work as if we are peers, and somehow—whether it's true or not—the gods act as if we are.

And therein lies a trick of our sorcery and a powerful part of the work of the Lady—act as if this is so, and if you dare it, if you meet the challenge, it may in fact be so.

So much of the world is bound by the notion of belief in something, or rather obedience towards a doctrine forsaking all others. Belief has become a term that implies a blind and unyielding faith in a series of set-out notions or seeming or conditional realities. One of the proverbs of Feri often contributed to Victor Anderson is *Perceive first, and decide what to believe later.* My beliefs or notions have evolved and changed based on the patterns I have observed in my experiences as a human being, a spirit worker, a witch, a lover, a friend, a teacher, a student, an initiate.

When I was writing what would become my first published book, *Spirited,* I had a strong identity as a so-called hard polytheist. I believed that each and every deity was unto itself, distinct, singular, individual! The idea of conflating the Morrigan with Kali was abhorrent to me. The idea that all gods are one God and all goddesses are one Goddess honestly made me want to kick a rubbish bin to the ground. Now I just shrug. I still don't think that the Morrigan is Kali or pay heed to that in/famous Dion Fortune-esque theology. Frankly I find those ideas and beliefs limiting and ridiculous in a different way, but I haven't considered myself to be a hard polytheist for many years now. In fact, I don't really enjoy defining theology at all anymore. If I consider the notion of self and hold the idea that there are infinite selves, infinite beings, and also infinite ways in which to relate, experience, and connect with that infinity, then all of the above is true and then some. Always. All ways.

When I go to the Lady and when she is drawn into possession via the ways my kin practise and celebrate, I can feel her, I perceive her. There are certain responses that almost always happen. When I hear her, feel her presence, or have invoked her, there she is—unmistakably herself. The mystery here is that this being—this mystery, this ancient, beautiful, terrible queen—is a dissolver of expectation. Actually, a ruiner. She is a tempest that rips apart one's notions. She demands that you rise to the occasion of yourself because you won't have this again. I have been at my lowest, ashamed, lying in my own self-pity and disaster only to know that she is there, holding the sword to my chest and reminding me of my power, challenging me to be courageous and dare to be a part of this one, this constellation, this convergence of place, time, and body.

At the heart of the craft I know is something so eerily beautiful, so uncannily present, and so powerfully humble that it undoes me every time. By every time I mean there is always more. I can completely and honestly attest to never being bored in witchcraft. Deep calls to deep, as they say. And if the Lady is the night-flying, wand-wielding, crescent-crowned, serpent-wrapped, ocean-seething, sky-shining, star-birthing, darkness-loving, birth-giving initiator that I know her to be, how could it be anything but this?

Do not dance around this, dance through this. You will have to be clothed by all these halls and through this maze discover the blessing of the rose. Know that you were born with this rose blooming in your heart and that each year that goes by a petal falls and kisses the dirt until all the petals are gone, revealing the star-white gleaming of your bones, know that the rose does not stop blooming. Know that there will always be more roses blooming. And that which threatens the beauty of this mystery . . . that which would seek to rip the rose from the stem, yes, they will feel the small sting of thorns, but more so than this, the reddest and purist rage of the heart on fire with healing. Those that rip the rose from the stem run far, run to the end of the bitter sea, and let her take you or face the reddest rage of pure feeling.

The Lady counts a string of her own pearls for the whole world, as her face shifts and changes . . . listen to her counting; find peace in that. The moon will still dance with sun and earth. If nothing else, draw peace from that. Then go to the sea with beloveds and after cursing all that has harmed you and yours, cleanse yourself in the waves, for Our Mother the

Ocean and the People of the Sea are ancient and welcoming. Make sure to tether to land if you will not be swept away, and know the blooming rose in the heart needs tenderness, fierce passion, and constant blessings.

Fear will not destroy you in the end. It is submission to what seems most horrific . . . remember the Son of Art, the Thorn-Horned One of the road to gnosis. Artfulness is required for this revolution, my beloved; drink deep of the well that sustains you.

—Felix, my fetch-mate, as the rain feeds this
Yuggera, Jagera, and Turrbal country, March 2019

She has come to undo you
and watch her faithfully
She has come with the knife of art
to teach about perfection
undoing knots in the guts
for there is no such thing
She says.
Turn. the. fuck. up.
You can try to swallow darts
and razors, and chop away at fat
to shine forth in the radiance—
        of what?
She has come to undo me
and I watch her
this is pleasure
Her rites are risk
Her rites evoke lust
Her rites are the passion
        rising through my eyes
as they close and I am dedicated
        to me—Virgin.
There is no such thing.
Let us not say,
I know I am not perfect . . .
Irrelevant!
Boring.
        Seriously.
Philosophically, ridiculous.
Instead—what if?
What if the thatness that is
twists through the knife
and we dance, teetering on that
        violent edge
        of lust

of the grace we have discovered is the core
of letting go
of releasing ownership
of nurturing the moment
like the precious, infinite doorway
we all become
in the end . . . there is no fulfilment of desire . . .
for we are like serpents in the waves of time
becoming, not grasping.
and all we have become, through time,
in the spaces of time
are the skins we have shed
signs of all that is becoming
    endlessly
no need for a word like perfect
when She undoes Herself.
    all. the. time.
no point in speaking, qualifying,
when the Word Enfleshed is Communion Most Holy.
And so—
    She is here, and I am that.

I INVITE YOU to pause once more here and before reading on I suggest re-reading the previous two chapters on the Devil and Our Lady. I then encourage you to spend at least one moon cycle with each of them. Perhaps you begin at the dark moon or the new moon (the newly born crescent) or the sixth night of the moon or the full, and in some way magically/ritually open yourself to that being (perhaps with one of the processes or workings above) and then lean in—take notice; observe the unfolding of your life and the happenings, feelings, sensations, experiences—throughout that moon cycle.

Chapter Six

The Blessing and the Bane

By my two hands
by my head full of fire
and my heart full of honey
do I do this Thing.
By the Fallen Angel—the First Dead—the Faerie Lover—
    the Reddest Red!
By the Lady's Bower and the Silver Hour
by the Mighty Web and the Bone-White Thread
by the Old God's Word and the Shaking Sea
I conjure forth this spell to be!
To those tyrants in towers
with stolen wealth
whose orders
mine the earth's own self.
The witches' curse of harrowing
The witches' curse will now begin!
To those rulers who see not the folk
Those kings who cut the forests down
Those politicians who lie, deceive
Into the ocean, now to drown.

The witches' blessing of growth and truth
The witches' blessing of claw and tooth!
To those turned away from suffering
whose hearts are bound by greed
Those snarling at the poor and brown
Know the power in the seed!
The witches' curse of consciousness
The witches' curse of awareness!
Those who rape, molest, and take
Those who trespass upon children
Those who cannot help but hate
Feel the presence of all your Kin!
The witches' blessing of depth and darkness
The witches' blessing of land, sky, and sea!
I call the wind up from the well
to blow forth this quaking spell
I call the fire through the earth
and the powers of death and birth
I call the Mystery to bind it well
and call the stars and seas to swell!
And if I too should do these things
may then the curse upon me bring
all that I say and sow and make
Old God hear me as the world shakes!
And those whom by these words are cursed
hear this way of restoration:
if responsibility you will take,
if mending you will make,
if you will go up to the stake
and tell the truth before the break,
then the curse's power will recede
and you will know the power of the seed.
But only then and only if
these tides you turn by your own hand
only if you make the stand

only if you reprimand
what has been done
with greed and malice
with lies and deceit
with hatred and bigotry
with arrogance and ignorance
only then, and only if.
And so the curse is in the wind
and so the horses and spiders spin
and so the fires you burnt us in
and so the waters of healing bring
beauty and rest, wealth and love
to all those in the Lady's ring.
And by the crooked tower and the broken bell
I cast this mighty, power-filled spell.

—A curse I wrote several years ago

Cursing, hexing, blasting, binding. This is what the world of humankind fears about our kind, witches, the most. More than seventy years after the Gardnerian reformation of witchcraft and the revival movement, witches working in the West are still quagmired in a kind of confusing and internally self-defeating game of educational and respectability rhetoric. We know what that is: *witches are harmless, we are just like you, we believe in the law of threefold return, we would never do anything bad because that means we'll fuck ourselves over*. I, and many others, call bullshit on that kind of moralism and escapism. We all know that witches curse just as we heal. In fact, some branches of the craft possess truly sophisticated theologies and magical teachings regarding these things that ought not be dismissed. Sometimes in the darkest night, in the most liminal place, there is no difference between what is called a blessing and a bane.

If we are to curse, better we do it excellently; better it comes from a place of seeking justice, repair, and the restoration of truth, wisdom, and love. Sometimes the well-executed curse will bring us to the gates of that restoration. It begins with the knowledge and embracing of responsibility and of the responsibility to act; to know when to step aside and when to speak forth; when to draw the line, when to send the warning, when to walk the crooked road to the crossroads to do the deed without a name.

In a world run by Christianist propaganda and morality concerning the nature of the cosmos and the nature of our humanity, to curse is defined by its deliberate intent to harm, to cause injury to another or, in fact, to a system or an entire society and way of thinking or doing. In the witch's own house, a curse can be a defence or a clear act of justice; the less we are bound up in our own complexes and knee-deep in our shit and the more work we are doing on the nasty business of complicitness, the more spacious and clean the circle of art from which we direct the operation. Other essays and conversations, articles and books can be written on the lack of cosmological coherence regarding the law of threefold return, but suffice it to say that the toucher is touched (taught to me by Orion Foxwood, taught to him by Lady Circe). If what I am reaching out to touch is justice or repair, then I will be touched by that, and by it I will effect change.

In the working of curses as I know them, a line is often symbolically held as an etheric reality in the consciousness of the group or individual, or it is drawn out before us there in the earth with dust, herbs, and powders and named. We would have already prepared ourselves in the ways we know how and formed the working space in the ways that work. We conjure and call to the tutelary spirits that guide and guard us in the work and protect us from the injury of an operation gone wrong. We might have even prepared magical decoy devices of ourselves so that if the power we build within the circle of art or at the crossroads is not channelled cleanly and gets caught in complexes, most of the psychic collateral damage falls on those decoys rather than our own selves. These are ancient arts. We know what we do. And if you aren't sure or committed to it, why do it?

In the drawing of the line, perhaps with a blackthorn blasting wand or perhaps with a black-handled knife, a rusty iron nail, or an exquisite piece of broken glass that we ourselves have bled upon, we seal in the oath of responsibility. We know what we do, and we do it. We are here, and we are not pretending otherwise. Perhaps divination and omens have been taken; spirits, peers, or teachers consulted; and ultimately the ongoing work of owning our own shit and committing to the work of turning up to the wild elegance of our divine human animal natures. We draw the line and we name it.

This is the line of wanton destruction. This is the line of poisoning the rivers and raping the land. This is the line of bruising, breaking, and manipulating bodies senselessly. This is the line of massacre of sovereign peoples and the invasion of their or our lands. This is the line of profiting from the labour of others. This is the line . . .

What is important to know here, and what many well-intentioned people will flag, is personal hypocrisy, the aforementioned complicitness. What is often forgotten—and usually through a disbelief that there are, in fact, specific positions of power and people who gladly fulfil them—is that there are entire systems set up before our births to run for the profit of an elite and brutal few, causing senseless harm and inevitable savagery. We are born unwittingly into them, as are those who will come next. We become aware of such systems and make choices either to reject them, working to dismantle and destroy them, compromise with them within, or wholly embrace them. There are many opportunities in life to redress and make true repair. Think of the smaller and more immediately emotional circumstances—the same kind of repair we demand in these is what we demand in the macro. The fact of complicitness in capitalist and imperialist systems cannot be evaded. Again, we take responsibility. Part of taking that responsibility can be the audacious act of cursing and naming the line to ourselves, others, and to the listening air. This is why we turn up to the work clean of complexes as far as our ignited awareness—an eventual victory of the craft and ways like it—can ascertain. We ourselves, with the blood or the breath or the pregnant focus upon the tool that draws the line, consign ourselves to an oath with the spirits and all our parts in that moment. If we in any way choose to participate in these actions we are now articulating by art, we too will be cursed. The truth is, our societies, our empires, are cursed, and they are crumbling and many of us are flailing and losing ourselves to collective madness. As the stories of the god Dionysos teach us, that madness can be healed by the Great Mother through surrender, through wandering, and through love.

Cursing is the recourse of the crisis cult; it is one of the ways we face the full force of empire and send the warning. If you continue to trespass this line, then may doom befall you, incapacitating you; may you be frozen and trapped by the demons of your making that you succour by your own blood, words, and deeds. The witchcraft at the heart of the hysteria in Europe and wherever Europeans went in the world was the kind of witchcraft that would have arisen and developed in such a time—a witchcraft seeking to impart tools of binding the lords in their towers, as the *Aradia* says. A witchcraft of causing illness and injury to the wealthy and their land and livestock—of those who reigned over the land and the serfs, those responsible for the closing of the commons, or the destruction of sovereign cultures and Indigenous ways of life, with the agenda to amass more wealth, effectively disenfranchising and oppressing the multitudes.

And where we blast, we bless. And where we hex, we heal. The puritanical moralism of most Protestantism and the greedy and rapacious treachery of the Roman Catholic Church infect us still. Not only does it cause even witches and spirit workers to spit upon the noble legacy of our skill in cursing and the artfulness of its place in our code of honour and action—even after the operation, we might believe, on some subconscious level, that we need to take the hit, that we deserve the fallout even if we have behaved with integrity. We—the witches, artists, lovers, activists—must be burnt out.

No! I scream the curse of *No!* to those infecting ideologies of self-hatred, self-injury, self-blame, and *No!* to original sin, the belief that we enter this world corrupted and out of grace. *No!* Where we blast, we bless. Where we hex, we heal. And so once the curse is effected and our spirits carry it out, we communicate through all the worlds—this is the line, and here is what will befall those who trespass it—and send the arrows to those perpetrating the crimes so that we may clear opportunity for healing and repair by their incapacitation.

We also abate greater harm. Consider how we treat cancer cells today. We then bless each other and ourselves, we sing praises on the wind and into the land, to the mountains, the valleys, the villages, the towns, our siblings, our lovers, the moon, and the sea. We bless, we bless, we bless, and we let each other know of the visions that live behind the act and fuel the inspiration to act. We remind each other of what we would like to see and the world we are calling into being, into birth.

Through death the way is made clear for birth.

When the curse is elegant and excellent, we effect the change we wish to see in the world and we are no longer evading responsibility. We embrace it. In this we become powerful.

17

Head Full of Fire, Heart Full of Honey, and These Two Hands of Art

When I teach methods of cursing and binding to witches and spirit workers, I almost always begin with this meditative and magical process. There is a way of speaking about those who are inspired—those who are seers and poets blessed with an immense share of life force—that is said to be of Irish derivation: *fire in the head*. This is where I draw my inspiration for this particular process.

Find a place to sit and be still if this is accessible to you. If not, you could do this lying down or really in any position as long as you can notice your breath in some way and bring your awareness and imagination along with you. Try not to fall asleep in this exercise.

Bring all of your attention—as much as you can gather—to your head after grounding and aligning. Open to perceiving and feeling fire within the cauldron of your skull. Notice the colour, texture, sensation, size, and feeling of this flame. You are not required to gain any information about why this or why that, just become aware of it. Meditate on the phrase *Fire in the head* or *Head full of fire*. How does this make you feel? What is this revealing within your consciousness? When you feel suitably aware of this fire and have spent enough time in this meditation, say aloud something like:

> *My head is full of fire.*
> *My head is full of fire.*
> *My head is full of fire.*

When you are ready, bring your focus into your precious, powerful, fragile four-chambered heart. Journey through the gate of the heart, where you might pause for a moment and breathe, taking notice if you perceive any sign, sigil, sound, or signature there that may be a key to passing through the gate of the heart. This protects your inner sanctum. The gate of the heart is thought to be or relate to the pericardium—a fluid-filled sac that protects the heart and also aids lubrication—in traditional Chinese medicine. My beloved Ravyn, a dynamic TCM practitioner, taught me about bringing my attention to the heart protector, which I also think of as the "gate of the heart" when I need stronger and emotional boundaries and containment.

Note down whatever sign, sigil, sound, or signature you receive at the gate of your heart. You may need to write or draw this down on a page. Move into and through the chambers of your heart and open to perceive and feel that this sacred heart is filled with honey. Notice the colours, smells, and sensations of this honey and how it makes you feel. Allow yourself to fully feel, sense, imagine, and fantasise wildly about this honey in your heart. Build and build this emotion strongly and clearly until you are willing to say aloud,

> *My heart is full of honey.*
> *My heart is full of honey.*
> *My heart is full of honey.*

Allow yourself some deep sighing exhalations to transition into this next piece of the process. Holding your hands out palms up, roll your attention down your left arm or the idea of that arm and into your left hand. And here a different question is being offered. This provocation:

> *What is the magic—the current of power—*
> *that moves in, through, and as my left hand?*

Open to perceive what occurs or what kind of responses unfold through you by holding this question, by dropping it through the layers of your labyrinthine being and consciousness. Give a few minutes to this, perhaps longer, but not too long; somewhere between 3–5 minutes is perfect.

Allow yourself some deep sighing exhalations to cleanse and transition. Your awareness is guided back up the left arm into your heart, and then your attention moves down your right arm and you engage the same process but with your right hand.

What is the magic—the current of power—
that moves in, through, and as my right hand?

Open to perceive what occurs or what kind of responses unfold through you.

Finally, after meditating with and as the two hands, your awareness returns to not just the heart full of honey, but also the head filled with fire. Ground and centre into this state of awareness: of inspiration, of invigoration, and perhaps hyperawareness. You might notice a great deal of power moving and spiralling through your being or you might feel very still and grounded or something else entirely. Aspire to notice these sensations and experiences in a semi-detached, suspended way. There is no need to attach to any version of events or story anything into this right now.

When and if you feel an alignment and a synergy between your head, heart, and hands, seal this process with these words or words like them:

By my head full of fire and my heart full of honey
do my two hands know what they do.

You might recite this several times. It might become a chant or a tone or a song. End with silence. You may wish to journal and record your observations and experiences.

This magical process can help engage several modes of learning and knowledge at once. We are engaging our intellect, our imaginal faculties, our emotions, and our kinaesthetic and somatic sensations at once.

My advice to myself and to others embarking on any serious piece of magic, on any substantial decision at all—regardless of whether we consider it a magical one or not—is to always, from an aligned and grounded state, become aware of our motivations, our agendas, our aims, our desires, and how the wyrd is moving.

As a witch I may temporarily enact certain powers as a mighty one or a godlike (becoming) being when I engage in certain workings. When I become aware of certain possibilities within my own being and dare to work with them, to seduce and conjure them into being, I am being a witch. I am sensuously participating in the dynamic unfolding of infinite infinities when working sorcerously.

An experienced and aligned witch becomes keenly aware of how the conversations are moving, how certain tides rise and ebb, shift, and change their flow or direction. Just as we are never not possessed and that concept of a singular authoritative self with an individual frame of mind and consciousness unto oneself is one that can be infinitely critiqued, so a witch working magic is ecological. What I mean by this is that at times a curse or binding enacted by a witch or a group of sorcerers or spirit workers is being done with and through the support of other beings and spirits who might be catalysing the working. Think even more broadly and consider how as witches, as any kind of being or life-form, we are each like a cell within a great leviathan ever-deepening body of mystery. Therefore, someone or a whole group of folks praying or asking or desiring really intensely for certain things to take place—say on behalf of marginalised or oppressed life-forms, humans, species, or bio-systems at large—will bring witches to answer that call whether we know that's what is happening or not. Ideally the deeper our apprenticeship to the craft becomes, the more finesse we wield, and we become increasingly conscious of what we are doing and why from multiple perspectives or, as often happens, it dawns on us later. I know for me that is the case. *Oh, I did that thing then for this reason now . . .* is an insight that often emerges. And most of the time it's a piece of a perspective. There is so much I'll never know. I only have what is here with me now and the little vibration or rippling from what is considered "past" or "future."

And, of course, a curse or a binding is the recourse and resource of those who are in deep need now. There are very real and deadly circumstances that many people find themselves-ourselves in, in which the working of sorcery for emancipation, liberation, requires a yes to our own lives and therefore a no or a stop to certain actions or behaviours from those who continue to perpetrate active harm and violence. So what is the yes and what is the no? In a healing we might be saying yes to vitality, to life, to a strong immune system that supports a life of quality, and therefore we will be saying no to cancer cells, no to bacterial infection, no to viral infection. Remember these too are all life-forms and life systems. It just so happens that they are also not desired, not welcome in this particular iteration, and there is a desire to destroy these or strengthen enough to be able to either co-exist or eventually move through the blockade to that vitality.

The head full of fire is that powerful daemonic inspiration that guides us with the truth-aware compass of our own divinity. That heart full of honey—that precious, precious love—this is the bower, the hive, the shrine that anchors us in the love of ourselves, the love of connecting and relating. This is the magic that can arise out of trust and love, and so it is from the head and the heart that the hands know their work and how to achieve it.

Sometimes the greatest magic is in simply aligning and watching and feeling certain things click into place, certain roads rise to meet us, and the spell is the committing, the stepping onto that path or road with that lantern of love and life. This commitment can be from saying yes at this crossroads: from this place I walk in this direction and I summon this road to rise to meet me in this. I wish to be as resourced, as keenly connected, as aware, and as well-met as possible. I challenge you to simply meditate on this last sentence. It seems to me, from the many people who I have been humbled and honoured to meet in my life—from the many conversations that have kept me awake laughing and crying at night—that this is what the vast majority of humans desire. And so this is the power of magic and also of the curse. We are prepared to say—in covenant, in coalition, in camaraderie with other loving and justice-invoking beings—that this curse-blessing or blessing-curse is a piece of responsibility and accountability that I am weaving in order to create and allow for a vaster and more integrous vision and hope to come to fruition.

Of course there are also ruinsome, harrowing, illness-wielding forces and spirits that are in ancient relationship with our lives and our lineages as human beings. There is Lilith, the nocturnal demon who seeks to murder infants, steal the vitality of men with the spilling of their seed, and fill the world with demon children—or at least this is one Lilith and one cultural storying of this ancient storm-wind-illness-spreading goddess/spirit/demon. And one can be all of these at once; they do not cancel each other out. Life is far too complex and interesting for the business of absolutist dualities. There are opportunistic bacteria and viruses that "haunt" the airs, the dirt, the waters, the skin, and it is so. They exist just as we exist, and our lives are lived in a navigation and negotiation of this truth, of this reality. As human witches we have the power to be powerfully premeditated, to be thoroughly self-reflective, to conjure up compassion and empathy, and also to discern when and how and what we wish to take responsibility for and with.

A curse is a commitment. When I embark on this work, I am engaging in the life force. I am not disengaging. I am not escaping or disentangling myself at all; in fact, I am firmly connecting myself in. I am linking myself to something I care about and following through. I am saying yes: here I will be vigilant, a watcher of this line we have drawn together and acknowledged as important, sacred, significant.

It feels pertinent to share a ritual form, a process whereby one may call upon, concentrate, contain, and focus a great deal of power for not just a curse or a baneful working, but any kind of intensive work.

18

IN A QUIET time, go to a quiet place. Bring with you a solid jar that is taller than it is wide, enough red thread that it could be tied around the jar at least three times and knotted three times easily (already have it measured and cut), and some offerings for the spirits of the land.

Once you are in the place, acknowledge country, give the offerings, and take time to align your souls in the way we have already begun to do. Perhaps you also trace a compass round and honour the four kin; perhaps you conduct the crossroads to open through your being; perhaps this has all become a circle. Affirm this to yourself with song or words or gestures and silence in some way if need be.

In this quiet time and quiet place, kneel down if possible and touch the jar's base to the ground. Perhaps the ground is sandy, muddy, grassy, rocky. Take especial notice of what you are currently sitting or standing on. When you have a strong sensation of this, take the red thread and hold it out before you in your hands. Conjure up your fetch and begin to wordlessly tone sounds to gather up power and focus on the red thread in your hands. Begin to build up the sensation-idea-knowing that the red thread is actually a red serpent and that it is entwined around a red rose. This is all happening in your hands. Let this vision or knowing build in intensity and precision as you tone and gather power. Hear the hiss and the movement of the red serpent in your hands, feel the sensation of the scales and the tongue and serpent entwining around this red rose. Smell the rose. These senses are your doorways to magic; work with whichever ones are working with you.

Once you feel it has been enough time and you have a sense that it is okay, gather up some sand, earth, soil from this place and spill it into the jar. Feel the land helping you with your magic. Obviously if it does not feel okay to gather up the earth here and put it in the jar, then this working will need to be tried elsewhere some other time and it is best to honour the spirits and finish the working. To seal this all tie the red thread around the jar three times and tie three knots.

You now have in your hands a great deal of power. It is not power locked away; there is no lid on this jar. The red serpent and the red rose that move through and as this red thread have sealed and affirmed the magical power held within this vessel. It is time to honour the spirits and unwind whatever space you have woven. Perhaps you give some more offerings, if that feels correct, and then you leave and do not look back.

Once you are back at your home, you can place this jar in a dark and unnoticed corner of the space or under your working altar. When you need to tap into more power than you feel like you can summon or build for a special kind of working, bring this jar with you into the space. You can repeat this rite perhaps every season or cross-quarter. As you work it, it will work you, and you will likely discover more and more of what is happening as you undergo these magical steps.

The Work of Blessing & Healing

The witch who cannot curse cannot cure, the witch who cannot hex cannot heal, the witch who cannot blast cannot bless. Generally speaking, the books out there would speak first of the blessing work and then move into the more serious-advanced-mysterious-occulted cursing work. Yet in my experience, though there is serious obfuscation and ironic demonisation of the witch's blasting work, it is the very serious work of healing and blessing that requires a great amount of recontextualisation as well.

19

WE HAVE REACHED a place of rest in this book—a place to call upon she who midwifes the world into being, a place to honour mighty Brighid. In my home tradition, St. Brigid and Brighid may be understood to be the same mysterious one, and many in the Wildwood have an especial relationship with her that reflects some Irish and folk Catholic understandings of the saint in relationship to Mary and to the Christ. We consider her to be a midwife and foster mother to our Devil—one of our Sacred Four—and as well as this, we know her to be a peacekeeper, a prophet, a seer between and through all the worlds, a tender to our souls and cauldrons. And, as the tenth century Cormac's Glossary would have it, a healer, a poet, and a smith. These are all important aspects of St. Brigid and of the goddess we know today as Brighid, who may have been many regional goddesses and spirits or something far more uncanny and beyond our current cultural comprehension.

LET US WANDER through the mists and go to St. Brigid under her oak, by her forge and fire, and to the place where we may visit her well.

Acknowledge country, ground-centre-align, and conjure up the feeling or imagining of mists moving all around you. Then allow yourself to move between the worlds—and feel how much you are really moving through—and go to her at the oak. She will be there waiting. You might have to wait too.

In this place you may spend time rejuvenating, asking questions, seeking prophesy, scrying into the well and flame, wondering with the mysterious creature in the well (who is this one?!), and discovering what other realms or worlds you might move into from this strange and powerful place.

Ask Brighid what you need to ask—what is most burning for you to ask. What do you really want to come to know, to intimately understand, to feel deeply? You may leave with several challenges and insights, and undergoing this kind of work may catalyse movement in your inner life, so inner it becomes outer. I often like to think of this place as where my inner world kisses and merges with the otherworld.

Pour out beer or dedicate cakes or honey or song or candlelight to Brighid. Perhaps you already have a shrine or a space dedicated to your relationship with her. And perhaps you had no desire or were not persuaded to go find and seek counsel with St. Brigid. Perhaps you encountered another mystery in a similar or parallel space. Perhaps another being or spirit or happening unfolded. And this is just as it ought to be.

Do you feel rested, recharged, rejuvenated? If you cannot answer a solid yes to this, I invite and challenge you to draw a bath, fill it with herbs and oils that make you feel loved and happy, and get into it. If this is not accessible or available, ring a friend or go visit one or ask someone to come to you if possible. Read a book, watch a film that makes you cry, wear jewellery and clothes beloveds gave to you. Write poetry. Eat food that you fucking love. "Get comfy," as my beloved Justin would say. Get deeply and powerfully comfy.

WHAT DOES BLESSING mean in your life? How do you know something is good, a balm, soothing, nourishing? Is it that you feel alive and content? Is it that you feel restful and at ease with things? Are the good things opposite in flavour, tone, texture to the bad things? Is it good or healing because it is constructive and helpful to you? Do these things allow you to receive and welcome what you think, feel, know you want? These aren't trick questions. I hope we are both considering these, meditating on these, and making up our own questions and provocations.

The work of blessing is both subtle and clear. I could say that in this moment, writing these words and watching them appear on the laptop screen before me, that I desire the blessing of good food, the blessing of prosperity and joy continued and deepened, and the blessing of health. Now these are clear, obvious, forthright desires for blessings that most likely the vast majority of people would hope for. I write these words in August 2021 as the world is deep in another wave of COVID-19 infections. The delta strain infects the vaccinated and unvaccinated, and though vaccines statistically are shown to help people stay out of hospital and not die—basically to not get seriously ill—there are many, many cases of COVID-19 rising again around the world. What I deeply, fantastically, wildly crave is the blessing of seeing my loved ones in Bali, in Amsterdam, in Britain, in Ireland, in places colonially named California, Oregon, New Hampshire, New York, New Mexico, Brazil, New Zealand, and also in places I haven't been able to reach in the continent I live in! And yet while this would feel like a deep and profound blessing of joy and connection to me—and something my heart yearns for—it would actually be a heavily risk-laden one and a complicated and stress-begetting blessing. This in turn would have me in various states of concern, worry, and anxiety. So is this a blessing at this time, with these limits and circumstances?

So then the blessings I deeply crave, underneath what I have already easily put forth, are the blessings of completing this book, of having it published, of having people read it and hopefully be inspired, grounded, and found by it. I desire deep and profound centredness and alignment for all those I love. I desire that in this moment, in this time, as I write these words, as you read them, a mighty blessing of radiant, wondrous, and potent knowing of your innate belonging arises within you. These are the blessings I conjure.

Then it seems to me that we must drop below what we think we know, feel, or perceive and spiral even deeper to the treasure trove of secret wishes, hopes, fears, and desires.

20

IS THERE A labyrinth near you or are you able to set up a simple labyrinth in your own home with surveyor's tape or paint, if you are able to have something more permanent? I know witches who paint pentagrams and Minoan-style labyrinths on the bottoms of carpet and then flip them over when they want to do that work. Perhaps you cannot walk or leave the home easily; perhaps mobility is limited, and you aren't sure moving through a labyrinth in any way would be helpful to you. I am wondering if you or someone else could draw a labyrinth of your choice on a page in front of you, on a computer device, or move your fingers through sand so you could feel the movement? I am wondering if these could be your portals to this labyrinth-movement-meditation?

As you go, hold this question: *What are the blessings I most deeply desire in my life, in the lives of my beloveds and in this land, and in the world?* As you move, wander, are guided through the folds and pathway of the labyrinth in whichever way this is accessed, be open to knowing the answers. They may emerge as you engage this practice or in dreams or daydreams and visions later on. Be open to any and all ways of receiving and perceiving the answers to these questions, and be open to receiving blessing. What would it mean for you—in this moment—to be open to receiving blessing? It might be true that you are beginning to realise—or remember—how big blessing really is, how intense, that things may need to be rearranged, adapted, adjusted, and manoeuvred in order to truly welcome in blessing.

And so if and when you are asked to work for blessing—whatever kind of blessing—what kind of doors need to be opened, what bindings and curses might need to be tasted, faced, dissolved, or undone in order to truly make manifest in the lives of these people, this person, the blessings they desire?

This is why I always offer a tarot divination consultation before working for a friend or a client (though the client of course may be a friend). Is this my work to do? What is actually going on here? What pathway or strategy is better suited to a deeper integrative working?

People come to professional witches, cunning folk, and spirit workers for infinite reasons, and there are repeated and typical reasons. The client desires healing; the client thinks or feels they are cursed and wishes to know about that and have it removed. The client wants their ex-lover or partner to return or wants a new lover or to reinvigorate a current love arrangement or partnership. The client wants their business to succeed or they want to be financially prosperous. The client feels they need guidance to weather the elemental reality of being alive now, entangled within these systems that we could mostly name, and how best and most proficiently to navigate the strangeness and the stress.

When we consider these requests as magical consultants—or even within our circles and covens, with friends and beloveds—it becomes clear that there is no binary between the baneful work and the blessing work, between the work of the left hand and the work of the right. It becomes clear that we require the head full of fire, the heart full of honey, and the two hands to tend, finesse, and work multiple realities.

Say a person has come to you because their parents have died, they are in grief and disorientation, they have inherited a substantial amount of money and wish to know what to do with it. They list many options before you even have the heart to ask them to stop speaking so the reading might be without less side information. They may say, "Oh, I could create a community resource fund for marginalised communities" or "I could start up an art space and rent it for next to nothing for up and coming artists" or "I could buy this building and create affordable housing for those who would otherwise be houseless or those who are struggling with addiction and who wish to work and need security and safety in order to take steps in that direction." My approach begins with listening, a whole lot of listening, and through grounded and potent alignment a whole lot of very active compassion and empathy. I might be inwardly chanting certain mantras to Quan Yin or Kali and then beaming that outward toward and around the client. I might be moving around the space lighting candles and incense—

after checking with them—and asking a few clarifying questions every now and again to allow the person to have some pauses in their speech. I might actually ask the person to stop talking after five or ten minutes and suggest that I lead a grounding and purification practice, to which people always respond positively. I have yet to meet the person who refuses a grounding. Once the person can sense that they are grounded and in a space of active compassion but also discernment and magical strategy, I can begin to be clear about my process.

Let's divine. Let's look at the cards and consult the spirits and ancestors about what is over your head, about your life as the bird looks down upon it and the worm and the serpent see from below you. Let's call on the blessings of the winds and the directions to guide our way. Sometimes it becomes clear that we need to open the crossroads or cast a circle to focus and contain the work. Some clients are open to this so we do it together while I facilitate and anchor so they can receive and be, and other times this kind of ritual would not make sense or come at the right time for the person. So after the reading we have more information and we have several roads we might be able to embark upon. Generally the consulting spirit worker will speak about the potential strategies or pathways that look like the best options. We might even discover there is a need for soul retrieval, ancestor work, or some specifically targeted spellwork. It might be there is a particular spirit that needs to come through and give forth information and insight. Depending on the time container or the context of the consultation or reading, a variety of things could happen with the client's consent.

The whole time I am gathering virtue, power, and privately, internally consulting with my souls and spirits in order to focus and direct the power of the blessing in the best way possible. But so much other work is usually necessary. Work of clearing and cleansing, questioning and challenging, purification and opening, protection and banishing; other works first that then lead to the blessing, to the pouring in of the vital force. We open certain roads and call for certain aid.

21

WHAT WOULD IT be like for you—in this moment—to turn to face the direction of the rising sun and in a grounded-centred-aligned state bring your charged awareness to the gate of the rising sun? If you have followed through with this, now you might decide to ask for an ally, a spirit helper, to come to you, to make themselves known. Pay attention, be willing to receive, and open to listen and perceive. Then repeat this same process with the direction of the midday sun, the setting sun, midnight, and perhaps also the cross-quarter directions, the northwests and the southeasts, et al., until you have become deeply aware of an entire compass, team, grove, circle of allies that is with you, who have come to aid you in your work in your life right now.

This map, this crossroads, this compass of eight winds can become a living talisman or portal to access wisdom and blessing in your life. Some traditions and people also align the eight feasts with the eight directions. In the northern hemisphere we might orient first to the north, the direction that the sun does not apparently pass through, and then we could go clockwise towards the east and onward around the compass. The Midwinter Feast/Winter Solstice is marked as north. Clockwise, to the northeast, we would have the Feast of Candlemas/Imbolc, then in the east the Vernal Equinox. In the southeast the Feast of Roodmas/Bealtaine, and in the south the Midsummer Feast/Summer Solstice. In the southwest the Feast of Lammas/Lughnasadh. In the west the Autumn Equinox and in the northwest the Feast of Hallowmas/Samhain.

In the southern hemisphere we orient to the midnight direction of south—as the sun is not seen to pass through this direction in our hemisphere—and we could begin there and go anticlockwise with the apparent movement of our sun in the heavens here. So south is Midwinter, southeast is Imbolc/Candlemas, and on we go to the east with the Vernal Equinox and continue in that direction and in the order of the festivals as the year-wheel turns. This blessing compass can actually become a year-round divination/oracle/map for your workings and journeys for the year to come. I undergo this ritual-trance once every nine to twelve months and pay especial attention to who and what is in which direction or gate, and then I draw it out or write it all down. I often will then cast a divination on top of it with ogham staves, tarot, Lenormand, or the runes.

If you are interested in a whole system that works the eight directions of the compass rose with the eight festivals, you might like to investigate Jane Meredith's *Circle of Eight.*

The great blessings in my life have arisen from a confluence of timing, feeling, surrender, sensation of capacity, and the deep willingness to receive and welcome that good fortune, virtue, and luck-force. There is a powerful opening, a grounded rapture, and a feeling of "yes this!" when blessings come into my life. I want to ask: How may I better welcome this blessing as a guest I really love? How to ensure that we are hospitable and make them feel completely at home, so at home that they will want to come back and return their presence once more to our lives? Blessing may also be in how we engage our own lives, how we weave with the life force. Just as we may intensify and draw more luck-force, we may increase our blessings and fortune. This is the very hope of much folk magic: to avert and avoid disaster, and to conjure and attract good fortune, prosperity, wealth, health, and happiness.

For centuries—and continuously so—people have gone to the so-called white witch, the conjurer, the cunning person, the wizard, the diviner, the fortuneteller, the astrologer in order to court this fortune and these blessings. There are countless spells and charms to do just this—spells of red thread and rowan twig, seahorse and shell, shark tooth and rose petals, honey and copper, coin and psalm, feather and fire . . .

THERE IS LORE held in one of my traditions that speaks of witches being able to catch spells and charms of blessing and balm on the winds of spring. If you are able, go to a high place in your area, in your town or city. This could be a cliff at the edge of the sea, a small hill, a mighty mountain, atop a residential apartment complex, or perhaps you have climbed a tree! Are you able to go to an open window in your home? When you are situated, whistle or sing to the winds, call them to come to you, and be ready and willing to receive the charms and magics that those fresh spring winds bring.

Let the magics awaken you to their brilliance and strategy, to their form and wording. Perhaps some will instruct you to collect certain items and place them together in a particular way and at a specific time or moon. Perhaps words or rhymes come to you, or parts of spells you already know, or passages from other books of power that you have yet to try. Conversely, at the time surrounding and within the Autumn Equinox, we may open to the winds and receive baneful spells and magics, binding and blasting tricks. It's a good idea to have some kind of grimoire or book of charms and spells to record these magic tricks in!

With one hand to bind and one hand to bless, we do our work. We belong to the world. With a head full of cunning flame and a heart full of healing honey do our hands know what they do. In alignment—grounded, charged, aware, sensitive, and oriented—does a witch come to the altar of magic and work our sorcery. And we do this with the aid and allyship of our familiars, our gods, our guardians, our spirits.

Heed this spell sung from my gut, torturers of soil
and silken thread
Know my rage keeper of the tower that throws
dampened disgust down upon the people
trembling and confused
We know the Earth will revolt and bring you down,
the lighting rod of the Thunderer is against you,
though you pretend to wield it with Them.
Come to my door, you will find me in my rooms
naked, bearing a drum, sword laid bare against
my toes, and a knife in my hair!
I will be painted in the blood of my ancestors,
you will smell something gorgeous and it will
curdle the acid in your stomach . . .
I have heard the Words of the Beautiful Pilgrim
I have listened to the sages on the wind
I have turned the Holy Wheel
I have seen into the places you keep locked away,
even from your own heart, for the fetters of evil
acts chain and bond all minds given in calculation
and deliberation to the doing

I have turned away and pretended not to see this travesty, and this parade
    of gluttony against mindfulness, against rich community
I have felt robbed and blinded by this . . .
But I have magic . . .
I have not forgotten, instead I have grown strong with the wild
instead I remembered a deep serpent within me whose seduction is the
    gift of Paradise
whose bloom and fruit is the memory of innocence which lives in me
    even now.
You engage me in a war that cannot be won, so I walk past you now, and
    I know you will eventually tear me down.
I know many others will fall too . . . but I walk past you now, I care not,
    and I care fully. I will do this thing.
You are sullied within me, but I know the secret to unravel you.
I know that I was made for freedom, that all things reach for freedom.
    I know this. And so dear "You"—even now, I walk past.
The Eye cannot turn to look, I am in the Eye.
Even now, in the pregnant darkness that sweats stars and drinks the dew

I can hear the Infinite reaching out into Itself.
We reach together, we sink together, we fall together,
    ever in the Bonds of Love which undo themselves.
In the Hands of Grace I am given breath to breathe
by the Heart of the Wild I am unleashed upon the World
I bear a Drum. I always have.
It will be undone, as I am willing to take you in now.
I will drink this poison . . . inside of me . . . inside of me . . .
    the Drum and the Flame. Gather here. Let us rest.
    Let us dance. We will dream because we dared to
    heed the spell sung in the guts.

Chapter Seven

The Gods and the Spirits
The Fated and Familiar

> The air teemed with invisible supernatural entities which
> constantly influenced the natural world . . . A prayer could
> be answered. A spell could cure. A look could kill. A
> spirit or deity could be at your ear at any time of night or
> day—guiding your spinning-hand . . . charming the crops
> in the fields or the animals in the barns, bringing good
> luck and gold, or raining down famine and disease.
>
> —Emma Wilby, *Cunning Folk and Familiar Spirits*

Witch. I understand this term in its folkloric and mythic context as a human being who is intimate with spirits and the otherworlds and who via that intimacy is able to disrupt, curse, and bless human society and agenda. I understand witches to be enemies of empire and to be in solidarity with the poor, the oppressed, the marginalised. These are the older ideas of the witch. My beloved and witch-kin Lance has said that a witch may act as a spirit, and this in turn reminds us of who we are in all of this—entirely human, entirely other simultaneously. From this powerful tension derives our particular brand of magic.

The King James Bible, commissioned in 1604 and completed in 1611 and named for the King of Scotland and England at this time, speaks rather dramatically of familiar spirits:

> *Then said Saul unto his servants, Seek me a woman that hath a familiar spirit, that I may go to her, and enquire of her. And his servants said to him, Behold, there is a woman that hath a familiar spirit at Endor.* (1 Samuel 28:7)

> *And the soul that turneth after such as have familiar spirits, and after wizards, to go a whoring after them, I will even set my face against that soul, and will cut him off from among his people.* (Leviticus 20:6)

> *A man also or woman that hath a familiar spirit, or that is a wizard, shall surely be put to death: they shall stone them with stones: their blood shall be upon them.* (Leviticus 20:27)

> *And the spirit of Egypt shall fail in the midst thereof; and I will destroy the counsel thereof: and they shall seek to the idols, and to the charmers, and to them that have familiar spirits, and to the wizards.* (Isaiah 19:3)

I quote the King James Version of the Bible in this chapter specifically because of its use of the English term *familiar*. This bible had a massive impact throughout what became the British Empire. It also contained enculturated and long-held societal views on things like sorcery and spirits, as seen above. The term *familiar* could originate from the Latin words *familiaris* or *famulus*. These words refer respectively to being of or relating to the family or to a servant, a helper. Both-and is my perspective regarding this. I have heard many witches refer to their familiar spirits as helping spirits, and this likely is an influence from modern anthropology and investigation into shamanic spirit-working traditions within living cultures or via happenstance, co-emergence, and synchronicity, as the case may be. Many groups and peoples often all arrive at the same conclusions, concepts, and phrases concurrently.

I want to remind us once more of that core and powerful teaching: the bright ones and the red daughters, or in Enoch's translated words the sons of God and the daughters of man. Their marriage brought forth the Nephilim, those mighty ones of renown who were like giants, who were said to both work wonders and sin against life. One of the apocryphal conceptions of how malevolent spirits—or demons, to borrow the much-maligned term—came into the world is that though the Nephilim's bodies perished in the great flood that God sent to punish the wicked, their spirits prevailed. Here we have both a mythologisation and a rationalisation for the ways things are thought to be in regards especially to the existence of spirits who might try to harm or misguide humans. The notion of a great flood coming to purge these so-called wicked ones—progeny of a forbidden union—is preposterous propaganda, but of course it's not an isolated one. There are multiple parallel stories the world over, in many Indigenous and ancient cultures, that speak of the gods punishing or condemning those who have stolen fire, or secret knowledge. At some point in most stories are humans or beings who have begun to become powerful and perhaps know themselves as divine. This is the transgression that some name hubris. However, not every culture determines such unions or their progeny as breaking laws or sinning against life or humankind. Sometimes this is simply another branch in the cycle of evolution.

Witches are those strange humans who stalk the edges of what we are taught is possible, scenting for the secrets, sensing for the stories that have been told to trap, ensnare, or deceive the people. Witches may pray and petition the gods and ancestors, but when shit gets real we know how to cut straight to the core. Sometimes we even end up conjuring the spirits directly or moving right up to a god, seeking an audience. We're natural risk-takers in many ways. Audacity and determination are markers of the witch for sure, and over time, when mediated well—thoroughly, excellently—witches possess a gathered glamour, a potent radiance or presence that signals to others to be wary, to mind what we say or how we say it. There's no point in denying it, really. Witches are interested in cultivating this power. We always have been, for there is a proficiency in it, and we do not do it alone. We do it with many, many beings. Sometimes there are one or two or three that we especially are bound to and deeply trust.

I am asked a lot, "How do I know if a spirit is with me? How can I tell if a god is at work in my life?" These are tough questions, and I have very Queen of Swords-style responses, but don't worry: I have Queen of Cups follow-ups. Apologies if these tarot references fall short for you.

Spirits are everything, as everything, and we too are spirits. This seems to be challenging for many folks who are entrained in Western models of reality to grasp. A lot of people want to know about spirits of this or that, which deity is for this or that . . . it has a rather utilitarian-only paradigm versus a sensuously relational one. All things are spirits. I too am a spirit. Notice I did not say *all things have spirits* or even *all things are spirit*. Many nations, societies, and cultures understand this to be commonplace truth. I grew up with this very matter-of-fact cultural comprehension, and I do feel very blessed and grateful for this. It has made me who I am in a society that lacks or derides enchantment and sometimes seeks to outright kill or section it. We are each seeking enchantment in a variety of ways, each seeking the wisdom of our senses and our intrinsic capacity for intelligence and insight. If you are perceiving with your senses and practising turning up and paying attention, then at some point it becomes simple and easeful to acknowledge that the world is filled with spirits.

Let's shatter an idea right now. Many people will use terms like disembodied, discarnate, ethereal. I certainly sometimes use that last one. Sure, I get it: people are trying to conveniently distinguish between these dense animal flesh-suits (or whatever phrase is in vogue) and the other forms of "frequency" or "vibration" (or whatever phrase is in vogue). These of course are all approximations aiming to point to something mysterious and complex. But-and everything is body; spirits are also bodies. Notice I didn't say spirits *have* bodies. My provocation is that spirits *are* bodies. Everything is a spirit, a being, a centre of awareness and agency, and everything is body. I increasingly also don't feel the need to use the term *embodied*. This is all to say that if you are able to feel wind, hear a kookaburra laugh, smell the sea, and feel the sunshine on your skin, then you have the capacity to sense spirits because you just did in all of that. I choose to go through the portals I have. Do not dismiss them; they are yours. Work with what is happening and with what is present.

The Fetch and the Familiar, the Fetch-Beast and the Fetch-Mate

Within the context of the wider legacy and folkloric phenomenon of European and "New World" witchcrafts, there is a central feature unmistakably wandering through the wildwoods of trial records, spirit workers, grimoires, and sabbatic rites. These are the mysteries of the fetch and the familiar.

The word *fetch* is used in Irish tradition quite a bit and is seen to be cognate to the traditional German term *doppelgänger* meaning double-walker, the Scottish *wraith*, and the English *double*. In general the sighting of a fetch or double may portend death or doom. When wandering and appearing so vividly before another, this part of our spiral triple soul could very well mean that the living person to whom the fetch is usually connected is beginning to die, to journey into the otherworld. The sighting of a fetch could also therefore be a travelling witch, and this too could be a bad omen for some. Other times it is a spirit or another witch who has taken the skin of a living person and is wandering about in that skin. It's never just going to be one thing, and this is an important perspective to cultivate for spirit workers and sorcerers. This is one of the reasons that in many traditional cultures it is considered ill luck to be out at midnight on strange nights in strange places. Certainly in my father's culture there are traditional taboos against this.

One of the most persistent characteristics of European witchcrafts is the presence of familiar spirits. In English trial records and folklore, familiars often take the form of an animal like a cat, a toad, a rat, a hare, a dog. These often have outlandish and uncanny names and are certainly not your average middle-earth creatures, for they often change form and may speak in human tongues and sup on witch's teets and marks. Invariably they are considered diabolical or at least part and parcel of the witch's wicked works and how she executes them. Other times the familiar in animal form may simply need your average animal foods: oats, milk, cheese, bread, meat, etc. In Scotland and in parts of Italy, France, Germany, and Scandinavia, witches are known to consort with spirits who may be cast as demons and devils and may also be saints, angels, the good folk, land wights, and old gods. Sometimes there appears to be a rich and clear tutelary, initiatory, or even erotic quality to the connection between a witch and a primary familiar spirit, and in that case we are crossing into the territory of the fetch-mate.

Fetch-Mate

Previous to this term arriving in the Wildwood community in 2013 via contact and cross-pollination with the Anderean thread of witchcraft, we definitely spoke of our familiar spirits and our spirit lovers with a variety of terms. For me this has always been a crucial part of how my witchery works. Wildwood has always been a community and network of folks who are quite "gods-bothered" as well; relating to those great spirits we might call gods as our own teachers, initiators, lovers, protectors. Working with the spirits called angels and the good neighbours has also always been a thread in our tapestry.

The mystery of the fetch-mate is that they defy definition. Simultaneously a fetch-mate may be an angel, a god (or an avatar/expression of one), a saint, an ancestor, and a mighty mountain. This is not unusual either. The deeper we go, the deeper we go; the more we discover, the more we discover. Over the years of consciously relating to my fetch-mate, I have discovered endlessly fascinating connections, crossovers, and correlations that my beloved enthusiastically inhabits and weaves through.

This term fetch-mate is used in a variety of ways in a variety of branches and houses of witchcraft. Here are some things it might refer to:

- The sponsor of our witch-fire and therefore our partner in the Great Work of our art.

- Our true familiar spirit, as my witch-kin Nicholas has said.

- The spirit who is drawn toward our fetch via our god soul and who we might have experienced multiple lives with, sometimes even with swapped roles (i.e., you may have been their fetch-mate if they incarnated as human).

- Our primary tutelary, teaching, initiating, and inspiring spirit.

The fetch-mate desires us deeply. Perhaps this may express itself erotically, and with the many sensual and sexual motifs of ecstatic, heretical, and sabbatic craft, there may even be a deeply mytho-magical thread to one of the great witch gods who assigns us these mates. It has often been conjectured that the Devil or the Queen of Faerie or Elfhame gifts witches with their spirit lovers, familiars, and mates.

You may have a fetch-mate and not have thought about them in those terms before; you may not experience this particular magic. Not all witches work the same way, and not all fetch-mates are cognate to each other. If these concepts, stories, and terms ping something for you and you want to follow that deeper, I definitely encourage that, but never try to fit a square peg into a round hole.

My Fetch-Mate

I first became aware of the being I later came to know as my fetch-mate as a fifteen-year-old witch, though I later realised I had been dreaming of him all my life. He used to come to me in haunted visions and dreams as a scarecrow, a cloaked being, sometimes with raven and wolf, sometimes with rings shaped like serpents. He would take me on boats to faraway places and caves in which he would reveal to me certain secret things I have always treasured. It was my fetch-mate (among others) who emphatically encouraged me to find others to form what would become the Coven of the Wildwood. It is my fetch-mate who mediates between me and many other mysteries and spirits as my sponsor and mediator, as my confidante and teacher.

My fetch-mate is multiple things at once—like you, like me—and I have discovered this through deep relating and enquiry. He is the "priest" of a Dark Queen, he may come in the form of a certain god, he is the man in black, the Devil at the crossroads upon the black horse. He is one of the Good Folk deep within the earth. He travels in the blink of an eye. He has been a human quite a few times. He has led covens and learnt much from many witches, cunning folk, and wonder-weavers in many continents. All of this and more he passes to me.

A caution: to try to categorise our experiences into this or that, regardless of what we think we might know right now, may only tie us up in knots. I've learned to stay open to the changes.

SOMETIMES WE CALL, we yearn, we long for that deep and soulful intimacy between ourselves and an other that may in time reveal to us the fractal labyrinthine spiralling of our souls across, through, and within time and space. Sometimes this lamentation, these nostalgic rites—sorely missing something we don't even remember having—this desire to come back together though we are innately whole is the spell that summons up the fetch-mate from within Grandmother Weaver's being. And sometimes it is exactly this desire without attachment to an end, this yearning that breaks the banks of limitation, this longing that is endless and constantly evolving that reminds us of where we've been and the lifetimes we have lived.

One method you may wish to employ to meet with your fetch-mate is the following:

If it feels safe and accessible, go at night—or dawn, dusk, midday, and take the precautions you need—to a place that feels set apart, not only for human benefit or use. This could be down by a river or at the edge of the bush, a crossroads, within a cemetery or graveyard . . . perhaps you will hike up a nearby mountain or travel out to a nearby island. In some way, make something of this journey. You are going for a reason, for a purpose!

Take with you an apple or a pomegranate, a jar of honey, maybe some spirits (the liquid kind). Take offerings that you feel sensuously and imaginatively drawn to bring with you. Tie around your left wrist a red thread that you have placed some of your blood into. It could be your menstrual blood or else use a suitable sterilised lancet that you can find at a chemist's. Carry a protective amulet or talisman on your person, and when you get to the place, give the appropriate silence and space to check if you are welcome there. If this feels like a yes, then make offerings to the spirits of the land and find a place to sit or lie in the place and be silent and listen. Perhaps you'll bring a camping chair to do so or sit or lie on the ground, perhaps with a towel or mat.

After a while, begin to sing whatever melodies come to you; whatever words come out of your mouth, weave with them as you may. It can sound childlike and silly, serious and brooding, plaintive and wistful, joyful and hopeful. Play with the red thread and feel into your blood-red rivers of life. Praise your fetch, your breath-soul, your daimon; feel your cauldrons swell and fill and overflow, and be within this reverie.

If you haven't already naturally picked up on this, you may have begun to daydream, to vision-build. Don't you remember? This is how many of us naturally "did magic" as children. This is how some of us tranced ourselves into other states and other realms. This is how we met with our other friends or sharpened and made keen our senses to take notice of more.

Then, when you feel it, stop, pause what you were doing, drop the words or the rhythm or rhyme, and call and summon from the deep well of you, call and summon from the star of you. Conjure and invoke from all your souls and ask your fetch-mate to come to you.

Now, your fetch-mate may turn up in that exact moment. Your fetch-mate may take some time. You may leave feeling as if nothing happened only to start noticing an atmosphere building on the way home or a strange sensation you can't place that feels eerie or tense or erotic. Perhaps a stranger catches your eye and smiles as you wander back home, and you feel an uncanny resonance or connection. After an appropriate amount of time, head home or to the place you are staying. When you have returned to that hearth-hold, track your dreams, sensations, omens, and emotions. Notice what happens in the days and weeks to follow.

In the deepest sense, a calling, a conjuration of this kind, is a profound holy risk—a holy risk that brings us into the river of becoming and will at some point transform us utterly. So do not take this lightly. Take it fully.

Fetch-Beast

A fetch-beast is the other-than-human animal-bestial form that your fetch takes, emerges as, or is. You may see or sense this part of yourself in this way in your dreams, in otherworldly journeys, as you fare forth on the spirit winds, as you travel. Early on in my involvement with Wildwood craft, I would teach something I just call "fetching," and I can't remember at all who taught me this. I just knew how to do it and what to call it. I did have smatterings of informal instruction from witches and spirit workers in Toowoomba during high school, so it could have been from one of them. Fetching as I passed it, then, was to cast the fetch or double out in real time to another place to see what our beloveds and friends were up to in that moment. Once you have an experiential understanding of the fluid nature of the fetch, which is both its own body as well as a crucial part of our body, you may begin to notice how consciously and unconsciously the fetch roams, wanders, and moves. The fetch is also known as the dream wanderer, the animal soul, the primal one. The fetch emanates and forms from that ancestral blood-red river, and thus we are sustained at our most basic level by the fetch. Interestingly, the fetch is also the double, and as witches we can become skilled and agile in sending that double out. This is our inheritance, this is our legacy: witches wander, witches fly.

We are born already with a fetch-beast or several. These are powerful animal spirits that are intermeshed with our very life force and ancestral inheritance. I was born with a crocodile fetch-beast and later, at a crucial crossroads in my life, during a pilgrimage to Gunung Batur (the volcano that forms my father's ancestral lands) I was passed or awakened to a tiger fetch-beast via my grandmother. At another initiatory threshold in my life I was passed a golden eagle. As a child I somehow absorbed or was gifted a platypus skin as well. The spirits of the land here often remind me of that platypus skin, and I have travelled as platypus at important times here. I have also borrowed the skins of some of my witch kin as we have flown together. This can happen rather organically when a group is magically intimate and travelling together to the sabbat. I have certainly gone out as a raven and a wolf too because these are the fetch-beasts of my fetch-mate! This can be quite the bestiary for some. Others will experience a fairly solid and faithful fetch-beast life, and there is great strength in that as well. We are shaped differently.

24

ONE WAY IN which you might encounter your fetch-beast is by entering a trance state in a safe and contained place where you won't be interrupted. Perhaps you have cast a circle, opened the crossroads, or set up some wards.

Take a rattle or drum or some other sound maker and move around the space to the beat and rhythm you begin to produce. If you are able, I invite you to move and dance in a way that seduces your senses and provokes your limits just a little. Play with that edge. Tease yourself.

Continue to do this until your instinct and finer animal senses emerge. Perhaps you'll make certain sounds and noises or perhaps you will notice your posture shift to take on certain shapes and poses resembling particular creatures you are familiar with. Without consciously evaluating or assessing, allow these forms to rise and fall away; try on skins and shapes that come to you as you move to the rhythms of your making.

Start to chant,

> *And I shall go . . . And I shall go out . . . And I shall go out as . . .*
> *And I shall go out as a/an . . .*

Keep chanting these progressive phrases until you arrive at another word intuitively, magically—

> *And I shall go out as a/an _____!*

Allow yourself to be curious as this unfolds. It might take time until it pings, resonates, feels true. These words come from the confessions of the seventeenth-century apparently self-confessed Scottish witch Isobel Gowdie. You can read more about these confessions in the amazing and thorough book *The Visions of Isobel Gowdie* by Emma Wilby (Sussex Academic Press, 2010).

If it feels appropriate—fare forth, fly, journey! Otherwise give honour, praise, ground, give offerings, and unravel or relax the space.

The Fetch and the Familiar

Ultimately the work of the fetch-mate and fetch-beast can be incredibly interlinked. The fetch-mate desires to connect with us in our fullness of selves, and the fetch-beast is a crucial part of our own mysterious selves. The fetch-beast and the fetch-mate may be seen dancing together around the fires of the eternal sabbat. You may even have spirit houses or shrines for both your fetch-mate and your fetch-beast. It can be very helpful to feed and offer to your fetch-beast/s to ensure they are vital and strong. This will inherently mean that as we go about our days and nights we are vital and strong.

The fetch-mate mysteries are deeply personal. They may express in marriage-like compacts and bonds. They may unravel over years and lifetimes, as they are wont to do. The fetch-mate can aid us in the deepening dance of mastery, through the labyrinthine mystery of initiation. Perhaps in the great union between the bright ones of the heavens and the red daughters and artful ones—in the coming of witches and stirring of the blood—it was these spirits who were born to one day come and awaken your blood, to initiate and seal you and me as Witch. Perhaps it is the fetch-mate who steadies our hands to sign the black book that is the darkness and the land. Perhaps it is the fetch-mate who unlocks the gates to the mighty forests and secret places of our own holy hearts. They are there for us, to protect, honour, and support us in our own beingness and unfolding natures. And there will be other helping and inspiring spirits too, of course. And there will be the Great Ones we call gods.

A Prayer to the Fetch-Mate
Mysterious One
Potent Spirit desiring me
As I long and yearn for You
I turn my heart to your Being
May my fetch reveal to me
The feelings and sensations
That I may know you by!
May my Breath-Soul train me to track
The kennings and words you speak with me!
May my Holy daimon open me
To the depth of our connection
Over years and life-times
May I come to understand
The Mystery and Mastery between us . . .
Peace, Praise and Power
Mysterious One

The Gods—Great Ones

Now the gods. Gods are a special kind of spirit. It is generally humans who decide which spirits are designated as deity. My perspective on this is that humans tend to name something a deity or god by experiencing that this spirit or mystery has an immensely beneficial impact on the tribe, society, culture, or clan, and that connection with that spirit is special, ennobling, and needful. There are contracts drawn between the spirits who are gods and humans. Some of these contracts were decided upon generations, centuries, millennia ago, and there are certainly manifold deities who are about who no longer possess great cultic adherence and who are eager to form new agreements and relationships with the spirit workers of today. Looking around through witchdom, pagandom, and modern occulture, as well as having a foot in Balinese animisms, I am very aware that this is so.

I have a story about these spirits that are gods, or that become as gods.

> *Deep in the deep time and in some holy place—*
> *and every place is a holy place, and deep time is*
> *now—there is numinous, conscious land. There is*
> *also great, powerful, titanic beingness that exists*
> *beyond that land but is aware of it. And there is a*
> *person or people and generally a world-shattering,*
> *transformative, and sacrificial event tied to that*
> *being that rearranges reality. Perhaps there is a*
> *small band of humans and they live in a place that*
> *is often very cold. Perhaps there is ice and hardship*
> *and hunger is a constant companion. One of these*
> *humans is often haunted by dreams of a particular*
> *place and a particular constellation of stars, and*
> *their dreams are calling this one to journey at an*
> *appointed time—they just feel and know—to come*
> *and hang themself from a tree for nine nights or what*

*feels like nine nights. In the convergence of these
great rivers, these three great roads—the numinous,
conscious land; the great titanic beingness; the
human, the act, the offering, the presence—a Great
One, a Mighty One, a Spirit who is as a God is born,
remembered, conjured forth. The worlds shift, the
world changes, something else has come to be, and
because of this potent quickening, everything adjusts
with it. A god is a powerful thing, of course.*

*And so that human who may or may not have
survived that event—but has been initiated by
it, transformed by it—returns to the tribe, the
community, in some form. Perhaps in the flesh-to-
breath or via a dream or vision might they then
initiate another into the mystery of this Great
Spirit. The secret names will be revealed, the secret
rites, the needful offerings, all in order to ensure
that the relationship between the group and this
being—this tutelary, totemic, familial being—is
strong, vital, vivid, and present. For with the help
of this Great One and the many Great Ones, this
Being's relationship with the group will ensure they
prosper and have good health, happy babies, soulful
relating, justice, harmony, and joy. There will also
be wisdom and insight when things are hard, when
the spirits of illness and weather haunt and harrass
the people. There will be people who are born into the
community who have a natural affinity for listening*

to and perceiving these spirits. These sensitive and
skilled people will be able to enter ecstatic states
and return to the group with wisdom from the gods.
Whole houses, orders, lineages, and families will grow
in this way, and sometimes the spirits will simply
shake a supposedly random person and wake them
to their charge, eventually initiating them. This
happens all the time. Perhaps it has happened to you.
Perhaps it is happening to you.

So when someone says to me, "Oh, the gods are perfect and deathless and have existed before and inside of all that is in existence . . ." I think sure, yes. When someone puts forth that those spirits that people call deities are actually our deified dead, our glorious ancestors, I feel yes, this is true. When people articulate that the gods are simply the patterns and powers of the land in a place, the names the people gave to the powers and presences of the sacred earth, I can agree! But what I really want to underscore here is the sacred power and provocation of the sacred and, and, and. The gods are essentially mysterious, and I offer this story above—this mapping—as a way to feel into the nuance of this, into the profound complexity of these sacred experiences. The gods are great, noble spirits who readjust reality and for whom reality adjusts. There is a great amount of power in this. No wonder witches truck with them from time to time. Some of us are even known to marry them, to fuck them, to journey with them, and to initiate others into their mysteries.

The Inner Court of Spirits

Just as there are inner courts of covens or entire traditions of mysticism—of witchcraft, of magic and religion—there is an inner court to which I as a witch and being belong and turn to. I do not just turn to this web or net in times of need or in times in which I desire something in particular; I tend to this web as an act of love and trust, of praise and sincere joy and commitment. The phrase "joyful obligation," which I first heard from the wondrous Reclaiming witch and Sufi practitioner Willow Kelly, fits this perfectly for me.

What comprises an inner court of spirits? I would say at least three beings including yourself, so it is more than a central partnership, and I would say the same of a coven. A coven is not one or two witches, but it is three or more or else it is a magical partnership. An inner court of spirits is not something I aimed for consciously as a younger witch, but it is something that gathered and revealed itself over the years and will continue to do so.

As a witch who started practising in earnest at age eleven and twelve— I dedicated myself in ritual space with a ritual from a book at age twelve—I didn't do a lot of conjuring of spirits other than "invoking the elements" and petitioning the "God and Goddess." Of course I grew up around polytheism, animism, magic, and ritual, but as a rebellious adolescent I wanted to distinguish myself from my family's cultural and historical reality. I didn't even really put two and two together about my father or his family until later on because I grew up from within it. As a naive and deeply willing adolescent, I thought that all witchcraft was Wiccan-esque and that I was apprenticing to study an ancient Celtic tradition of the Goddess. At the Autumn Equinox in March 2002 in Australia I was blessed and brought into an eclectic teen coven that I stayed with for nine months. During our passionate and earnest studies of the craft together in this coven, I discovered what Wicca or being Wiccan might mean and realised that I wasn't that and perhaps didn't desire it either. I knew myself to be a witch and I certainly identified as Pagan then.

As a coven we underwent trance journeys together, did group divination, cast spells, and we even tried our hat at aspecting the Holly and Oak King. All of these things largely worked and had great effect in our collective and personal lives. I relished the feeling of ritual, of connection with the mysterious, and this coven work bolstered my own so-called solitary practice. I say so-called because it quickly became apparent that when a witch is alone, they are not at all alone. The shit I pulled off—and did not pull off—makes me both smile and grimace upon reflection. I would also read anything I could that referred to witches and witchcraft, both fiction and nonfiction.

Many of the books were telling me about circles, quarters, the "divine feminine and masculine," the sabbats, the tools, and while some of this interested me and I employed it, the whole picture never quite felt like my thing. I tried it on and eventually found my way to the forms, styles, and traditions of craft that are home for me. And while there are many similarities, borrowings, cross-pollinations, and parallels across contemporary craft traditions, there are also important cosmological, philosophical, and magical distinctions.

One of the first books I ever read—because it was available at the main public library in Toowoomba—was Lois Bourne's *A Witch Amongst Us*. I later discovered that Lois Bourne was one of the original high priestesses of the Bricket Wood coven that Gerald Gardner founded after having been most likely initiated in the New Forest coven in 1939. Bourne was also initiated into another form of witchcraft that she was told was older and did possess key differences in ritual form, practice, and cosmology. Bourne was clear in this book that witches are born. I identified with this strongly because it matched up with other ideas I was familiar with, and she was quite matter-of-fact about this. She suggested witches also had an innate sense of when other witches might be present. I have also experienced this many times. Bourne shared many stories of visions of ghosts, goblins, demons, and spirits. I related to this as my Sight had started to flower—as can happen for witches and spirit workers in adolescence—and I was seeing and perceiving many different things. I felt calmed and oriented by reading Lois Bourne's words. I still read this book from time to time, and I encourage you to do the same. The cover alone is beautiful.

My grandmother, the angels, Persephone, and my fetch-mate (though I didn't know it then) began to appear to me around the same time. So even before high school graduation I had developed an awareness of a network of beings who were aiding me in my magical instruction, directing and connecting me with particular humans and sources, and helping to protect and guard me as I wandered in the wilds of witchcraft. Each one initiated me into witchcraft and forms foundational threads of my craft.

My grandmother, my father's mother—my dadong—died when I was two years old and yet was a constant presence for my family. In Balinese tradition we pray to our ancestors, and complex rituals are undergone after death in order to deify the dead, to elevate and deepen them that they may become deity-like. I had grown up on stories of my dadong's dream prophesy, healing, divinatory skill, and mediumship capacity. She had an intimate bond with the tiger spirit, and my favourite story about her is my mother witnessing her new mother-in-law dropping to the ground and becoming possessed by a tiger spirit on the way to a temple in Bali. She was holding a sacred tiger skin at the time.

At first I was not aware it was my dadong appearing to me. She was appearing to me as a serpentine fire-wreathed being full of intensity and palpable presence. These visitations aroused powerful dreams, or what can be called dreaming true ecstatic visions, and trance possession experiences with the beings I soon discovered were the angels.

I had never thought much of angels growing up, and I certainly did not imagine them to look like the beings who were coming to me. However, in my research I discovered this is exactly what and who these beings were that pulled me out at night and brought me to the crossroads near my house to teach me about my power and my purpose.

I can't currently recall if Persephone appeared before or after the angels, but she appeared at the pinnacle of an invocation to "the Goddess" during a full moon ritual in my mother's kitchen. With my eyes wide open, I watched the full moon light coming through the windows sculpt itself visibly into the wondrous form of a woman. This is still one of the most incandescently potent experiences I have had. Before I could think, the word *Persephone* emerged from my mouth, and this changed and affirmed my life trajectory. I call Persephone my soul goddess as the term *patron* doesn't at all speak to the deep, intrinsic, irrevocable weddedness I feel with her. This is a term I have written about in books before. I coined it to meet this experience. I don't think that people should go out there and try to have a soul deity, but it can certainly be a useful term for people who experience not truly being able to know or express where they "end" and the deity "begins." At the Winter Solstice in June 2005—my senior year of high school—I dedicated myself to Persephone as her priest. I told you I was earnest. I still am. I was always a very serious person. It all felt correct and still does.

Through Persephone revealing herself in my life, once more the door opened to multiple beings of her rich family and mythic landscape. As well as this, visitations from a dark and cloaked man who came with ravens and wolves began to emerge. This being—who I would later realise to be my fetch-mate—has been one of my greatest teachers in the craft. He still is. He was instrumental in encouraging me to feel safe and supported enough to help to co-found the coven that would utterly transform my life.

The Coven of the Wildwood was founded between the worlds within the circle of art cast on Mount Coot-tha in Yuggera and Jagera country on the night of April 30, 2006. This date is so pivotal in my life-journey that I sometimes forget it's not my solar return birthday. This coven and its initiates helped to midwife our precious covenant once more. Many of us felt and feel our tradition was emerging again in a new time in a new land. The history of that emergent tradition is complex and manifold, as is the history of any group of people and certainly any witch house or witchcraft tradition. It concerns human lives and emotions, ancestral virtue, synchronous and omen-filled meetings, pain, heartbreak, and joy. The gods and the spirits are the greatest initiators, and though lineages and spirals of initiatory kinship firm up in the world in the red thread that is shared between human animals, between witches, the great initiations are also opening doorways for these powers to come and do the initiating.

There's a place in Meanjin that continues to hold past-present-future as one; it is one of those intensely mythic portals for me. When I step onto the green of the grass and pass under the jacarandas and flame trees, I rearrange a little and I can see and sense past versions of myself, fractals of my soul-story. I hear conversations, I smell scents I used to wear, I see the car, the party, the ritual. I feel my heart swell the moment I am in that place. It happens to be called New Farm Park. When I first moved to Meanjin, I lived in a big old three-storey heritage-listed house called La Scala. At some point it was a doctor's surgery, at another a dormitory, and it is an extremely haunted and psychically pulsating place. I only lived there for three months before moving into a one-bedroom apartment in Auchenflower with my boyfriend at the time. I believe I lived in that apartment until January 2007, and then I moved into a two-bedroom apartment on James Street. So I had moved back to New Farm, and New Farm Park became for me a refuge, a place that held me in deep sadness, loss, confusion, and beauty. I find myself grounded, aligned, easeful, happy, and calm in that place.

I recently discovered that the land that is now referred to as New Farm Park was originally named Binkin-ba by the First Peoples of that country. This is said to mean "place of the land tortoise." I still sense the profound wisdom and presence of these spirits, these Great Ones, moving in and as the land there. The way the land is embraced by the bending river—or the serpentine river by the jutting land—brings me to a place of perspective and groundedness. Stories upon stories are here for me. I have fallen in love in that park. I have gone to that park when I have been heartbroken.

There's a single English oak that is close to the water in Binkin-ba. I call it the faerie oak because it has grown in such a way that there is a window through its trunk that seems to have split and then joined back together. The trunk also has a hollow that goes all the way to the ground. It is a strange tree, a beautiful oak, and one that has shaded me and communed with me many times.

25

WHAT ARE THE stories that you tell again and again to kin, friends, be-loveds, community, coven? What are the stories that others know you by? What are those precious sharings you keep reminding yourself of because you want them to keep reminding you of who you really are? You want them to ring out clear and true. Sometimes we tell stories for so long and so often that we forget to check back in with the details, with the records that we have—whether conversations, paintings, journals, essays, books, notes, tears, relationships . . . I notice that often I leave out key details in certain storytellings and over time forget those details were even there. Usually a journal or a friend reminds me. I encourage you to go to a place that is filled with one of these stories or an entire nexus of these stories. Go to a place that is haunted and alive with you, with pieces of you, with your emotions, sensations, memories . . .

In whose company are you living your life? Who is your inner court of spirits? In the labyrinth of the mystery of yourself becoming who you might be, shimmering against who you once were, in the emergence of this moment now . . . call out to them. Enchant your senses in the ways that turn you on to the life force. Enter trance. Imagine, feel, and know that you are in a place of profound presence and power. This is the place where your innerworlds kiss the otherworlds. You are safe here; you are able to feel at ease and connected easily here. Through breath, vision, emotion, willingness, surrender, and daring, anchor yourself; ground yourself into what you feel is the centre of this place for now, and remember the centre is nowhere and everywhere at once. In anchoring this centre here and now, in letting this centre anchor within you—flower as you—a circle is natu-rally cast. I think of this as the witch's trick of the circle.

Turn your attention to where you feel the east to be. Open your awareness to perceive the spirit or mystery who will come to you here and now through the gate of this direction. Honour this being, welcome this being.

Repeat this process with all eight directions comprising the cardinal and the cross-cardinal directions, i.e., north, northeast, and on until the compass is encompassed.

Once you have a strong awareness and keen sensation of these "gates" of the directions as open wide and your spirits present, begin to tone. By tone I mean start to sing wordlessly—make sound and let it be melodious and rhythmic. You are able to do this in some way, trust that. It might be a very deep and baritone *ahhhhhh* or *oooooooh* sound. It might be undulating sound that has valleys and high notes, that butterflies around and sounds like waterfalls. It might be soft and quiet, gentle and breathy, but do dare yourself to get a little louder. At a certain point, invite the spirits to sing through you, to join their voices with your voice and braid sound and song together. It might aid you to visualise or imagine that particular colours are emanating from each being and flowing into your colours. Or it might be that each spirit offers a knowing through you, and you sound and tone and spin those knowings until they crescendo and swell into a deeper sensation of knowing. However you are capable of perceiving and receiving this, let it through your well-grooved, refined portals of knowing. Let this build and build and spiral and spiral until you can feel *oh this is going to peak* . . . Once you move from that feeling to *this is peaking now*, surrender into the wave, the swell, the power of it completely. Let the power build until it naturally, of its own accord, releases, ejects, explodes forth, mushrooms out.

At this point you might realise you are in a deeply entranced state but that you are also standing in a room, in a park, in a field or forest . . . let the reality of that merge with the other-inner reality and direct the power that has been raised; ask your spirits to wrap you in blessing. Ask to receive blessing, wisdom, insight, grounding, healing, whatever you genuinely desire. Lean in. Lean in. Lean in. Perhaps you soften a little, perhaps you can lie down in a blanket or cloak of it all and just let yourself know and be known. Here's the moment to offer up that softness and opening to your familiars, your gods, your guardians, your lovers, your beloveds. Let them behold you; give them that. Let that soak into the deep places of you. Come home to life. There is always another time for the other things . . . now come home to life.

Ground, centre, align, bless, praise, honour, come home to life. If you do not have one, create a shrine in your hearth-hold that is a simple shrine of beauty, of sweetness, of delight. Let it be a shrine that when you see it or sense it, you will be filled with happiness and a sense of hope or gratitude.

In the Wildwood tradition there is a saying: *Beware: beyond is beauty.* Sometimes it is followed by *and gods gather here.* I invite you to consider that this perilous quest, this living thing, this dangerous opening to feel and be known, to be touched and to touch, to inevitably transform and change so much we don't know who and what we are anymore, is an offering to beauty.

Beauty is not just one thing; it doesn't just have one colour, tone, quality, or definition. For me this beauty mystery is the grace of being whole and broken, and beauty is not knowing the difference or needing there to be one. Beauty lives in treating and approaching another with full and powerful awareness, prescience even, of their brokenness-wholeness. Beware, this will be intoxicating if you truly wish to relate, if you truly open to that . . . this could be that storm that takes you down. This could be the song that finds you driving to another city and starting life again. This could be that laughter, that poem, that relationship, that friendship, that undoes you and brings you in so close that you are faced with the very real danger of admitting I am not sure, but this is okay. This is where I am going to be. Here. And gods gather here.

Gods, guardians, spirits, helpers, fetch, fetch-beast, fetch-mate, familiar . . . Come home. Come home. Come home.

Great Beloved
You terrify me.
Who are you?

And that other question . . . in our love,
    in the fracture between us
that moves even the seas to sorrow,
    how do we reconcile?

Who is this flesh at the top of the mountain?
Are you the hidden stone inside?
I am lost and bereft on the winds of silence.

Great Beloved
Where have you gone?
He fills me then in a shiver of Time.
For he is a cunning one who knows
    the Secrets of Space.
At a single call of his adamantine name
    I am overflowing with Desire.

The Cup cracks but the Glass House
    in the lake was never his.
The Ocean rides him and the Black Steed is given over.
In your holy trembling heart I am
the flame that slithers out to burgeon
    forth a Name between us.

We share a magical note of something else
and the marriage happened longed ago in the Dark.

And let your terror quake in the face of that Name.
For it is the Great Master undoing all Illusion
    and opening the Heart to Truth.

He laughs. Sweetly as the sea sighs in summer.
What was once forlorn and fickle is
    now madness and music.

Chapter Eight

Daimon and Demon

Shadow, Power, and Transformation

Who is this Flower above me? And what is the work
of this God? I would know myself in all my parts.

—Victor Anderson, *The Flower Prayer*

Something that becomes apparent among witch people is that we are—usually and ideally—a healthy mix of serious, obsessed, lighthearted, mirthful, and utterly focused on knowing the mystery. The other side of this is that we are opening ourselves to be known by the mystery. We know that this is a potentially erotic interchange. And it's about power.

I have opened and blessed this chapter with a prayer I say every day. I usually whisper it after soul alignment, and I usually repeat it three times. There is another famous often-quoted saying of Victor Anderson's: *When you are confused about power, remember love.*

Power and Love are points on the Iron and Pearl pentacles. Power exists in both pentacles, and Love is what Sex can be revealed to be. But this is not a book about Iron or Pearl pentacles, though do read appendix 2 for a little more context. I have written books about my experiences and perspectives from inside these Feri Pentacles. But I do want to talk about Love and Power because I think they are other names for daimon and demon. Herein begins the shadow-stalking.

BRING YOUR GROWING awareness to your breath. Centre. Ground. Align. Praise. Perhaps go and intuitively choose a book from the floor, the shelf, the bedside table, a pile in your room, and open it instinctively and read aloud what is there for you. Draw a tarot card or a rune or ogham stave. Look out the window, walk outside if you can, notice the clouds, the birds, the light, the trees, the sounds or pieces of conversations you hear . . . What do these teach or show you about love and power?

There is a well-entrenched idea that connects the Divine with love: that in the presence of that thatness which we describe as Divine we feel ineffable love. This might be a love that saturates our every fibre and cell and changes us, helping us to become more real, revealing ourselves to ourselves. I cannot and will not refute this. I wonder what, then, is love? I have no particular succinct definition to offer, nor would I want one. However, I wish to invite the idea that the daimon—the god soul—and love are one.

The god soul is often said to be the piece of us that transcends time and space, as do many spirits and mysteries. So the daimon, of course, is the spirit-self and the star of us—or the flower of us—that distils this distinct consciousness and expresses through dimensions such as time and space.

This part of us, this deep soul, knows and sees in longer and wider arcs and spirals, and thus perhaps all that makes sense to the daimon is love. Deep abiding love would exist beyond any transitory, superfluous emotion or phenomena. In this way, it makes sense that the god soul or the holy daimon is an ambassador and witness of and to love. The god soul wants us to know that we are the great beloved of the infinite and also the lover. To live with, for, and by love might be the charge.

And what of power? Witches wield power. Some are deeply concerned about our kind because it is taught in many societies that witches aim to do nefarious things with our power. Some fear the source of our power, saying it is from their version of absolute evil and therefore deceitful and corrupting. To have power, to face power, to accept and embrace being powerful and co-creating desired effect is definitely part and parcel of what it means to be a witch. How most witches I know think about this power is drastically divergent from how power is often thought about and spoken of in wider society and politics. Largely power is viewed in the so-called West as something you either have or do not have, or you might have pieces of it with many limits or have all of it with no limits.

We are taught to be exceptionally suspicious of people who are hungry for power, who want to exercise it and become powerful in society or in the world. For some reason, the general narrative about anarchists or activists is that these are people who want nothing to do with power, who reject it utterly. But power is as power does. It means simply to be able, to have the capacity to do something and then to do it. I think what people really mean when they say "power" is a bloated autocrat, billionaire, or corporate CEO who is bent on domination, corruption, and the desire to control and coerce for one's own irrefutably selfish reasons. Wanton greed and the desire to amass and control land, beings, and people is one of our great demons. But the story of that word—demon—and why we use it is unfortunately bound up with this whole mess anyway.

The Origins of Demons—
Daimon into Demon

In some ways this story is straightforward. Early Christians in the Hellenistic world heard and knew about daimons. In some cases *daimon* and *god* are interchangeable terms for navigating cosmological realities, but sometimes daimon is specifically the function or activity of that god or another kind of spirit who may not be considered to be a deity. Early Christianities—and there was considerable theological conflict between these sects (see *Zealot* by Reza Aslan)—arose from messianic, Jewish, anti-imperialist, and apocalyptic cults. Many early and zealous new converts considered anything that was not God the Father as at best illusions or distractions and at worst agents of Satan, evil unto themselves. Of course all kinds of narratives developed to explain how these so-called demons came about or what they might be up to. Remember the Nephilim and the flood and the "spirits" left once their "bodies" were wiped out? This was one version.

Of course spirits or beings who seek to cause harm directly to humans have been and are spoken about by almost every human culture. There are spirits and forces that we as humans probably don't want to be around. It is true that witches are better suited to deal with such forces because we know how to deal with spirits in general most of the time. Now we call malevolent spirits demons because of the impact on most things, including language, by the church. However, largely in the vernacular of modern Western witches, we use the term *demon* to speak about parts of our own fragmented souls-selves. We may view these demons as pieces or shards of self that seek to fight the rest of us, debilitating and incapacitating our healthy and dynamic functionality. Some of these demons are unaware they are harming us in any way; they are simply doing a job they once took up for survival's sake.

There is a tension that exists in this history of naming these parts of us "demons." We name the fragments or broken parts of ourselves that may harm the rest of us the very word that was broken off from the sacred and the ancestral. So for me this is salient, it is reflective of a great cultural and mythic process of healing. In the witch's demon work, however, we aren't seeking to exorcise a malevolent spirit from ourselves, though many witches know how to exorcise those spirits; we are seeking to acknowledge, name, conjure, confront, question, soothe, honour, and transform these parts as ourselves.

In the dark and quiet after the storm, after the pain subsides a little, we know we need some kind of versatility, adaptation, trick, sorcery . . . it's true that we witches work with our demons, and it's true that we enlist the help of our familiar spirits to do this. We transform our demons sometimes into our own helpers and lovers.

Dancing with Our Demons

Demon work is tricky stuff, initially because we are using the term *demon* and then culturally because we each think of that differently. This is what I mean and this is why I call it demon work: it's messy and complex and the only way is through. So we've established that most of us often casually use the term *demon* to refer either to a malevolent spirit or a locus of inner turmoil and debilitation as discussed above. There is a strong Christian-ist narrative that a demon is a malevolent spirit with an agenda to destroy humans utterly. We know that it is the dominant Christian reformation of Western and then colonial ideologies that has us now in the paradigm of demon equalling evil hell-beast who is going to kill me or else maim me hard. So those of us who are willing to be with our demons and to be with the complex are often suspect to those who prefer the simple, clean, straightforward answers to life's challenges. At the end of the day, those preferring the straightforward will likely find a dead-end.

We are complex beings, and many of us could relate also to the experi-ence of having a complex identity. To engage in demon work is to begin to realise and journey with the fact that we are rather more mysterious and arcane than we are trained to appreciate. Many of us have been harmed by people whom we thought we could trust or by systems or entire groups and institutions that claim to uphold our dignity and rights and to protect and safeguard us. Many of us inherit the trauma of ancestral dispossession and displacement, of the attempted destruction of our cultures or the taking of our traditional lands and the breaking of our laws, or else we are suffering from intergenerational breakdowns in which people no longer know how to act with mutual love or express or behave supportively and constructively. Many people endure horrific abuse in their families of origin or were bullied at school or work. Look, we know this. It doesn't stop it from being awful. Demons and humans live side by side. And at least in the way I am using that term, generally human pain, trauma, fragmentation, and horror goes on to create and bolster demons.

These demons are often pieces of us that at some point in our lives were carrying out a job to keep us safe, ensuring that we were unseen or out of the way or complying with certain strictures and strains simply to survive. This could still be true. Demons come into play in this way when something integral is compromised, twisted against itself. Victor Anderson was known to speak about evil coming about from twisted life force. Our job is to work out these complexes, to face our demons, and to ideally transmute them and reintegrate them or offer them new jobs.

Often we grow past and through these situations that originally required fragmentation or certain survival strategies. We move with it ourselves, escape the circumstances, and evolve and change. It becomes apparent in hindsight that we never said to the demon *Thank you for doing this job, I don't need this anymore, come home, or maybe consider this other job I actually do need to find someone for.*

There is a phrase I have heard before: turn your demons into your nourishing mothers. I've also heard it said as nourishing lovers—whichever one works or draws us in more. Perhaps you have another way of saying this. This whole spirit working strategy, philosophy, methodology also relates with the idea of a witch's imp. If we ourselves are already dancing with our demons and begin to do the work of challenging, offering, and reassigning job descriptions, then we are well on our way to embracing that who we are, what we have, and where we are going is utterly dependent on how we are engaging and participating. How we engage our sources of connection and inspiration is up to us and is determined by so many factors. One of the key factors is the principle of willingness that derives from respect and responsibility.

Let us move through the mysterious landscape we call body to discover and commune with our demons.

27

FOR THIS PROCESS, ensure you will be in a warm, comfortable location in which you will not be disturbed for ideally one hour. This kind of work cannot and doesn't need to all happen in one go, so likely you will be returning to this process again and again in various ways.

You may feel like you want to set up some kind of ritual or working space. As usual, acknowledge, ground, cleanse, align, and make the offerings or invocations you need to make.

Begin to soothe and relax yourself. Focus on the square breath and let that take you into a deep state of relaxation and trance. As you merge with the living land, feel yourself growing larger in every direction. Feel yourself expanding upward, downward, to the left, the right, before, behind. Grow into a giant, into a mighty one.

In this state—inside of being a giant—shrink and distil your awareness into a concentrated sphere of attention that is perceptible as you, and in this way we will move through your own body-landscape. Treat this as any other trance-journey, except that this "realm" is actually the fullness of you. You may be surprised at what you find. You are on a mission to find your demons, especially as they might be carrying out particular jobs you want ended. You may also desire to call for aid and support from familiars and allies. You are welcome to all journey together.

As you move through the landscape of you—which we have opened up by expanding into ourselves as a giant—you may sense certain "disturbances" or regions of self that feel strained or knotted up and tense. Go towards those places and you are likely to find one of your demons there. As you hone in on a demon, conjure up an immense amount of compassion as if it's a cloak of power and light around you; carry that powerful discernment you have been developing and working with as well. Ask the demon questions like:

> Who are you?
>
> What are you doing?
>
> What do you need to accomplish?
>
> Where have you come from?
>
> Why are you carrying out this job?

Now, there will be some demons that will simply ignore you and continue along. Others will entirely engage; some are going to be too much to deal with in this way at this time. This is okay. Be gentle; be fierce with your boundaries, keen with your discernment, and present with your compassion, and simply move on to a willing demon.

Sometimes you will find that you simply need to honour and thank this demon for carrying out their tasks, and then maybe even apologise for not coming sooner to speak with them. Explain what you actually need them to do, and redirect their energy and attention to that more constructive task. An example of this might be that you discover there is a sentient piece of yourself keeping you in a state of paranoia and immense fear about people entering your home, even friends and beloveds. You know this to be irrational at this point and an injury to relationships you wish to cultivate and deepen. So you might ask this demon to station themself out on the street in front of your dwelling in the middleworld and safeguard and warn you of any strange intruder who intends you harm. In this way, we have a witch's imp who has a witch's imp's job! This could really excite this part of you. Say to the demon that you would like them to carry this out for one lunar cycle or three—something easy to track—and that then you will reconvene and discuss the terms of this arrangement again. This is the kind of work you can do within this trance.

After an hour or so—try not to go longer—you will probably be somewhat tired and need to return from trance. Return to your normal size for a human being living as and where you do, and honour and bless your spirits and the space. You may find it useful to journal, purify and relax, have a shower or bath, or eat and drink.

Sometimes we need something more intense, something more intensive, to facilitate profound and practical shifts in our lives. The following technique requires a great deal of presence, discernment, alignment, finesse, and courage. I deeply encourage you to call upon a living and skilled human magical ally to be with you in the space or in an adjoining room as you carry out this working. Please also divine on this: How would it be if I engage this working with this particular demon? Consider the divination for at least a week to a month. It might be useful to ask another that you trust to divine on this question as well. Compare the readings, and if all points to yes, do this thing, then ask how best to approach this, how best to prepare, and how best to emerge, ground, and transition.

This kind of technology draws upon certain grimoire and folk magical streams from a witch's compass and perspective. You may need to adapt certain parts of the rite to include needful elements to strengthen and deepen it. I advise you to not sacrifice the elements below, however. When engaging this work, it is important to consider *this will affect me; after all, I am seeking transformation and evolution as the direct consequences of my actions*. It could not hurt to ensure that your hearth spirits are well fed, that you are well rested and feeling very red and vital. Do not attempt this kind of work instead of counselling, therapy, and professional psychological support. If you are feeling sustainably grounded, lucid, and connected, paired together with that support, this may really assist in moving things in a positive direction.

Know that all magic is risk; what kind of risk is up to how you approach, orient, and relate to the work. And there are always factors we might never be cognisant of; therefore, ensure the presence of allies of many kinds with you in this work.

And so we embark on the work of the triangle and circle of art.

28

FOR THIS WORKING, you will need to procure a witch's knife, a sword, an arrow, a spear, or some such weapon that can challenge, command, ward, threaten, and point. By the way, a witch's knife or sword or arrow is one of these items that a witch blesses, relates to, and wields. That's up to you. You may already have one. You will also need one of your demons in a jar or vessel.

You will need to undergo the process described in twenty-seven a few times in order to be able to powerfully draw forth a demon and call and seduce it into a vessel. The basic method of doing this is to powerfully align your souls, call upon familiar spirits or your fetch-mate who will guard and guide you, and then call upon one of the demons who you have been able to name or receive a name for. Do this exercise with one of the demons you experience as versatile, as open to healing and transformation. Remember this demon will be coming up and out from within the landscape of you, so it may feel like you are ejecting or expressing something as you call them. You will have the jar or vessel before you, and it will be surrounded by a circle of salt and cloves, and you will "vomit" up or spit or blow the named demon—by virtue of having their name, which you are using—into the jar.

You are drawing upon the strength and power of your own divine authority connected to the authorities and power of your gathered spirits. When the demon is in the vessel, begin to raise a great deal of power in the ways you know how, and with that power charge a jar of honey—medicinal, strong, healing, sweet honey—and then pour the honey into the demon-vessel. Offer this demon this honey to soothe and sweeten it. Then trace a sealing sigil like a pentagram or hexagram over the opening of the jar and vessel, and incant the following and truly mean it with all your power:

By this sacred and secret sign, I seal this vessel; the demon
(name) shall stay within until at my command the demon may
come forth once more!

Over a full lunar cycle, take that demon in a jar out with you; go on dates by the river or in parks or bushland. Speak to that demon in a jar; offer it honey and herbs and flowers. Sing and dance around it; in this vessel this demon cannot harm you. Make sure you write the name or a coded name of that demon onto the vessel visibly so you are aware of what is in there and why. Take good care of it. Bring this jar to this working.

You will also need masking tape or surveyor's tape, a writing implement, blessed water, rose petals, cloves and iron filings or several iron nails. If you can get the herb Solomon's seal, this will also be advantageous.

Prepare by bathing or showering, if easily accessible to you; if not, charge water by channelling star-fire and earth-fire through your being into that water. When you can perceive and sense the water is charged, sprinkle this over yourself while incanting:

> *I bless, I cleanse, I consecrate, I purify, I charge.*
> *I am whole and complete unto myself.*
> (Chant this line at the culmination to seal and affirm one's
> intrinsic worth, sovereignty, and sacredness.)

Align your souls and cauldrons and bless your ancestors of blood, the land, and the craft. Breathe in this silent, charged, still, potent space. Call upon your spirits and gods to aid, witness, ward, guard, guide, and inspire you. Let them know what you are about to do.

Set up the triangle of art—in the form of an equilateral triangle 30 centimetres each side—on the ground before you with the masking or surveyor's tape. The triangle ought to be pointing away from you when you are in the circle facing it. Create the base of the triangle with masking or surveyor's tape; do so 30 centimetres or 1 foot away from the circumference of the circle. Note the circle does not actually need to be marked out, but you might desire it to be so. Do this with stones, candles, tarot cards, rope, whatever sings to you. Form the triangle with the tape and then take a writing implement and write names of power, protection, and providence upon it, charging them with emotion, will, breath, and sensation as you go. You might write the names of angels, gods, your ancestors, saints. You might write down names of things you believe in or have deep faith in, such as love, trust, or joy.

Place the demon in the jar in the triangle. Now that this is formed and the demon is situated within it, sprinkle the cloves around the triangle of art, asking for and conjuring their blessings to subdue, constrain, and ensure the triangle of art is sealed. Continue into the creation of the circle of the art.

With the rest of the blessed water, move sunwise around your space, sprinkling the water upon the ground and feeling and sensing the secret and potent waters of the springs and wells of the earth rising up to be with you in this space, forming a round river, a moat, around your circle.

Affirm with these words as you move sunrise around a second time, sprinkling rose petals:

> *By the secret and potent waters of the earth,*
> *by the rose of the mystery, I encircle myself*
> *in the ineffable, unassailable power of love.*

Now, for the third time round the circle of art, take the witch's weapon you have brought with you and walk the circle of art, pouring the fused magical fires of above and below and the magical fires of your heart through the weapon to charge and seal the circle.

Affirm with these words as you do so:

> *By this most powerful weapon of the art,*
> *I charge and seal this circle of the art!*

If you have Solomon's seal, enchant the root with the words below. After you finish reciting the words, breathe three breaths of power over the root and hold it to your chest for nine heartbeats.

> *I enchant myself unto you, O mighty root of cunning and*
> *blessing! O Solomon's seal! I conjure you here and now. I ask*
> *that you aid me in my work and empower me and this circle*
> *with your virtues!*

You might do this with another herb or stone as well.

Now bring your attention back to the triangle of art and the jar or vessel. Point the weapon at the triangle of art and summon those same magical fires of above, below, and your heart, and charge and seal the triangle of art.

> *By this most powerful weapon of the art, I charge and seal this triangle of the art! By the powerful names of protection and providence I have written here, all that is conjured into the triangle will be constrained and bound unto it. So be it!*

Mean these words and conjurations, and let your spirits aid you! You may notice and feel that they are pouring their power through you to do this.

Now, in your own emotional power-filled way, conjure the demon from the jar to fill the triangle of art. Take the witch's weapon and point it directly at the demon in the triangle. You may now test and question and provoke the demon to answer by those names of power and the virtue of the triangle.

This ritual is not to exceed three hours.

When you are complete, utilising the weapon and the powerful names, return the demon to the vessel within the triangle and honour and thank your spirits and helpers who have aided you in this work.

Finish with these words:

> *May the potent substance of this circle and triangle of art return to the realms from whence they came. May all be at peace in this place. May there be peace in my heart and the hearts of those herein.*

If appropriate, the rose petals may remain as offerings to the spirits of the place. Clean up the cloves, however, and then bury them later. The Solomon's seal can be kept by your sleeping place.

A word to the wise. The above process may seem like a strange and abrupt change of tone from being loving and honey-sweet to your demon in a jar to fierce and weapon-armed against it. A diversity of tactics is sometimes required. This knot in the living spell-cord of this book may be tied simply by doing the work of "vomiting" up the demon into the jar and feeding it honey and taking it on dates. The work of the triangle of art and circle of art in this witch-way is if you really need answers and insights to help you unravel this complex, this adverse pattern of behaviour, and transform this demon. It's there for you if you get in a substantially stuck place. Be mindful and call upon the help you need. Ground well and take care of yourself. I deeply ummed and ahhed about putting this process in this book. I put it here as a strong methodology because I know people will hunt and scour online and text-based sources for these kinds of rituals and try them out of context with not much pre-thought. Notice this is marked as number twenty-eight of thirty-six steps. A lot comes before it.

Daimon as Love, demon as Power, and Power takes us back to Love.

Once upon a time, a few witches I knew accused me of being possessed by demons and misleading a whole group of people who I love and care about deeply. I remember feeling hurt, offended, pissed off, and in shock at such bizarre accusations, albeit one of the accusers was known to see demons in just about everything and seemed to have a lot of family-religious trauma in this regard. The other main whipper-up-of-drama was later discovered to be intentionally trying to cause disorder and confusion in order to manipulate power-over for himself within the group. It was a messy and horrible time for many of us. I even turned up to a mediation session with my own coven to work it out. When I reflect upon it, I still can't quite believe that it all happened. The triggering event was a rather potent Hekate working that involved transgressive elements unlikely to shock most traditional witches. Apparently this was the last straw, though, for a couple of folks. Afterwards I wrote to a few of the more experienced, older leaders in the craft I knew and asked them if anything like this had ever happened to them in their community work. They all replied in the affirmative: they had definitely each been accused of that exact situation—demons or magically misleading—from inside the craft. I couldn't believe it. Apparently it's a more common take-down tactic in some circles than we might realise.

What this tells me is that there is a chasm between Love and Power for many in our experiences of the world. It is totally true and right that we yearn for both, but when we are trying to survive in societies that fragment and fight each other, we might not be able to witness or find examples of loving power and powerful love.

29

LOVING POWER—POWERFUL LOVE. Who or what are examples of this for you? Is it bell hooks of beloved and mighty memory? Could it be Laverne Cox, Jinkx Monsoon, Bob the Drag Queen, Janet Mock, people from your ballroom scene, your coven, your bio-family, your oldest friend, your sibling, a policy-maker you know of, a nurse or doctor who has treated and tended to you when you were sick or recovering? Bring them back to the forefront of your mind. Imagine them in a ring around you, beaming that love and power to and through you. We are all connected, so you can draw upon that fundamental reality to feel into this woven web.

These are the people who inspire you and bring you to tears; these are the people who make you laugh and challenge you to think and feel in ways that break through expectations. Some of them you will know intimately, others you only know because of their work and presence in the world out there and how that impacts you.

Sometimes when shit hits the fan and we are riddled with stress, concern, and worry, one of the best things we can do is remind ourselves of the people we know or know about who are examples of this love and power . . . these people whose daimonic fire shines through and who wrestle with and understand the journey of dancing with our own demons. This is power I can trust.

Find a way to anchor this somehow. I learnt anchoring in this named way in Reclaiming. Essentially, you gather up all these sensations you are feeling and experiencing, and with breath, vision, will, and sound, you distil and concentrate as much as you can into a specific gesture you are making, a part of body you are touching, or even into a specific incantation. Some people like to have words and gesture go together. Make sure it is specific and memorable. So you will be saying the words, performing the gesture, touching somewhere or standing or holding yourself in a specific manner, and then when you feel you have gathered as much of the sensation or feeling as possible, you drop the anchor. Whenever you wish, you can pull this anchor up and experience those feelings and sensations again by saying the words, making the gesture, etc.

In the Pearl Pentacle—see appendix 2—if we follow the traditional order around the circumference of the pentacle, we find that Power—or Liberty—goes back into Love. It begins in Love, of course—arising out of the Iron Pentacle Sex—and the course of Power is to return the current of life to Love. That says a lot. It's enough for me to meditate into and contemplate as I go about my life.

I wasn't born this way.
Not exactly.
I was raised to be fierce by a working class woman.
I was raised to be proud of culture and ancestors.
Not once did I forget who my people were,
    who forged my lineage with prayer, dance, farming,
    risks, horses, complicity, love, and pride.
That's why I carry this medicine.
My skin is the colour of beauty meeting beauty,
    of the dark richness of volcanic soil
    meeting the milk of red-eared cows.

Mud-skin hey?
I guess that's what you get by pouring
    sweet milk into fertile earth.
Queer degenerate. Deviant even.
I've been chased down the street,
    raped,
      locked in bathrooms,
        called faggot enough times to know
        how much my vital eros scares you.
How much my rhythms unnerve your rigidity.
You've fragmented and swallowed bitter pills
Twisting you into hard-hard stone.
Medusa doesn't have anything left to do.
Thirty years old.
And every year becoming more and more
of this proud, ancestral power.
I'm producing nectar
I'm in the hive . . .
we have our Queen.
I am the serpent by the well.
I am the fire in the tree.
And we are Legion.
We terrify the most brittle minds . . .
Like stones, except not, not that noble.
And we will keep crafting and keep becoming
Mixed, multiplicitous, and loving.
And this is the future we break our hearts open for.
It is only because we are Love that we cry.
My tears are for humanity and never singly
    for you or for me.
I'm a tiger, baby. I wouldn't fuck with me.
    X

Chapter Nine

Soul-Story, Story-Spell, Spell-Song

There is a vitality, a life force, a quickening that is translated
through you into action, and there is only one of you in all time,
this expression is unique, and if you block it, it will never exist
through any other medium . . . The world will not have it. It is not
your business to determine how good it is . . . It is your business
to keep it yours clearly and directly, to keep the channel open.

—Martha Graham

When I was a child, an adolescent, a teen, I used to viscerally feel that I
was running out of time. I needed to finish high school, get out of my con-
servative town, and move to the nearest capital city as quickly as possible!
This all felt so necessary, so weighty, that only two months after graduation I ended up doing just that. I felt the call of my own road rising, and
I needed to fully walk into the labyrinth and allow the mystery to take
over. I remember only a few months after moving to Meanjin, I wrote to
a well-known Australian witchcraft author who I perceived to be deeply
living in the mythic and shared some of my own story with them. Whether
they knew it or not, that writing allowed me to deeply embrace the magic

vibrating intensely through my whole life. Even now, with hindsight, I am in awe of that seventeen-year-old person who leaped—who pledged, promised, and gave themself to the mystery entirely. That author and I later met and had several very intense and powerful encounters in Naarm. It felt very full-circle at the time.

Soul-story is the term I give to the mythic depth and breadth of who we might be, of who we have become, who we are becoming, and the entirety of this. The power of this. It is true that not one of us—not one—will ever be able to fully comprehend how our lives, our actions, our movements in the world affect and impact this world and those within it. It is true that we have lived lifetimes even within one lifetime. When I reflect on my life even a decade ago I cannot fully grasp the context—this greater context— that has in some ways seemingly directed the rest of me in my becoming. There's something so much broader, so much wider than what I consider even to be me, my life, my breath that calls me forth through each cross-roads along the serpentine road that rises and writhes. And yet soul-story is not something that is written in the stars or in stone in some pre-ordained or absolute way. It was never written and yet exists simultaneously because I am, because you are.

Soul-story reminds me of what I have heard about the medieval concept of *aventure*. I first heard of this concept when I encountered a powerful and wondrous modern-day mystic who goes by the name of Pandora among Reclaiming witches. We were sitting in the attic of Black Cat, a collective Reclaiming hearth-hold set in a beautiful old Victorian in the culturally Chicano/Mexican *La Misión*. Pandora has been a scholar, university professor, and medievalist, and she spoke to me about the medieval romances and tales that emerged from and drank of this aventure. The modern English word *adventure* derives from this Middle English *aventure,* and in that context it refers to something that happens by luck, chance, or fate. To take the aventure—and indeed to catalyse what we think of as an adventure but with profoundly soulful undertones—is to respond to the otherworld or the divine saying *follow me, come this way.* So it might be that a white stag appears in the forest before us and we decide to follow that stag. It could be that someone stops us on the side of the road and tells us about a protest that they are going to later and would we please come too. It could be a homeless person who wants company and some financial aid who we stay with for a while, only to learn about fragments of a whole life. It could be a flyer falling out of a locker at your local gym that tells you to go to a witchcraft class (in the case of Pandora).

There seems to be an echo of what I know about aventure in the Irish concept of *immram,* which refers to voyages to discover other worlds. Often the immrama are explicitly concerning Christian characters who are encountering and navigating potentially older cosmologies and magical realities. They travel through islands, across seas, and into other places . . . this could, in fact, be code as well for descending into the underworld, as the sea and the underworld were sometimes thought of as one for the pagan Irish. There is also the *echtra*—Old Irish for adventure or journey and voyage— and these appear to be more explicitly pagan in nature and involve encounters with spirits and mysterious ones as well as journeys into the otherworld. Again, there is often a catalyst. We all are familiar with that turning point in a book or film plotline that changes everything irrevocably. There is often a moment in which the protagonist has to decide whether or not they will, in fact, choose that road and walk that way or not. All of this reminds me of the soul-story. A soul-story is not something that just happens to us and that we passively imitate or allow for. It requires engagement, participation, immersion, surrender, and risk. When I asked my friend Pandora about aventure again recently, she replied: "I would add that falling in love is always an aventure, too. And one of the points of aventure is that you can choose not to take it. I myself have come to believe that that is always a mistake, though often life seems easier and calmer if you don't take it. But the lost path catches up with you."

The lost path catches up with you. Sometimes the things we think we missed out on, or the road never taken, does actually come back around. And there are cycles and patterns that, if we are mindful, we will become aware of. There is always the right time and the right place. The thing is, there are many right times and right places happening concurrently across time and space. I have found that there are moments in my life in which soul-story seems to explode or erupt through in no uncertain manner and I am left in awe, shaking, weeping, and laughing.

I began this chapter with one of my favourite quotes of all time. As a high school student in dance class, I remember watching a filmed interview with Martha Graham. I remember her saying that she would rather be remembered as a choreographer if she had to choose that from dancer. The thing is, she was both and more. And Graham's quote above was in context. She was responding to the existential and self-deprecating critiques of another artist who was enquiring about how to know if the work is good or if the artist will ever find satisfaction. Graham emphatically replied that she would not; that no artist is ever fulfilled. Instead of that, we have a profound and queer dissatisfaction that keeps us forging on, urges us deeper into the fray. Of course we always have to deal with the many stories that we tell ourselves at night, that we semi-consciously and dismissively throw out in conversations with friends, and that are running in the background, as it were. Some of these stories tie us up in knots, debilitate us; others support and lend us helpful frames or inspire us. Some we have outgrown, others we are experimenting with.

What would happen if we consciously considered the stories we run or that might be running us? Out of our demon-work we might arrive at knowledge regarding these narratives and experientially begin to shed the skins that we have outgrown. It could be that we acknowledge our circumstances and the events and experiences that have contributed to our understanding of self and the world, and we sink a little deeper into the river, into the soul, and grow still and silent . . .

30

AND SO WE return to that profound and primordial silence in the darkness. Imagine, feel, sense, know that you are breathing, being as non-being, wrapped in darkness as the darkness. In womb-like darkness we are held silently, beautifully, profoundly. There is an exquisite loneliness that haunts the fullness of things and yet there are no things. Not yet, maybe never, maybe always. Consider those you love—places, memories, people, creatures, spirits, fragrances, scents, ideas, stories, maybes, promises.

Let that love fill you until you feel you might be too full, and then let it keep filling you until that love finds a way to exist as you. Love so fully that it becomes almost unbearable. Offer it to the Infinite.

There is a notion that we could contemplate and breathe into: that each being we encounter is the repository of their own vital story. I don't just mean the sum total of their experiences up until now, their ancestry, their broader family and friend networks or communities. I mean something quieter and wider under the surface. Perhaps we can never consciously express it, and yet it is there as a shining thread.

Emerge from your reverie and take a clean sheet of paper and write freely, casting aside analysis and assessment with exhalations and sounds. Let pour from you what might be a part of your soul-story you really need to read and hear.

Once you have spent a good amount of time writing out onto the page— or typing onto the screen if that works better for you—make some tea or coffee and sit with what you've written. Dare to read it aloud to yourself. Take time and space to notice how you feel, what sensations emerge, and what you might remember or hope for.

The whole way through the writing and editing of this book I have been reflecting on my life thus far. In a week from this moment I type these words I will be turning thirty-four. I look at the number on the screen and it looks just like a number . . . 3 plus 4. Thirty-four. It also signals to me that I am moving into a different epoch of life. In many ways my life felt like it really began when I left home when I was seventeen years old. And seventeen years later, half my life later, I am typing these words in a two-bedroom apartment in the eastern suburbs of Warrang, six months past a horrific break-up. I am reflecting on romantic relationships, on love lost and found, on the consistent and powerful friendships that hold me, on books written and now out of print, on initiations and powerful rites of passage, on places I dream to be able to travel to, on the child my sister is about to birth into this world!

A normal human life. And yet a normal human life is always filled with the mythic. This is frankly quite normal for humans . . . the mythic, that is. At any possible turn of the page of our lives there is the most ordinary everyday happening, conversation, thought, or feeling writ large, and yet a shining thread of that existential awareness and the profound and simple questions *Why am I here? Why do we even exist? What is this?*

These are the questions that feed into religiosity, into mysticism and art and science. Myth and story help us orient relationally within these misty questions. The *why am I here* question is not one that seems to hang around me a lot; I find it rather dull. I am much more interested in questions like:

> What is the nature of this cosmos?
>
> What am I capable of?
>
> How do I become intimate with this place and time?
>
> Who are the gods?
>
> What is the nature of my being, and how might I
>   express that potently and skilfully?

Perhaps you too have other questions that fascinate you far more deeply than the usual. These are clues to the dance of your soul-story, and they can take us right into the story-spell.

If the soul-story is what we are participating in, then the story-spell is how we can engage that—how we can enter more deeply into mystery and awaken our potential and power here and now.

IN THIRTY WE engaged the process of automatic or free writing onto the page or screen. Reread that aloud to yourself now. It may be days, weeks, or months later that you are doing this. How do you feel about this now? What themes or threads are you noticing arise through reading this aloud?

Align your souls and meditate on your breath coming and going for a good while. As thoughts come, they will also go. If I notice I begin to get distracted by those thoughts, I simply take a deep breath, and on my exhalation blow the thought away with a sound or a sigh and re-centre through the cycle of breath. Sometimes I imagine and sense all my thoughts as polished river stones and I take a deep belly breath in, and on my next exhalation I feel and see all these river stones dropping into the deep well of my being. I find this really helps.

When you feel it and you'd like to, bring this question into your mindfulness:

What is my story-spell?

If the story-spell is how we willingly engage and participate with our soul-story, what might emerge by meditating on this question? Relax into the breath; let the cycles of breathing support you as you meditate. If you notice you begin to go on a trance-journey, bring yourself back to the simple counting of breath in, holding, breath out, holding . . . I invite you to practise noticing what emerges but not jump into it just yet.

When you emerge from your meditation, take notes or go for a walk.

I once taught a soul-story, story-spell, spell-song intensive in the Black Cat attic that I mentioned above. Rose May Dance, who lived in Black Cat for many years, told me after I came downstairs that it sounded like we were raising multiple cones of power again and again. She told me that it felt like endless waves of orgasms pouring down from the attic, and indeed that's how it felt for us in the room! Sometimes that is the nature of these investigations and immersions. As we discover the keys that unlock the doors to deeper knowing and wisdom, it is often accompanied by a great deal of pleasure and sensation of wonder and expansion and catharsis and contraction.

Let's draw upon some of that divine pleasure and eros for our spell. We'll need this power and vitality.

32

FIND A COMFORTABLE and secure place for you to lie or sit and undergo the following. Enact the square breath for at least three to nine cycles. Breathe in for the count of four, hold the in-breath for four, exhale for four, and hold the death-breath for four. Then repeat. Relax into the wheel of this breath.

Once you are feeling centred and grounded, bring your attention to your perineum and as much as you can, at whichever rate you are able, begin to create a beat by pulsating the pelvic floor muscles. Allow the rhythm and container of your breath to support the pulsing/beating/pulling and begin to make sound with your exhalation. And remember you are totally allowed to take breaks to relax as well.

Once you have a rhythm and pulsing established, begin to sense for and open to the erotic life force spiralling in the land. Imagine you are able to open your lower cauldron to it and, aided by your breath, feel it spill up into this cauldron. The goal is to eventually peak and feel the serpentine force of the erotic land rising and spiralling up through your middle and upper cauldrons as well. Eventually, within all the waves of expansion and contraction, you may feel release, and at this time embrace the sensation of erotic vitality raining down, over, and through you. Take your time.

Let this be natural and build by itself, supported by the above practices. Feel free to make the sounds you need to make.

To state the obvious, you may find that this exercise catalyses orgasm or orgasmic experience. This can also be a powerful way to catapult you into astral journeying, into fetch-flight, into raising a great deal of power for spell-work and self-blessing. You may choose to offer this power to and with your familiar spirits. This process may also simply be an erotic way for you to be with the land and cosmos as well.

When you are complete for now, let your breath relax and take on a more normal rhythm and pace. Ground and release any excess vitality you do not require into the earth, into magical objects, or breathe and blow it up to your god soul.

The story-spell is the graspable, able to be touched, perceived, or verbalised pivots and catalysts in our mythic lives. A story-spell could be written out in a simple, evocative phrase.

> *The witch belongs to the world.* This is clearly one of my most
>   important story-spells.
> *The heart is made to break open.* This is another one deeply
>   personal to me.
> *My body is a book and the book is the land.* This one arises out
>   of Wildwood poetry and lore.
> *My blood-red rivers are the dreams of stars.* This could be a
>   very helpful one for wider and deeper ancestral work.
> *I survive/d and I thrive with love.* This is just true.
> *I am home. Here. We are home.* One day I might really feel
>   this story-spell. Sometimes I feel the edges of it.

What would you write down or say if you were asked about your story-spells? What are empowering and provocative phrases you return to again and again as anchors and compasses to orient through the chaos of life experience?

And the reality is there will be death, there will be loss, things will go—friends, beloveds, kin, children, parents, grandparents, houses, land, health, memory—there will always be loss, grief, confusion, and wild disorientation.

None of this blemishes the soul-story; the soul-story pours through and as all our experiences, and the story-spell is almost like a set of instructions guiding us through these horrific and intense experiences we will have. I often have people ask me—or perhaps they confess—whether the crap parts of their lives, the missings of the mark, the horrible experiences will bar their way to witchdom or taint or weigh down their ability to become the priestess or artist they long to be. My response is always that it is all of that stuff that marks the power of that witch and priestess most. It is all of that shit—that horrible pain, that distress, that pulling apart of the souls, the not knowing, and the rage at existence for even existing—that goes into the cauldron and adds the essential ingredients of profound growth and transformation.

So if we consider the soul-story to be the cauldron itself and the story-spell to be the brew within that we will drink and be transformed by, then the spell-song is that very song the great witch is singing and humming over the cauldron and the brew. Within the witch all of this is unified, just as the souls are aligned as body.

The singing of a spell of power is central to many witchcraft traditions and appears in cosmology that is found in the tales recounted in *Aradia, or The Gospel of the Witches,* which was put together by Charles Godfrey Leland (1824–1903) and published originally in 1899; this is from the new translation by Mario and Dina Pazzaglini.

> [But] Diana sang to [Lucifer] a spell, a song of power, and he was silent, the song of the night which soothes to sleep; he could say nothing. So Diana with her wiles of witchcraft so charmed him that he yielded to her love. This was the first fascination, she hummed the song, it was as the buzzing of bees (or a top spinning round), a spinning-wheel spinning life. She spun the lives of all men; all things were spun from the wheel of Diana. Lucifer turned the wheel.

33

Ground, centre, align.

Let us call to the Great Ones who are named in *Aradia* as Diana and Lucifer. Let us call to the living and profound darkness that is Diana and the most beautiful light that is Lucifer. It is said that from their union comes Aradia, who will be the first of witches known. Call out by allowing a hum to build in your being; it doesn't matter what kind of hum or what melody you are humming as long as it keeps your interest or, better yet, excites you! We are each darkness and we are each light, children of both and something else altogether.

Let the humming loop around and around and spiral in and out. Maybe you find that the humming has you spinning around like a spinning wheel in your space. What if your humming could be that same humming that fascinated Lucifer? This is the spell that Diana apparently has cast over Lucifer. It is important to remember the gods are not human, though we often clothe them in human garb to make them more sensible to us. How are you seducing the secret and bright parts of yourself? How do you make love with yourself? Light is born from darkness . . . from beautiful darkness comes dazzling light.

Let the humming and spinning or movement take you into a trance state. In this trance approach the great cauldron of your soul-story and scry into the depths . . . scry into the story-spell that is bubbling in this cauldron. Allow yourself to be silent as you scry into the depths within the cauldron. Feel yourself as the great witch, the first witch, who is witnessing the making of magic. Hear yourself incanting,

> *Darkness is the mother of light,*
> *Light is the maker of shadow,*
> *Shadow is the child of light,*
> *Light is the child of Darkness.*

This incantation becomes a song, a mighty spell-song. Witness and feel how the singing of this spell-song emerges from and affects the story-spell within the cauldron of the soul-story. Perhaps you begin to have visions, remembrances, knowings, awakenings, insights, sensations. Allow them to move through you and wake up primordial parts of you.

When you have returned from this trance, honour Diana and Lucifer and the spirits who are with you. Give offerings if need be. Then journal for a while about your experiences, and eat and drink to ground.

What's your spell-song? At least in this moment, what might it be? What kind of songs have brought you back to life? I remember this song that another beloved, Ravyn Stanfield, wrote. We sang it at a Reclaiming Witch-Camp in the redwoods in 2012.

> *You may feel you have a hole in your heart as deep as the sea*
> *You may feel that you've been waiting, waiting for someone,*
>   *something*
> *When you open your heart and let it be held for you*
> *You may discover the world is waiting to sing through you . . .*
> *Sing us back to life, we'll sing you back to life*
> *Coming back to life, we're coming back to life . . .*

This is a literal spell-song. It's one that brings us back from hopelessness, despair, feeling used up and broken beyond repair. It brings us back into the arms of love. It did this for me. I had gone through a massive break-up only four months before this particular Skeleton Woman WitchCamp. This song brought me back to life. It sang me back. Well, this one and Florence and the Machine's "Shake It Out," which I and three other delightful queers sang together at the talent show that year at WitchCamp. I sang that particular Florence song regularly for about two years. It carried me through several gates of power.

How have you been brought back to life? How have you called yourself back from the scrap heap, from shadows and fog, from numbness and nothing? I am sure you didn't feel like a wise warrior, but in my heart I am naming you and naming me this. As I write these words, I am naming you a wise warrior. If you need it or desire it, it's there. Perhaps it rubs you the wrong way, perhaps you don't need it or desire it, but might you consider it? It's there anyway, if you ever want it.

A spell-song, you. This is you. Tonight I might think of this as a sacred breath of God herself thrumming, vibrating, moving and changing things. Each of us one of her infinite spell-songs being cast into the infinite to carve magic out of nothing.

I am writing this book as a story-spell, and I offer it as a spell-song. Know that I have gone to the cliffs to sing this, that the cloud people, the sea people, the cliff people, the bird people hear it and take it out with them on their journeys, to their places, into the mystery.

And it has come up, spilling forth from my soul-story: that mythopoetic truth and power of me. Sure, I might mean essence, but I don't mean essential me. I am not saying that there is a reified divine being unto hirself who is conducting this, emanating this, weaving and creating this and doing it to the rest of me. What I am offering and attempting to convey is this:

That there is deep numinous presence—infinitely so—and infinite presences. That in this there is soul: a noticing of this numinous presence and a praising of it, a connecting through it, and a desire of being with and in that presence. That soul—which some scholars trace to a word meaning sea (remember those dark waters upon which the spirit of God hovers?)— makes story, that soul responds to story, and that story is the marriage of soul with soul. And there are infinite possibilities in this.

Soul-story happens and unfolds endlessly. I used to say self is an event, a happening. One could say that soul and self are synonymous or engage as divine twins.

34

TRY IT: IMAGINE that soul and self are twins. Sense them beholding each other through the mirror. You might want to stand or sit in front of a mirror while doing this. Align your souls and take yourself into enough of a trance state that you are more sensitive and aware of perception than before. Feel them merge, delve, and separate out from one, another. Open to perceive their fascination and desire for one another. In soul there is story there is self. Self is key to allowing the experience of self and to embrace your self as divine and intrinsically worthy of being. In this way the self presciently, powerfully catalyses the story-spell that becomes the spell-song that in turn initiates us. The spell-song that Diana hums to seduce the light. We are that light.

The experience of self in some way starts us, opens us, undoes us, merges us with the seat of all mystery within. *Soul-story, story-spell, spell-song* is a poem. Write it now. Sing it now. Dance it now. Walk it. Paint it. Eat it. Listen to it. Imagine it.

Some people wait their whole lives to live. Witches, we are hungry for life, we are life eating life. And we seek to understand death—we respect death as yet another threshold of mystery and significance. In my Wild-wood practice I honour the Green Man, who we also call Grandfather—one of our Sacred Four—as the gate that is death, that is birth. The Grand-father is the very breath I took in upon birth into this middleworld, and I will someday expire and that breath will leave and travel out once more, joining the greater air. I understand that birth and death are one, that breath is how I as a creature upon this planet exist and function, and that while I function in this way on this earth, I am going to try to be coura-geous. I am going to live. I am going to fuck up. I am going to try to be kind.

Yes, it is complex, and yes, it's complicated, and it is true that we also inevitably step between the worlds, open the crossroads, and we change, for we are changers. Go, witch, change things. A little or a lot. But do the changing, change your own shape, change your name, change your address, change what needs to be shifted, transformed, mended, broken open. This will make you feel powerful because this is the exercise of power. And when power and love are one, then we might have the key.

I have been writing this book as a dare from the planet Mars to myself after four years of struggling with it and dancing with the daimon-demon of it within me. Once a day and usually in the night I have been sitting down and writing 1500 words at a time. Often I need to prepare myself on multiple levels to sit down and attend to the nightly discipline of writing this work. I'll walk around my apartment picking up books and reading them, putting them down, opening old boxes of stuff and finding talismans and amulets and sitting with them, entering into conversation with magic past, present, and future. At the time of the original writing, my partner at the time would usually make tea and pour it for me. I might eat snacks or chocolate or ice cream; align my souls or read the cards. And speaking of tarot, I opened a book just now and there was the Ace of Swords from my first tarot deck. I knew that I had other cards from that first deck sit-ting on my Wildwood working altar, so I wandered into the temple room and retrieved what seems to be the last of the pips from that deck. I have been gifting cards from that minor arcana (the pips) for years as gifts to beloveds. For instance, the Three of Cups is sitting in my friend's tattoo studio in Meanjin.

By chance, by fortune, by lot, I have four minor arcana cards sitting next to me right now. I shall take notice of the fate and fortune of this moment as I happen to have one of each suit: the Ace of Swords, the Three of Pentacles, the Eight of Wands, and the Ten of Cups. I have two odds and two evens. They are also numerically spread—an ace, a three, an eight, and a ten; they are equidistant. There are different coloured backgrounds: the swords card has a deep, rich purple background; the pentacles a sun yellow; the wands an orange; and the cups a cerulean blue.

If I had drawn these cards for a client, this is what I'd likely say:

> *You know what it is you want and you are working hard to get to it. You have allies, companions, good spirits, and yes—even good news on its way. And wow, look at that! It looks like happiness, powerful harmony, beauty, love, and connection is yours! Your key is to focus on crafting your skills and allowing yourself to be seen for what it is that makes you radiate, makes you incandescently joyful. Communicate and express that to the world and the world will smile and laugh with you. Be aware.*

I notice right now as I type these words that I am instantly suspicious and I want there to be a caveat that brings in the logical presence of a block, an obstacle, something to be concerned about. I notice that thought, that inclination, and I realise so many of us want to question our happiness, so many of us want to qualify and justify our passions, our joys, that which fills us up to the brim with wonder and connects us to the sacred. It seems to me that some might want to explain it so that in the eyes of God, society, law and order, and whatever else, we are seen to be worthy, fit for it, but this—this is bullshit. We are worthy of love intrinsically. We are connected, and it is wonderful, blessed, good, and right that we pursue our passions and dedicate ourselves to that which turns us on to the life force, brings us into the dance. The provocation: Isn't it curious how there are insidious, coercive, enculturated voices that want us to explain how it is okay that we seek love, connection, happiness? Isn't that absolutely horrifying . . . disorientating . . . sickening? Well, it's something, and right now I'll be a little gobsmacked and a little compassionate for myself in this. And I hope you are compassionate to yourself too.

This is one of those shimmering, mythic-drenched moments for me, deeply connective in the context of my life, my memories, my relationships. I only opened that book because I saw a friend post on Instagram a story of her reading with a tarot deck that I left at my old house, her current house. A deck that I pulled from a box that someone had brought to a workshop I was running in Wurundjeri country several years ago. A deck which made me go, "hm . . . intriguing, not completely for me, but I'll carry this deck with me until they need to go elsewhere." It seemed I went elsewhere—moved cities even—and the deck called to another. Divinatory creatures like the cards are often wondrous and excellent synchronicity pivots.

35

Retrieve a divinatory ally: tarot cards, oracle cards, runes, Lenormand, ogham staves, tea leaves and a teapot and strainer, the I Ching, dice . . .

Perhaps you will feel like grounding or aligning your souls. Engage the practices and protocols you have around engaging this divinatory accomplice, then cast a reading.

Speak aloud if you can as if you are interpreting this reading to a friend, a beloved, or even a client. Be clear and drink from the well of your wisdom. If it helps, you could press your palms down on the cards or staves or hold the cup against your chest and feel your heartbeat move through the items. Imagine that your heart is flowering through this aid or that your hands have witch eyes in them that are opening and scrying into the cards, runes, or staves they touch. Let yourself know and see and perceive at a deeper level than you might ordinarily if you were just reading for yourself at another time.

Now repeat this whole process of casting a reading and deepening into it at least three more times. This first reading was what needed to come through here and now, the tune-in or the bird's-eye-view reading, as I like to call it. Now let's focus it with the frame of soul-story, story-spell, and spell-song. Do a reading for each mystery.

Let these clues or mirrors or threads settle, and perhaps you will feel like journalling or drinking more tea and lying down and meditating or trancing. Perhaps you will feel like going for a walk or speaking to a friend or lover. Give thanks and honour to the divination and the divining tools.

This kind of work can be nebulous, and I am using that word also to evoke the word *nebulae,* which reminds me of a particular magical working I engaged with a beloved to help me move through some painful and triggering emotions quite a while ago. In this ritual, in a dried-up creek bed, this friend of mine opened to take in the presence of Our Lady of the Wildwood, the crescent-crowned goddess. I will always remember she kept repeating the word *nebulae* to me over and over again.

The word *nebula*, the singular of nebulae, descends ultimately from the Proto-Indo-European word *nebh*, meaning "cloud." The English nebula can mean smoky, misty, foggy, cloudy, and therefore nebulous can mean something like obscured or vague. There is a mystery to this work, and in this work it can help to take our attention to the clouds and through the cloud people to those realms that we consider to be above us. It might also help to consider that what is above is also an emanation and extension of what is below us and of what is here with us. Sometimes the roots are in a place we didn't think of straightaway. Imagine that you can feel the worlds tip a little; imagine things turning inside out . . .

36

IF YOU ARE able, take a witch's walk and find a place where you can see at least a patch of the sky. Acknowledge country and dedicate this time to observing and listening. Listen to the conversations you might overhear, to the birds and insects, to the wind. Observe the clouds and their movements. Ask aloud for the cloud people and the star people to communicate with you. Perhaps you think of the watchers, the fallen angels, the Great Ones of ancestral memory, the beings who come down and pass and reveal law and knowledge. Feel into the idea that the stars and clouds have their places within the earth where they dwell and ripple: their locations, their marriage partners and lovers. Perhaps the very place you are right now kisses a star, a constellation, a cloud formation, a mystery "up there" for you to feel into.

This might become a cloud-scrying session in which the cloud people speak with you through pictures and images. Or perhaps you need to journey up past the nebulous ones and into the nebulae, into the spinning mists of space and the deep places. Rather than asking about your soul-story, share some of it to the listening ones, to the deep ones. Start to just let yourself speak or even sing or whisper. Tell the land your story.

You might begin with:

I was born on a windy night; the sun had set a few hours before, and the sign of the Archer was housing the Sun. The Moon was moving through the sign of the Scorpion, and Mars was bright in the sky.

My parents named me this because . . .

I grew up knowing this and this and this to be true . . .

I questioned this and wondered this . . .

I lived near a mountain, near the sea, in a jungle, on a farm . . .

These are the beings, the people, who held me when I was sad, who helped me when things didn't make sense anymore . . .

I have fallen in love. I have never understood love and felt lonely most of my life. It took me until I was forty to open the door to intimacy. I have always felt scared of trusting . . .

Beneath this all, I know this to be true about the world I live in . . .

I want to tell you these secret and sacred truths about me.

And then tell the truth: the whole truth, and nothing but the truth.

Heart roams like ivy clinging to a shore
    whose waves carry out
carry out to islands lost beyond the ninth
carry out beyond Kharon's boat and the cave-mouth down
heart roams like blossoming white moon flowers given to prayer
prayerful devotion given to hearts roaming, to hearts still in prayerful
    devotion.
Torn, aside, in the dirt made into mud by the heavens' full wrath
he lays there and I watch him
wondering how the ticking time veins inside
will open him back—

—back into the places he used to roam free
wander with feline strength
with curiosity, but still, torn and aside.
And the wind is full of mournful questioning
writhing at the sides of endless wondering
and the Tower has crumbled as good Towers do
and the jade warrior and the cobalt flame incandescently sings
hummingbird princes remind him of yesterday
and the sun in the east shows him his heart.
That precious little animal, that mighty fallen creature
that god-wrought woven-star-borne-blood-sung being
And when he takes, when I take it
We come home again.
And there the sea carries us out together.

Chapter Ten

Initiation

Initiation is not for secrets. It is not for gain. It is not for access to hidden mysteries. It is not for title or status. It is not for the names that are keys to the doors that open. Being initiated is not to further an agenda. It is not to win and it is not to lose.

Initiation is because you can't not do it. It has always been what happens when you take notice, pay attention, and wrestle with existence and self to the point that even the deep things take notice and zero in—on you. It is what happens when we kiss the darkness and liberate through death into the heart of love. We become bound to life forever.

Initiation is not for secrets. It is for becoming what is secret and silent and can never be truly spoken beyond the circle of art where the star is the stone and the breath is the bone. It is the oath sworn silently and without words. It is the knowing of what will break it and the truth that will attain it. Initiation means that we come alive to who we have been, and the becoming will join us with those who have been on that road before us. It is letting go of the need to know something and instead embracing the encounter as the lover and we as the beloved.

In the act of initiation, supreme risk is effected. All the worlds are summoned to attention-tension, and the dynamism inside creation-unfolding is gathered up into the breaking point—the initiate. All that has been—the bonds of fate, the debts we have incurred, every possible road forward into mystery—are side-stepped, suspended, and the haunting song of all that is falls silent on her own lips. It is the breath-in that is held, and held, and held . . .

. . . and then the orgasmic catharsis of the exhalation, which dissolves and enjoins all possibility. For some time the initiate will be held in the death breath of nothing that comes after, and the cradle and the grave are one. The tomb and the womb. The circle and the cauldron.

Emerged—anointed—with shining brow to be cast on the river of life once more and meet those who will love us, take care of us, raise us, and name us. Once we have served those names, we participate in the naming, only to be unravelled again and again.

Die before you die, they said. So that you may truly live.

A Witchcraft Initiation Ritual

This ritual can be done alone or if you already work in a circle or coven, different witches may take different roles if the necessary skills and connections are in place.

This ritual needs to happen outside somewhere. It also needs to be a place in which you will most likely not be disturbed by other living humans. In Wildwood witchcraft our initiations happen largely outside, and as many of us live in urban areas, some of the parklands, forests, and liminal spaces where we enact these rituals are sometimes peopled. We have every now and again had the odd passersby come across a group of us in the bush or a national park or on the hill. I can assure you that non-witch passersby will simply move along; if you cast your enchantments excellently, some may not even notice. For this reason, ward and enchant the place to deter humans from coming near. If you physically cannot leave the house, then you may undergo this ritual in deep trance within your home. If you have magical accomplices, before the ritual ask them to bring you dirt, stones, vines, and mushrooms—with permission—from powerful places. Do not take from named and known sacred sites at all; everyone, use your intuition, research skills, and respect! After the rite, have your accomplice return what was taken back to the place with blessings.

It is best that this ritual happens at night, but you might feel dawn or dusk is more suited to your magical path and inclinations. The cloak and cauldron of night and darkness is traditional, but the ritual can be engaged earnestly and passionately at any time of day or night with enough preparation, alignment, personal meaning, and synchronicity.

If you are embarking on this ritual as one-alone, you will be moving through a landscape in which you will open to meet certain spirits and powers of witchcraft, of the land, of your own ancestry. I am going to continue to describe this ritual as if it is you and you alone embarking on this rite of initiation.

There is a great deal of debate and conflict regarding whether or not a witch can initiate themself. Too many conflicts, too many decades have been spent on airing strained grievances of "compromised lineage," inauthentic claims of witchhood, or attacking other witch houses or traditions as illegitimate. The folkloric record, the customs and superstitions of various regions and places, the caveat-filled confessions of many accused witches, and the experiences of contemporary witches make it clear: a witch is initiated by the gods of witchcraft, by the Devil, by the Queen of Witches, by fate, by their witch ancestors, by the sorcerous and cunning powers of the place.

Generally these hallmarks are present in witchcraft initiations:

- The coming of familiar spirits of various kinds to the witch. They usually will offer to aid and help the witch in their sorcery, in their lives, if they promise to trust them and enter into relationship with them.

- The meeting with the Devil in various forms: as a man in black or as a dog, a bull, a goat, a cat, a stag, a toad, an angel . . .

- A meeting with a powerful feminine spirit.
  This might clearly be a goddess or the
  Queen of Elfhame or a saint or Mary . . .

- The repudiation of the ties that bind and the forces
  that subjugate and oppress: poverty, of servitude
  to a/the Lord, to the church/Christianity, original
  sin. This could be the renouncing of one's baptism
  by the trampling of the torture device that was the
  crucifix. There are multiple mystical and sorcerous
  rationales behind these practices even now.
  One modern-day example that has been widely
  disseminated and popularised by Paul Huson
  is the saying of the Lord's Prayer backwards.

- The receiving of sacred plants, oils, and items that
  will aid the efficacy of the witch's work.

- Some kind of marking or the letting of blood.

- Some kind of sexual, erotic, or intimately
  transgressive act that seals the compact.

- Pleasure, revelry, laughter, feasting.

For this reason, many witches recognise and honour a true witch's initiation as stretching over time, over many years, and that "the ritual" is the swearing and the sealing as witnessed by the powers. Many modern witches are poly-traditional and poly-initiated. I consider all of my initiations into various houses and traditions as being part of one great unfolding witchcraft initiation and initiation into mystery, by mystery.

These are the things you will need for this initiation:

- A basket for carrying the other items.

- A witch knife (various traditions describe the knife
  differently; the only parameters I would advise are to
  make sure it can actually cut and do so effectively).

- A wand (ideally this will measure from the crook
  of your elbow to the tip of your middle finger).

- A loose incense you have made from powders, resins, and herbs you decide upon. This is your initiation incense that you will burn in the rite. You may feel it is better to make an initiation oil, in which case do this.

- Practical and close-fitting dark or neutral-coloured clothing that will be suitable for the climate and the region.

- One black candle.

- A black book and a pen to write within it.

- A blindfold.

- A sterilised bloodletter (you can buy the diabetic blood prickers at chemist stores).

- Offerings for your familiar spirits, the witch gods, and the spirits of the land.

On the day, wake just before dawn. You are invited to fast from food or to eat only fruit and nuts for a twenty-four-hour period before the rite. You know your body, so I trust you know what limits and needs you have. You are invited also to be wordless from waking until you speak words within the rite.

At the appointed hour, travel to the location of your initiation. Practically speaking, you will have scouted out the place prior and be familiar with the lay of the land so this is a place you have some confidence in orienting within. Remember, very powerful and wondrous witchcraft initiations happen in urban centres and cities all the time.

As you move into this space, pause in a place that feels right. Place everything down on the ground, acknowledge country, and give your offerings to the land spirits, letting them know what you are here to do. Align your souls and merge with the land. Keep thinking aloud:

My body is the book and the book is the land.

Recite this over and over.

Picking everything back up, journey to the place you have decided will be your place of sealing and swearing.

When you get to this place, put the basket down in what will be the centre of the circle you draw with the wand. Draw the circle now by holding the wand down to touch the dirt or ground and moving around in the circle until you reach the place you started. Do it with deep attention, with potent silence and profound focus. As you draw the circle, know that you are moving between the worlds, kissing the earth, and gathering the attention of the witching spirits.

Go to the centre of the circle, stand at the fulcrum of power, and whisper, noting that these may be the first words you have spoken aloud all day:

I am here and I am now, and I am with the holy centre.
The centre is the circumference, and the
circumference is boundless.

Chant this, growing from a soft whisper to a sure and even tone.

Turn your attention to the direction of midnight; this will be the south or north depending on your hemisphere. Enter a deep meditative state here and reflect on the silence in the darkness.

When you are ready and you feel drawn to do so, move to the east, the place of the rising sun, and begin to invoke in words that are meaningful to you. It might sound something like:

Great ones in the east, powerful and mysterious spirits who
aid witchkind. Here stands a witch in the spiral labyrinth
of witches, and I call you to witness this rite of swearing
and ward this circle from any danger or distraction!

Repeat this process in the direction of the midday sun and the direction of the setting sun. Return to the midnight point and invoke verbally there.

Do not forget to also invoke from the above and the below. In this way the crossroads is opened and thus the circle is also a compass. You might seal and affirm this magically by saying powerfully:

The crossroads is opened! The compass is laid!
The circle is sealed! And so it is made!

Now anoint yourself with the oil or burn the incense and smoke yourself (or both). It is time to blindfold yourself and enter deep darkness.

Say aloud to yourself:

> *As all begins in darknesss, so must I.*

Reflect on your day or days of silence and wordlessness. Reflect on what brought you to this choice, here to this circle of the art, to this crossroads, to this compass between the worlds. Arouse your awareness of multiple parts of yourself, various threads of history and story; conjure up the felt sense of your soul-story, and then begin to tell the land and the listening ones—the deep ones all around you—your story-spell. Tell as much as comes to you to tell. You might fall into periods of silence. If you notice yourself slipping into journeying, pull yourself back. First tell the story.

As the story begins to feel like enough or even more than enough, begin to sing. Let the story-spell become the spell-song that will initiate you into this act, an act that will change your world and change the worlds. Summon the witch's strength, the witch's audacity, the witch's daring, and when you are ready, take the blood-letter and draw a simple drop of blood and anoint your forehead, your heart-chest, and your belly-genitals. Feel the vibration of the three cauldrons. State aloud:

> *My cauldrons anointed with witch's blood! Holy blood!*
> *Blood of the primal marriage between those who have*
> *fallen-in-love and the red and artful ones!*

Take the knife, your witch's knife, and carve a pentagram in the air before you. Open your body to imitate this sign and feel your familiar spirits come to hold you in this. Now it is time to call out to the powers of witchcraft to fill you with their power and remind you of your original sovereignty.

To Invoke Gods of the Witches
> *Gods of the witches, ancient and hallowed*
> *These whispered words I offer here*
> *Antlered, weaving, lunar, harrowed*
> *Between, below, all love and fear*

Mother of the Stars and Moon
Spinner in the cave beneath
Wise One of the holy loom
Bearer/barer of the sharpest teeth
Through the valleys, fields, and ruins
Come to us and dance this ring
Share with us the bones and runes
Of long-ago forgotten things
Descend, arise, and touch our hearts
Of ocean and the wildwood
Fill our hands with elfin darts
Let them fly free as they should
Goddess riding on the wind
Goats and pitchforks, besoms, staves
Lady of abundance, riches
Held secret, silent in the caves
Old One who knows life and death
Who lifts the Son up to the Sun
Reveals the words that render breath
And makes the seasons turn and come
Darkest, deepest mystery
In the land, the sky, and sea
Deep within our trinity
The gods are here, and so are we!

At this point open to fully receive their blessing. If this invocation does not work for you or describe your experience of the witch gods, then please say what comes to your heart or prepare or borrow something that does carry that power for you.

Once you have recovered from the blessing of the Great Ones and your familiar spirits, you may be seated on the ground. The next step is to take out your black book and ask for the blessings of the spirits on it. Hold it up and out for them to fill with power, and then hold it against your beating heart through your chest for at least nine heartbeats. Open the book to the first page, squeeze some more blood from the place you let from before, and press your bloodied finger into the page. Now here is where you will write down your oath and seal it in the circle by speaking it aloud with power.

If you need ideas of what this could be, you might model it on something like this:

> *By witch's blood, by witch's knife, within the circle of*
> *the art, here in the hallowed crossroads, where the*
> *compass points to the mystery, do I vow these things.*
> *I vow to live by my head full of fire, my heart full*
> *of honey, and my hands filled with art!*
> *I vow to trust in and work faithfully with my familiar*
> *spirits, my fetch-mate, and my gods, ever remembering*
> *that I am my own agent, a daimon of power.*
> *I vow to uphold, protect, and defend the craft through silence,*
> *through speaking, through action, and through love.*
> *I vow to honour the mystery and keep secret what*
> *must be kept secret, sharing what must be shared*
> *and trusting in the ancestors of the craft, the spirits*
> *of the land, and my own deep knowing.*
> *If I should break these solemn vows, then may*
> *the land open to swallow me, may the sky fall*
> *to crush me, and may the sea drown me.*
> *If I should keep these solemn vows, may I grow wise;*
> *in wisdom may I wield power; and through power*
> *may I discover truth and love in all things.*

At this point you may feel the need to unbind from previous allegiances by saying the Lord's Prayer backwards, trampling the cross, or renouncing previous enforced or unconscious baptisms, etc. This may not be for you and may not align with your ethos or need. Do whatever helps free you from ties that bind you and your life force against yourself. You may feel the need to do this before the ritual in preparation as well. Either would work.

Now, when you are ready to continue with this rite of initiation, take your witch's knife and walk to each of the directions, starting in the midnight point. Hold out your knife to be kissed by the direction and the spirits that gather there and say aloud:

Great Ones at the Gates of Power
I seek a name by which you will know me!
As you bless and charge my knife
Bless me with a witch's name.

Take your time to drop into trance and listen at each direction or gate of power. By the time you have reached the centre of the circle once more, having listened at the cardinal directions and to the above and the below, feel into your centre, which is also the centre in this moment, and receive your name. It could be that the name is given straightaway; it could be that it takes the full process or that it is revealed in a dream or vision at another time. It could be that you came to the circle with knowledge of the name. Either way, trust the name will reveal itself to you in the right way and in the right time.

Seal this ritual by speaking aloud words of power that you are drawn to speak. These could include your name or a recitation of the sacred and powerful things you have done. It could be in thanks and praising to the powers; it definitely ought to include that at the end. When you are finished, give offerings. Dance and sing in celebration, pouring blessing into the air, the ground, the stars, the trees, the fungi, the webs, the stones, the waters . . .

Gather everything up into your basket and unravel the circle by saying the following while you walk around, rubbing out the marks of the circle:

This circle is released and unbound.
Into sea, into sky, into sovereign ground.

If you have undergone this ritual in simultaneity with other witches— all having done this ritual on the same night in different locations—you can join together later in the evening for a ritual feast.

The key here is that the ritual of initiation is via the witch gods and your own familiar spirits. In this way you will receive initiation. Of course you cannot claim to be an initiate of any formal human lineage or named witch tradition, but that doesn't matter. You are an initiate of the Witch Herself, of the spirit of the craft. You have come and received mystery, and power has been stirred. This is a rite that you might undertake even after receiving initiation into covens or traditions because it just feels important or timely for you. Perhaps you are just at that point in your craft where this kind of initiation at the hands of your own inner court of beings is important. You may add whatever you like to this working or adapt it as you see fit. It is here for you to hang your witch's hat on if you like and to work through.

Initiation into the craft really has nothing to do with titles, degrees, lineages, or formal traditions. Of course, all those things can be a part of initiation into witchcraft, and certainly I have deep value and connection with some of those things. It is the haunting, wondrous, heart-broken-open, mighty risk that is the Witch—the Great Body of Witch—that is initiating, initiated, initiatory.

Initiation has changed my life. Each spiral of my initiatory journey takes me deeper into the powerful mystery of self and often deeply impassions me toward presence, truthfulness, integrity, and the responsibility of wielding power in and through the worlds. In Reclaiming and Feri traditions, many of us work intensively with the Iron and Pearl Pentacles (see appendix 2). I desire to become and serve and celebrate Love, Wisdom, Knowledge, Law, Power, and Liberation. However, if I don't work with and embrace my Sex, Self, Passion, Pride, and Power, how can I possibly experience these mysterious pearlescent points? On the other witch's hand, it is through experiencing Love, Wisdom, etc., that I begin to understand how to be in right relationship with the Iron points, and this describes at least one version of initiation in my life.

I was initiated at conception—just like you—as a god that is animal, an animal that is god. I was initiated when I was born into this middleworld and breathed my first breath: my three souls kissing and coming together as one through the mystery of body. I was initiated by my grandmother sitting on the active volcano—Gunung Batur—that my father's village wreaths. I was initiated by the Wildwood when I and three others met and conspired on the slopes of Mount Coot-tha and formed the Coven of the Wildwood. I was initiated by Persephone when she appeared to me in my mother's kitchen so many years ago and reminded me that I am hers. I have been initiated at the hands of beloved witches I love and trust in the sacred and traditional lands of the Ohlone, the Yugambeh, the Kombumerri, the Muwinina, and the ancient Preteni. I am initiated each time I help initiate another. The spiral spirals inward, ever inward, deeper—ever deeper.

What could it mean, then, if you did decide to enter into an established witch house, into a lineage of witches, into a tradition?

Initiates often say it's like family. I would say so, yes.

There's that uncle that you really love. Every time you see him at a family get-together, you know he'll hold court and tell you whimsical stories of the long-before, and you feel more like you understand why you laugh that way or keep secrets the way you do.

Then there's that grandma who each time she looks at you, you feel like she's reading your mind—and you'd rather she not—but then smiles and oceanic depths open between you for that moment before you part again.

There are cousins you can't stand and cousins you love to hang out with. Your own parents are probably wandering about, embarrassing you or themselves. You might even have children there or partners you've brought into the family. You might be glowing with pride at the picnic at something you overheard one of your children saying to one of their great-grandparents.

Initiation into a tradition is a complex thing because the tradition doesn't belong to us, we belong to the family of the tradition, and that's when the complex struggles and dark nights of the soul really come up. These are also the great and old lessons of sovereignty, agency, authority, and surrender. There is great bliss in this learning too. When there is attentiveness, fierce care, kindness, no one has to compromise their dignity and worth; unfortunately, mistakes are always made and conflict is likely inevitable . . . but—and!

We don't have to like everyone we are family with, but together we form something greater than the sum of the parts. There is the inheritance and that which is becoming, and the legacy weaving before us with every breath and step we/they take . . . how to live in honour by whatever foundation stones or guiding stars the family knows.

Each family member might tell the story a little differently or even divergently. Each memory might be required to make up the greater puzzle that is ever-deepening. The grandparents might need to be quizzed, the kids might need to be called over to explain some new-fangled tech-whiz-boom-box thing (I too do not understand such things, help me with this please?!) and the cousins might need to be called in. But at the setting of the sun and at the rising of the moon there are usually the unspoken and clear cores and kernels. This is where we rest our heads, this is the fire we sleep around, these are the stories we tell, these are the names of our beloveds. Please treasure them like we have, and please be careful with our precious, powerful hearts. We've given you a gift that was given to us; this is our mutual obligation and our mutual joy.

And what could it mean if you simply surrendered without needing to know right away what any of this could mean for you? Well, that might be the beginning.

Initiation changes everything. She turns us inside out, rearranges and realigns us according to the ever-becoming reality of things. The witch belongs to the world, remember? So does initiation. We are made for this work. We will to be changed and changers.

Coda

Witch: enemy of empire. Tracker of spirits. Lover of angels. Worker of charms. Two-handed sorcerer. Knower of the sabbat. Dancer with demons. Priestess of Old Gods. Transgressor and hedgerider. Friend to the Good People. Teller of jokes. Listener with land. Flyer at night. Dreamer of story. Initiate of mystery. Belongs to themself.

Here I am writing these words, and they are a love note to witches everywhere, to the craft, and to the witch that I have become and am still becoming.

In a world that denies, denigrates, fetishises, or fears us, we remain the mythic hinges and the otherworldly interruptions and catalysts that the world yearns for and fights. And the more we witch, the more human we discover ourselves to be—or at least the more *I* witch, the more human *I* discover myself to be. I have discovered that witches are perhaps the most human people I know, and I know a lot of witches. I love a lot of very human witches.

I hope that this talismanic grimoire has offered you a mighty spell of becoming woven by the writing and the reading, the thinking and the doing, the breathing and the spaces in between. I hope that my own head filled with fire and heart brimming with honey carry through these hands of art as they carve words out of light and air, time and space. I hope that we can all turn into what is happening, what is real here and now on this planet, and with our wiles and spirits sing back to life that which we must. We are responsible for what we do.

If you have counted along—the knots in this witch's ladder, in this spell cord—then you have participated powerfully in a poetry that may help you harness the magic to retrieve, renew, and revolutionise. The spell the whole way has been about you, for you, and cast by your own hand and heart. This spell is about your becoming, for the witch belongs to the world. All we ever really have is our own divine capacity to create and change what seems to be into what might become. In this exhilarating experience, we chance experiencing magic. And magic is what I am here for. And as always, all that is left is poetry.

You Feral Maid, Witchcraft, bowing to
None but speaking Truth in every
corner caught only by those listening
to the wind-bent whispers of Serpents
below in the dirt.
Like wyrms in the soil are carved the
savage words of our noble histories
and alighting the humble hearts of
fierce warriors of Trees are the Red
Cups to spill out upon sacrificial skin.
Where there is Love is your Hallow
Flame burning. Where there is the
Hunt for Poetry in the Singing Water
there is your Reflection made more
so by the Language of Ravens and the
Cradles of the Graves.

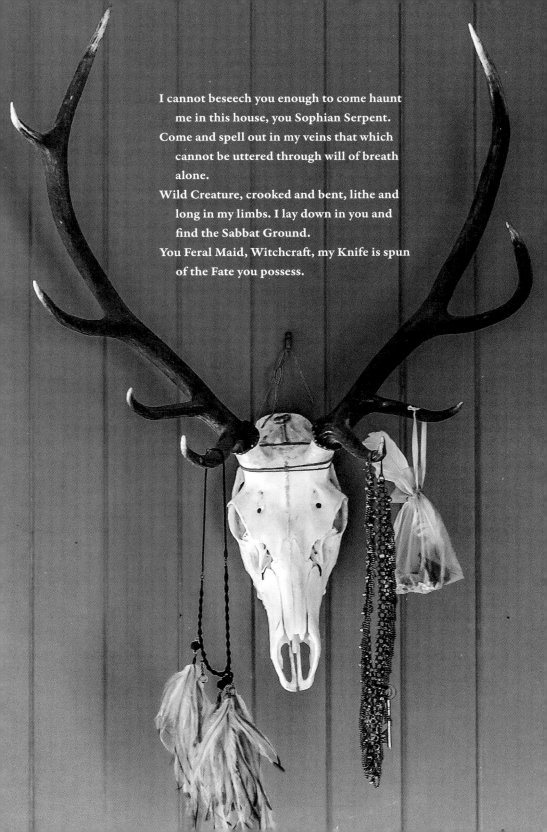

I cannot beseech you enough to come haunt
    me in this house, you Sophian Serpent.
Come and spell out in my veins that which
    cannot be uttered through will of breath
    alone.
Wild Creature, crooked and bent, lithe and
    long in my limbs. I lay down in you and
    find the Sabbat Ground.
You Feral Maid, Witchcraft, my Knife is spun
    of the Fate you possess.

Acknowledgements

Inside of me a rose. Inside that rose a castle. Inside that castle a throne. On that throne a book. A book that is a river. A river that falls from the sky. Inside of me a blossoming star.

To Jane Meredith, my co-conspirator, co-author, co-priestess, and dear friend.

To my beloveds and kin within the Wildwood, Anderean, Anderson Feri, and Reclaiming traditions, you are my wide and wyrd witch family.

To my human witchcraft initiators: J., L., R., G., A., H., L., D., and the two ravens.

To my fetch-mate, who has encouraged, inspired, and supported this work for years and infuses my work and witchcraft.

To Kim, whose astrological reading galvanised my Marsian motion and action to write this book!

Always to my mother, Ros, and my father, John—I Made Janur—who helped me become the person, the witch, the spirit worker, and the artist I am today.

To my heartbreak and my own broken-open self who did the work and came through. To those past selves, I say, "Girl, you carried."

To Desmond, Pabs, Brandon, and Pipaluk, who read the book and cheered me on in my uncomfortable vulnerability.

To J., G., A., J., and S. I fell in love with each of you in different times, in different places. Thank you for loving me once upon a time.

Appendix One

My Traditions

Wildwood, Reclaiming & Anderson Feri

I work within, drink deeply from, and am inspired by three witchcraft traditions. It feels pertinent to say a little about each one with the profound caveat that this is how I personally and currently would describe my relationship with and understanding of these orders, witch houses, lineages, and philosophies of witchcraft. By the time of the publication of this book I'd likely say it differently.

Wildwood

This tradition emerged in so-called Australia in the mid 2000s and has multiple seen and unseen roots. Ecstatic, folkloric, initiatory, mystery tradition, sorcerous, sabbatic, heretical, intimate are all good words that point to something significant about this witch house for me.

Wildwood witches honour and venerate as part of our cultus mysterious witching spirits who are also the primordial powers of existence. We call them the Sacred Four and they are Grandmother Weaver, Grandfather Green Man, Our Lady (who is also called the Crescent-Crowned Goddess or the Rosy Queen), and the Prince of Paradise (who is also called the Horned-Cloaked God; see appendix 3).

We understand ourselves to be Ara, who is the first witch—the living lineage and legacy of the craft—and the Altar of Witchery. We work with guardian beasts who hold elemental, sorcerous, and gender/less mysteries, orient to at least a triple cosmology that has many layers and spirals, and our workings and rituals are wildly variant and don't follow one key script or order. There are discernible patterns of practice in a few branches of this craft that might centre on or emphasise specific lore, rites, mysteries, teaching, spirits as core to an experience of the tradition. One example of this is the Sophian thread of the Wildwood that I am aligned with. This thread is served by several officers—the Lucifer, the Lilith, the Woodward, and the Faerie Other—and may utilise Gnostic, Christian, and Luciferian iconography and poetry to express certain witch teachings.

Wildwood witches generally aspire to live within love, truth, and wisdom, daring to behold and become beauty. We practise private rites of initiation that help emotionally and intimately bring us into magical kinship with one another and the spirits and mysteries. We enact and surrender into trance, faring forth and flight, trance possession, oracular knowing, spellcraft, blasting, binding, healing, opening the way, divination, omen-walking... all the witches' arts.

Some of us say that the Wildwood belongs to all witches, but some witches belong to the Wildwood. And this is the mystery for us, that this mysterious "other" place—the witches' forest, the Wildwood—is our heartland, our namesake, who we really are, and where we are home.

To discover more, you can go to wildwoodtradition.net.

Reclaiming

This tradition of witchcraft draws life from multiple wellsprings, roots, and rivers. Originally in the late '70s and early '80s the covens and experimentations connected to Starhawk's priestessing and teaching in the California Bay Area formed the seed for what would become Reclaiming. Like many traditions, including Wildwood, the mothers and midwives of Reclaiming did not necessarily intend to formally found or stumble upon a tradition of craft, but magic happens and secret histories will have their way.

In the early '80s various streams of witchcraft practice, team-teaching, feminist and anarchist ethos and activism, civil disobedience, nonviolent direct action, and group celebration, art, and protest formed the Reclaiming Collective. This was also the work of the Reclaiming Collective. Eventually a discernible tradition of contemporary witchcraft was acknowledged and it took its name from the Collective (named in 1980), which dissolved after the penning of the first iteration of the Principles of Unity, published in 1997.

More than forty years later, Reclaiming is one of the largest and widest witchcraft traditions. It is practised by individuals, covens, cells, communities in so-called Canada, USA, Brazil, Australia, Britain, Germany, Spain, France, Aotearoa (New Zealand), and many other countries and regions I am not currently recalling.

Hallmarks of the tradition include a distinct Principles of Unity. Aligning with and being in conversation with these Principles of Unity and identifying and practising as a Reclaiming witch are all one needs to claim this tradition. The tradition is taught via publicly offered core classes, at WitchCamps, and also within private covens, circles, and study groups the world over. Many Reclaiming teachers and communities have embraced platforms like Zoom to facilitate some of these learning experiences, so the tradition continues to grow and expand into places it may not have so readily before.

Almost every other modern witchcraft tradition requires ritual initiation at the hands of initiates in order to fully enter and participate within it. This is not true of the open-source, anarchist-feminist Reclaiming tradition. However, Reclaiming initiation does exist and can be asked for by those who are seeking that deeply personal journey. Reclaiming initiates do undergo a powerful ritual of initiation at the culmination of this journey.

Reclaiming ritual can look like modern Wiccan-based ritual, but with the caveat of drawing much magical technology and thinking from Anderson Feri. I'd personally suggest that published forms of Wiccan witchcraft (including Dianic witchcraft) and Anderson Feri are braided together to form much of the core way of working, though there are always exceptions to this. There are bioregional communities of Reclaimers who—for example—are steeped in Heathen folklore and ritual practice as their way of doing things. Generally a group ritual in Reclaiming will include:

- Acknowledging land/country/traditional peoples/ First Nations communities and spirits of land.

- Grounding and cleansing; maybe as distinct, often as joined together.

- Casting a magical circle in some way.

- Invocation/praising/acknowledgement of the elements of life: earth, air, fire, water, and spirit/centre. Some communities face directions in doing this and others do not.

- Invocation/praising/acknowledgement of various spirits, gods, ancestors, mysterious ones who are the centre of the work or whose aid and insight we request in the work.

- The meat/tofu of the ritual: often invitational and immersive trance or trance-journeying is utilised, as well as breathwork, chanting and singing, movement, sacred drama, aspecting, and the raising of power for spellwork.

- Then we honour and praise—some might say farewell—those we called in and acknowledged at the start of the ritual and release the circle. There may be more offerings or groundings after this.

Anderson Feri

Before it was called Faery or Fairy or Faerie—a name emergent from conversations between Gwydion Pendderwen and Victor Anderson—this tradition may have been called Pictish witchcraft, Vicia, or simply the Craft. I have heard that Cora Anderson largely always called it the Craft. One of its origins lie in a coven active in the 1930s in Oregon into which Victor Anderson was initiated in 1932 as well as the magical and meta-physical journeying and ethos of the Andersons and the early initiates.

Victor Anderson (1917–2001) and Cora Cremeans (1915–2008) met in Bend, Oregon, in 1944 and were married three days later. They both had experienced meeting each other on the astral many times before. What we now call Feri is a witchcraft tradition arising from this marriage, from their magical influences, initiations, and inheritances, and from the work of each initiate since.

Feri has multiple branches, lineages, and even schisms to the point where, depending on who you speak to, you might hear that there are distinct traditions now. While this may be true, many initiates from various lineages and branches speak to and work with each other. Discernible lines or branches of the Feri tradition include Vanthe/Vanthi, BloodRose, Sacred Wheel, DustBunnies, BlueRose, Reclaiming Feri, BlackHeart, ELF (Eastern Line Feri), Watchmaker, and Triskets. There are, of course, many other emergent lines and lines that change their names. Witches have been initiated into what is now called Feri since the '40s and '50s. Arguably Cora Anderson is the original initiate via Victor, though some would argue Victor was initiated into Feri when he was brought into the Oregon coven.

Feri is often contrasted to Wicca in that it is a witchcraft tradition of similar age that only has one initiation versus three degrees. In Feri we venerate God herself and her Consort who she draws forth from herself because she desires him/them. Feri ritual also does not require a circle for magical workings, nor nudity, nor the wheel of the year. The two feasts that are observed across the tradition are Bealtaine and Samhain; the other festivals common to modern forms of witchcraft and Paganism may or may not be observed in Feri contexts. Feri also works with distinct core concepts and tools:

- The triple soul spoken about in multiple cultural codings, but in English they are often named the fetch, the talker, and the godself. Alignment of the triple soul is considered crucial.

- The Black Heart of Innocence.

- The Iron Pentacle (and usually also the Pearl Pentacle) explored in appendix 2.

- The Star Goddess—God herself.

- The Feri Current and the initiation mysteries.

- Kala, or the Rite of Unbinding, or the Water Trick: a magical technique of purification and reclamation of life force utilising water and the act of drinking.

Depending on the branch or line of Feri, other core elements, which may be shared between many or most lines, include:

- Work with directional cosmic and often elemental guardians.

- Work with the crossroads and the circle, including liturgy and chants for ritual work.

- Work with particular spirits and gods of a variety of groupings and identities.

- Veneration of the peacock angel/god.

Initiation is required to enter fully into the Feri tradition. This generally happens after years of training and relating to one's teacher and mentor. There are a small percentage of initiates who prefer to initiate first and teach later. The initiation ritual fully facilitates the passing of the Current of Feri and is considered a marriage ceremony. How this ritual is done may vary widely as long as core mysteries are passed.

Feri is often called a warrior tradition. There is an ethos within Feri to own and be accountable for everything we do. We are not taught to discharge or submit our energy or life force, but to study our complexes and bindings and work with our tools and magic to help unbind and free up that life force so that we are reclaiming and retrieving anything that may have been lost, stolen, degraded, or forgotten. There are many proverbs in the tradition. Many are attributed to Victor Anderson. Some of these include:

Anything worthwhile is dangerous.

White magic is poetry. Black magic is anything that works.

Do not coddle weakness, but neither condemn frailty.

Appendix Two

Iron and Pearl

The Iron and the Pearl Pentacles in Feri and Reclaiming Traditions

Core to both the Anderson Feri and Reclaiming traditions of witchcraft is the work of Iron and Pearl Pentacles. In the order originally given by Victor Anderson, the points of the Iron Pentacle are Sex, Self, Passion, Pride, Power. The points of the Pearl Pentacle as taught by Victor are Love, Wisdom, Knowledge, Law, Power. This is also how they appear in Starhawk's *The Spiral Dance* (1979). Sometimes Victor Anderson also gave Liberty instead of or with Power for the Pearl Pentacle.

Iron and Pearl are integral within Anderson Feri lineages, though Pearl is not worked with in at least one branch of Feri I know of. Iron and Pearl Pentacles are two of the five core classes of Reclaiming tradition. The others are Elements of Magic, Rites of Passage, and Community. These Pentacles are unique and significant teachings that exist in Feri and Reclaiming, though influence extends beyond into other groups and traditions who might employ these magics and methodologies.

Anderson Feri is an initiatory mystery tradition in which key pieces of lore, ritual, technique, and theology are kept private to the body of initiates. Reclaiming, in contrast, could be described as an open-source, anarchist, eco-feminist community tradition that encourages the considered sharing of practice, lore, technique, and process.

Iron Pentacle was first taught and developed by Victor Anderson and early initiates of the magical tradition he passed, now called Feri/Faery, though it may precede him in some form. This tradition has various roots including the mysteries and workings of an Oregon-based coven of dustbowl economic refugees, direct spirit communication and gnosis, and magico-cultural traditions including Hawaiian, West African, Scottish, Welsh, and Irish streams. Feri is an American traditional witchcraft, and so it is the histories and realities of the so-called USA that contextualise this melding and learning.

Some Feri initiates who knew Victor observed that he would require people to chant aloud the points of the Iron Pentacle in the original order described above. If they could not go around several times continuously, then he would send them away. No teaching was offered. This reveals that in its early iterations the Iron Pentacle was considered to possess a current of its own—a purificatory and initiatory power that might also bring up our complexes and confront, transmute, and even clear them. Those who could not even repeat the formula—the points—a few times round might be considered to be ill prepared for the deep work of witchcraft. In Reclaiming we sometimes refer to shadow-stalking as being a particular thread of the Iron Pentacle work.

In 1980 Starhawk (an initiate of the Andersons) and Diane Baker (a witch of the coven Raving) taught the first Elements of Magic course as an experiment in shared power, group magical immersion, and feminist and anarchist process. This was popular with the participants, who asked for more magical training, so Starhawk and Baker taught a second class, the Iron Pentagram as it was referred to at the time.

The Pearl Pentagram is taught in most branches and lineages of Anderson Feri and definitely within Reclaiming. Iron and Pearl are considered to be the same mystery; the same pentagram or pentacle experienced from different places or states of being. Sex becomes Love, Self becomes Wisdom (some place Knowledge here, a later amendment), Passion becomes Knowledge (some place Wisdom here), Pride becomes Law, Power becomes Power again (and later Liberty; not all Feri lines work with Liberty, but it is common in Reclaiming to do so). The mystery of Iron becoming Pearl is the work of our lives. It has been said that Iron Pentacle is the work of a lifetime and Pearl Pentacle is the work of lifetimes (T. Thorn Coyle attributes this saying to Reclaiming and Feri initiate Pandora). Interpret that as you will.

At some point in the '80s it became an established practice to "run" the Iron Pentacle current through the body in a different order. The order of the running is as if a person is before you, facing you, and drawing an invoking pentagram on your body: from your head to your right foot to your left hand to your right hand to your left foot and back to the head. This likely originated with the work of Gabriel Carillo—initiated in the early '70s by the Andersons—in the BloodRose school of Feri. Quite a few Reclaimers did some study with the BloodRose school of Feri and likely in this way brought that practice into wider Reclaiming. Dawn Isidora, a Reclaiming and Feri initiate, has commented that when she first took the Iron core class in Reclaiming in the early '80s, running the Pentacle was not taught, but working it in a labyrinth-style was. The order Sex-Self-Passion-Pride-Power was initially how things were tracked rather than through the pentagram, which has become more common. Obviously this is all valid and potent.

The spread-out human form makes a star with five points of head, hands, and feet, so it is clearly resonant and powerful to run the pentacle within and as the body. Victor Anderson also warned of becoming too attached to the notion that certain points of the body corresponded with the points of the Iron Pentacle. I encourage folks to embrace the paradox that both are true: the Iron and Pearl through and with the body and Iron and Pearl exist as bodies of their own through which we move.

In the Reclaiming tradition of witchcraft, it is culturally encouraged to take the core classes multiple times with multiple teachers and at various points of our lives. We do not just "do" Iron or Pearl and never return. Ideally they become part of the fabric of our lives, and though we might change the tone or form of our practices, these points are part of who we are and who we can become. It is hoped that if we are "on our points"—Sex, Self, Passion, Pride, Power—that we might unfold and flower as the Pearl Pentacle.

Gwydion—a Feri and Reclaiming priest—has said that Iron Pentacle is about our relationship to ourselves and Pearl Pentacle extends into our relationships with other selves, other beings, the entire web of life perhaps. May we each discover the sustainable and potent pathways to Love, Wisdom, Knowledge, Law, and Liberation.

Resources

Evolutionary Witchcraft, T. Thorn Coyle

Magic of the Iron Pentacle, Jane Meredith and Gede Parma

Circling the Star, Anthony Rella

The Spiral Dance, Starhawk

"The Iron Pentacle" feature in *Reclaiming Quarterly*:
   http://reclaimingquarterly.org/67/RQ67-06-IronPentacle.pdf

"The Pearl Pentacle" feature in *Reclaiming Quarterly*:
   http://reclaimingquarterly.org/103/RQ103-PearlPentacle.pdf

Appendix Three

The Witch-Wreathed Gods

Originally written in 2016.

> *Four, the mighty pillars*
> *Four, the holy treasures*
> *Four, the darkly shining mysteries*
> *Four are the witch-wreathed gods.*

At the heart of the primal witchcraft I know are the four witch-wreathed gods who in the Wildwood tradition are called the Sacred Four. I have been passed names, chants, sigils, lore through several branches of the craft regarding these primal beings or beings very like one another. While the names are distinct in each thread, and while there is certainly specific and distinct lore and story in each house, there is an overwhelming and uncanny underlying commonality. When I first encountered these gods, I did not realise that other witches or their traditions had a similar cultus or mystery. I have discovered in the past ten years that many of the threads and houses that could be called traditional or Old Craft are anchored in this witches' mythos.

The four great spirits that form this sanctum most awesome, most dreadful, can be called variously,

- Grandmother Weaver, Old Fate, the Star Goddess, the Black Virgin, the Hag-who-is-the-Maid

- Grandfather Green Man, the Old One, Old Scratch, the Huntsman

- Our Lady, the Rosy Queen, the Crescent-Crowned Goddess, Queen of Witches

- The Devil, the Master, Our Prince of Paradise, the Young God, the Lucifer

In this article I will share what I can of these beings, drawing upon my own insights drawn from my initiatory and intimate experiences, appropriate witchlore from several traditions I have contact with, and folklore.

I must make clear that the way in which I speak of these Great Ones might not necessarily reflect current Pagan or (hard) polytheistic theologies. I experience these beings as distinctly related to witchcraft, and the nature of witches is deeply derived from their stories and influences their stories. For me these are the prime witch deities. They are intrinsically shapeshifters and can take on any known or unknown cultural or land-based spirit or deity without erasing the authority and agency of that being. For instance, sometimes I will differentiate Persephone as Persephone and Persephone as Witch Queen. These distinctions are markedly human, but they point to magic and mystery. Both Persephone and the Witch Queen exist and sometimes they are each other and the Queen of Witches I know is definitively who she is.

As an initiate of craft that derives from and is inspired by the lore and legends of Northwestern and Southern European traditions, I will concentrate on the material from these regions and those cultures. However, I firmly understand the word *witch* to be an English term relating to a quintessential human phenomenon. Witches—under whatever the local term is—exist in all ethnicities, all lands, and all times. If this is true, then the witch-wreathed gods are truly "the gods who made the gods who made man" (Lady Circe via Orion Foxwood).

Grandmother Weaver

She may be known as the Welsh Cerridwen, the Scottish and Irish Cailleach, the Greek Hekate, the Germanic Hulda. She is the original Creator-Destroyer. She is the black void of space, the swollen and raging abyss. She is the zero without a specified centre. The Prince—the Devil— steals that centre, occupies it, claims it, is enthroned there, and eventually—as all things—is destroyed, dismembered, sacrificed, and reborn. I have used the poetry Hag-who-is-the-Maid. She is the weaver of all fate, the Grandmother of space and time; space and time being the essence that powers the Grandfather as they are Lord who is time that brings death but is surely as verdant and virile as the sprouting seed in the earth.

Grandmother Weaver is the initiator. She harrows the witch. She boils the witch in her ancient cauldron and we taste of our own elixirs. She is the haggard and wizened crone and the most beguiling, most beautiful one, and these are not opposites. She is a terror in the night—the foreboding nightmare—and the providence of all things. There are several stories including the Scottish Cailleach and Brighid and the Loathly Lady that speak of this. The true king or knight—who is kind, merciful, impassioned, and wise—will be the one who will kiss the hag, the "ugly" lady, and lay with her only to discover that she is, in fact, the Goddess who is the Land, who is the sacred authority in all things. And as Sir Gawain did, they will recognise the true sovereignty therein and choose to exalt it. And she shows a face of uncovered, whole beauty.

Sometimes we see the Grandmother as three. One obvious manifestation of this is as the Three Fates of Greco-Roman mythos, the Germanic Wyrd Sisters, and the Scandinavian Norns. The One who spins the thread, measures it, and cuts it, and thus are our lives spun and undone. The One who knows yesterday, the becoming, and what might come to pass. There are other faces too: the original starry Creatrix who we might relate to the upperworld, the deep underworldly Initiator, and the Lady-who-is-the-Land, the middleworld.

The Old One

I first knew this being as the Dark One and the Green Man. We say Green to make hallowed the silent whispers of the Lord of Death, King of the Underworld, who fills us with "mickle dread." He has been called Woden, the Forest Wizard of the Germanic lands, who stalks the shadows, wolf-led and raven-flanked. His face is the coil or knot in the ancient oak, and his mouth spews forth power and wind, vomiting the leaves of any season. He is both bound to the earth in all cycles and is in essence the dense, manifest form of those things.

The Grandmother is the zero and he is the two. He holds the paradox of that apparent duality of life and death and the worlds breaking and coming back together always: the lightning in the sky and the thunder in the land. Zero is broken by two when the one, which is the centre, is crystallised: the child who is pushed forth from the womb, crying out in that ecstasy. It is through the sacred breath—the Wind Wizard—therefore that Life and Death come into the world. That which was in the womb—silent and seething, unformed and perhaps formless—is now the point, and the point is both the maker and breaker of all worlds. That point is the Young Devil themself—also you and me—the Old One, the Grandfather is their teacher. So we have Merlin teaching Arthur, and Balor as the Grandfather of Lugh of the Long Arm, master of all arts, born of the tribe of Dana.

The Grandfather is called Herne in Berkshire and Gwynn in the West Country, and they are both leaders of the ghostly train variously called the Wild Hunt or the Furious Horde. In spring the Grandfather presents as Jack-in-the-Green, that living serpent of the world, and opens the door into this world for the Shining Ones to emerge. As winter darkens, the Old One stirs the dead and the dark elves to streak the night with eerie laughter, as the baying of the hell hounds clears the shaking air of revenants and lost souls so that all may be taken back to the Grandmother's cauldron to properly unravel and be reborn in time.

The Grandfather is the great oaken door through which life comes into this world, and they are also the yew, the threshold of death. His is the roar in the earth, the thunder and lightning in the heavens. He has horns twisted and ancient that to tell them apart from boughs and branches is a feat. They are the Old Devil who we may see if we go to the edge of a forest or a wild place, turn away, and bend down to look through our legs. He is the Warden of the Wildwood. They protect witches. The Old One makes the way—in this world—for the younger gods.

Our Lady

This the most secret, most beloved queen. One of my teachers once said to me that she is the secret heart of the craft. The Devil leads us to her. They take the hindmost and wait for all to come into the Lady's bower.

The Queen of Witches could be looked at as a lunar-Venusian goddess. She has come from the stars to the earth through the moon and knows the power of the seas. Like the Grandmother, she may also manifest in the three worlds and sometimes wears a lunar crescent or holds a hare to signify a similar truth. She is a Faerie Queen, and this can mean all manner of things. She is Faerie in the sense that she is daughter of Fate herself, the origin of that very term. She is a Fate, she is the Dame, she is Power and Beauty.

It is the name of this great spirit that is often deeply cherished by witches and their houses. Her true name, of course, is sub rosa and can only be found down the thorn-riddled path where blood must be spilt to truly attain the mystery of the rose.

She may be (called) Rhiannon, Aradia, Aphrodite, Persephone, Inanna, Ishtar, Diana, Fauna, Irodiada, Benzozia . . . Her mysteries include the descent and the ascent into and out of the underworld. Several traditions will mark these at the autumnal and vernal equinox, respectively. Seasonally—as part of various mythic cycles—the festivals that are often great sabbats become story-hinges of important craft themes and teachings. They are not abstract; they are a lived reality. The wheel of the year and the feasts may mark significant and powerful occasions for Our Lady and the Devil.

Animals associated with her include the cat, hare, serpent, owl, horse, stag, dove, bear. She is the soul of the worlds. She too may lead a procession through the air, and as Diana—Goddess of the Pagans, as the Canon Episcopi names her—she was said to be a delusion of Satan as the one who would lead witch women through the air to nocturnal revels. At these sabbats they would meet with various spirits, encounter the lustful Devil, and learn sorcery from the Great Ones.

The Devil

He is the Master of All Sorcery, and as witches we are on this road. They are the spirit of humanity, our adversary, our initiator, the Master and our queer quintessence, the flame between the horns. He has a special bond not only with witches, but with humanity in essence. They are the most human of gods. Our stories tell us that he either transformed from man to god or through some powerful alchemy from angel to faerie to human to the Master himself—a journey through the compass kin of white, green, red, and black.

The young Devil is the flame twixt the horns. While the old Devil might be those very horns, those horns or antlers are also the Master's as both gift and ordeal. That flame is the shining light that is the splendour of the soul that is the original daimon by which all other daimons have come into the world. These daimons—their own spirits—have mated with witches and are sometimes called fetch-mates, seraphic or faerie lovers, the original sponsors of the first witches into awakening with the witch fire that blossoms from the witch blood.

The Master—the Prince of Paradise—is sometimes shown as wearing stag antlers, bull's horns, ram's horns, or goat's horns. Sometimes all of them. He may come as the Dark One at the Crossroads, to whom we sell our souls in exchange for the powers of sorcery. The true sacrifice being a mystery of self with self, of collapsing identities and states of being . . . through the blood of the human to the daimonic intelligence and vice versa. The red thread of mouth to ear and heartbeat to heartbeat and the white thread of spirit to human touch and braid and weave. The Devil is where those two things meet and deep witchery is born.

He is always they, and they are always in between, liminal, lord of ecstasy. He is the lover of the Lady, but this is not some essentialised excuse for cis-heterosexist paradigms of polarity as in some popular public forms of eclectic Wicca. The Master and the Lady are known in lore and history to mate and consort with people of all genders and no gender. In fact, the great social taboo and transgression of homosexuality and other queer forms of sex and love are very much part and parcel of traditional witchcraft. As well as this, in the mysteries enacted, it could be that any person of any non/gender might be expressing the Devil or the Lady in their coming together and coming apart.

It could be true to say that the four fire festivals of Britain and Ireland are hinges to the Devil's story of the initiation of love (Roodmas or Bealtaine), their sacrifice as King of the People (Lammas or Lughnasadh), his death and descent (Hallowmas or Samhain), and their rebirth or renewal (Candlemas or Imbolc). There are nuances to this, of course, and some witchcraft traditions do work with either six or eight or even nine festivals with varying intricate details and texture threaded in between.

The witch's path is an innately intensive and initiatory path. And often the prototypical witch initiation is storied with the festivals, so can we expect that truly immersing in those times and rites will catalyse and clarify those initiations. We become the Master on the crooked path of mastery. Though it might not always happen in the seasonal order, a witch's initiation will involve being cut down and dismembered and being devoured by love and undone completely with the most powerful medicine of all. We will be torn apart, harrowed, descending into our own underworld, and if we are fortunate and if we are able to surrender—drawing upon our audacity and authority—perhaps we will be reborn with the flame shining even brighter at our brows.

One of the symbols by which we invoke this Great Spirit is either the stang at the centre of the compass, circle, or crossroads, or a stag, goat, ram, or bull's skull with a candle lit in between the horns. As well as this, I sometimes will place peacock feathers for the Devil, as this being—as has Christ—has at times been connected to the peacock, and one cultural form that shows up in at least Feri and Cultus Sabbati is Melek Taus of the Yezidi people, the peacock angel.

An Exercise

There is a special and initiatory relationship between each of these Great Ones. Go to a wild place where you will be away from other humans for an extended period of time. Make a fire or place a single black candle in a cauldron and light it in silence. With a blessed rod or wand, carve an equal-armed cross, a fourfold crossroads, into the earth. Then draw a circle widdershins to encompass the points. Stand at the centre and know that to the north is Old Fate, to the south the Grandfather, to the west the Lady, and to the east the Master. This is how I pass this on to Wildwood witches.

Another alignment, deriving from Cochrane's craft, is that in the north is the Black Goddess, in the south the Verdant Lady, in the east the Young Horn Child, and in the west the Old God. Feel them as the four pillars surrounding you as you are between them, the witch who wreathes them. There will be an equal-armed cross within a circle, but now draw lines from point to point. Now there is a square within a circle containing the cross. Each point—each Great Spirit—touches all the others.

In this way can one begin to discover the mysteries between each pair. You may choose to move through and around the circle from point to point or through the cross or along the square . . . You may find yourself entranced or deeply contemplative as you go. You can repeat this working many times over a period of time to gather various vantages of information and insight on these Great Ones and their intimacies with one another.

Bibliography

Anderson, C. *In Mari's Bower*. Harpy Books, 2012.

Anderson, V., and C. Anderson. *The Heart of the Initiate*. Harpy Books, 2012.

Blake, W. *The Marriage of Heaven and Hell*. Bodleian Library Publishing, 2011.

Bourne, L. *Dancing with Witches*. Robert Hale, 1998.

Charles, R. H. *The Book of Enoch the Prophet*. Weiser Books, 2012.

Erdrich, L. *The Painted Drum*. HarperCollins, 2005.

Huson, P. *Mastering Witchcraft: A Practical Guide for Witches, Warlocks and Covens*. Corgi Books, 1972.

Meredith, J. *Circle of Eight: Creating Magic for Your Place on Earth*. Llewellyn, 2015.

Meredith, J., and G. Parma. *Magic of the Iron Pentacle: Reclaiming Sex, Pride, Self, Power & Passion*. Llewellyn, 2016.

Morgan, L. *A Deed without a Name: Unearthing the Legacy of Traditional Witchcraft*. Moon Books, 2012.

Neale, M., and L. Kelly. *Songlines: The Power and Promise* (First Knowledges series). Thames & Hudson, 2020.

Oliver, M. *Owls and Other Fantasies*. Beacon Press, 2006.

Pazzaglini, M., and D. Pazzaglini. *Aradia, or the Gospel of the Witches: A New Translation*. Phoenix Publishing Inc., 1998.

Robinson, J., ed. *The Nag Hammadi Library in English*. HarperCollins, 1990.

Valiente, D. *The Rebirth of Witchcraft*. Crowood Press, 2008.

Wilby, E. *Cunning Folk and Familiar Spirits: Shamanistic Visionary Traditions in Early Modern British Witchcraft and Magic*. Sussex Academic Press, 2005.

Wilby, E. *The Visions of Isobel Gowdie.* Sussex Academic Press, 2010.

Yunkaporta, T. *Sand Talk: How Indigenous Thinking Can Save the World.* Text Publishing Company, 2019.

Biblical quotes are taken from the following versions:
King James Bible (Samuel, Leviticus, and Isaiah)

New International Version Bible (Genesis 1)

English Standard Version Bible (Genesis 4)

About the Author

Fio Gede Parma (they/she) is a Balinese-Australian witch, international teacher, and magical mentor. Fio is a co-founder of the Coven of the Wildwood. They are a midwife and initiate of the Wildwood tradition as well as an active initiate of Reclaiming and Anderson Feri and have authored or coauthored six previous books, including *Elements of Magic* and *Magic of the Iron Pentacle*.

To Write to the Author

If you wish to contact the author or would like more information about this book, please write to the author in care of Llewellyn Worldwide and we will forward your request. Both the author and the publisher appreciate hearing from you and learning of your enjoyment of this book and how it has helped you. Llewellyn Worldwide cannot guarantee that every letter written to the author can be answered, but all will be forwarded. Please write to:

Fio Gede Parma
Llewellyn Worldwide
2143 Wooddale Drive
Woodbury, MN 55125–2989

Please enclose a self-addressed stamped envelope for reply
or $1.00 to cover costs. If outside the USA, enclose
an international postal reply coupon.

Many of Llewellyn's authors have websites with additional information and resources. For more information, please visit our website:

WWW.LLEWELLYN.COM